Studies in the Psychosocial Series

Edited by

Peter Redman, The Open University, UK
Stephen Frosh, Centre for Psychosocial Studies, Birkbeck College, University of London, UK
Wendy Hollway, The Open University, UK

Titles include:

Stephen Frosh
HAUNTINGS: PSYCHOANALYSIS AND GHOSTLY TRANSMISSIONS

Uri Hadar
PSYCHOANALYSIS AND SOCIAL INVOLVEMENT
Interpretation and Action

Margarita Palacios
RADICAL SOCIALITY
Studies on Violence, Disobedience and the Vicissitudes of Belonging

Derek Hook
(POST)APARTHEID CONDITIONS

Garth Stevens, Norman Duncan and Derek Hook (*editors*)
RACE, MEMORY AND THE APARTHEID ARCHIVE
Towards a Transformative Psychosocial Praxis

Irene Bruna Seu
PASSIVITY GENERATION
Human Rights and Everyday Morality

Lynn Chancer and John Andrews (*editors*)
THE UNHAPPY DIVORCE OF SOCIOLOGY AND PSYCHOANALYSIS

Kate Kenny and Marianna Fotaki (*editors*)
THE PSYCHOSOCIAL AND ORGANIZATION STUDIES
Affect at Work

James S. Ormrod
FANTASY AND SOCIAL MOVEMENTS

Jo Whitehouse-Hart
PSYCHOSOCIAL EXPLORATIONS OF FILM AND TELEVISION VIEWING
Ordinary Audience

Bülent Somay
THE PSYCHOPOLITICS OF THE ORIENTAL FATHER
Between Omnipotence and Emasculation

Julie Walsh
NARCISSISM AND ITS DISCONTENTS

Wendy Hollway
KNOWING MOTHERS
Researching Maternal Identity Change

Stephen Frosh
PSYCHOSOCIAL IMAGINARIES
Perspectives on Temporality, Subjectivities and Activism

Candida Yates
THE PLAY OF POLITICAL CULTURE, EMOTION AND IDENTITY

Studies in the Psychosocial Series
Series Standing Order ISBN 978–0–230–30858–9 (hardback)
978–0–230–30859–6 (paperback)
(*outside North America only*)

You can receive future titles in this series as they are published by placing a
standing order. Please contact your bookseller or, in case of difficulty, write to
us at the address below with your name and address, the title of the series and
the ISBNs quoted above.

Customer Services Department, Macmillan Distribution Ltd, Houndmills,
Basingstoke, Hampshire RG21 6XS, England

The Play of Political Culture, Emotion and Identity

Candida Yates

Professor of Culture and Communication, Bournemouth University, UK

palgrave
macmillan

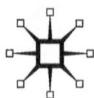

First published 2015 by
PALGRAVE MACMILLAN

Palgrave Macmillan in the UK is an imprint of Macmillan Publishers Limited, registered in England, company number 785998, of Houndmills, Basingstoke, Hampshire RG21 6XS.

Palgrave Macmillan in the US is a division of St Martin's Press LLC, 175 Fifth Avenue, New York, NY 10010.

Palgrave Macmillan is the global academic imprint of the above companies and has companies and representatives throughout the world.

Palgrave® and Macmillan® are registered trademarks in the United States, the United Kingdom, Europe and other countries.

ISBN 978–0–230–30252–5

This book is printed on paper suitable for recycling and made from fully managed and sustained forest sources. Logging, pulping and manufacturing processes are expected to conform to the environmental regulations of the country of origin.

A catalogue record for this book is available from the British Library.

A catalog record for this book is available from the Library of Congress.

Contents

Acknowledgements

This book was written with the encouragement and support of colleagues, friends, family and institutions. I began writing this book at the University of East London (UEL), where I spent many years working in the Psychosocial Studies subject area, housed in various schools and finally in the School of Social Sciences. I am grateful to UEL for all the support that it has given me over the years and I want to thank the many colleagues and friends at UEL who have encouraged me to write this book and especially, the staff team and students on the UEL Psychosocial Studies programme. Special thanks go to David Jones, Corinne Squire, Heather Price, Nicola Diamond, Darren Ellis, Angie Voela, Lurraine Jones, Cigdem Esin, Bethany Morgan Brett, Helen Powell, Siobhan Lennon-Patience, Jacob Johanssen, Julia Dane, Robin Stinson, Andrew Calcutt and Giorgia Dona. Particular thanks go to those friends and colleagues who have read draft chapters, including Caroline Bainbridge, Helen Powell, Mastoureh Fathi and the Palgrave reviewer, who provided such helpful feedback. I would also like to thank and acknowledge other friends and colleagues as supporting and encouraging me on my journey as an academic and researcher including, Michael Rustin, Lynne Layton, Shelley Day Sclater, Susan Greenberg, Heather Nunn, Anita Biressi, Deborah Jermyn, Andrew Blake, Marta Rabikowska, Iain MacRury, Barry Richards and Joanne Brown.

This book began its life during the period of the AHRC Funding for the Media and Inner World (MiW) research network, which I set up with Caroline Bainbridge at The University of Roehampton in order to develop a new Psycho-Cultural field of enquiry. Many of the ideas in this book were developed at MiW events and through its publications. A number of colleagues and friends associated with MiW have been influential in shaping my ideas for this book, including Brett Kahr, Carol Leader and Michael Maynard and also colleagues at the Freud Museum, including Ivan Ward and Carol Seigel. Thanks also to David Aaronovitch and Dan Chambers for their thoughts on Boris Johnson and the emotional theatre of politics more generally. My dear friend and research partner Caroline Bainbridge deserves special thanks and acknowledgement and I remain very grateful to Caroline for her ever-present support and insight and also for sharing her wit and fabulous sense of humour when needed!

I completed the book in my new institution, Bournemouth University, and I am grateful to my new colleagues in the Faculty of Media and Communication and in the CMC group for the very warm welcome that I have received and also for encouraging me to finish the manuscript. My thanks go to Stephen Jukes, Richard Scullion, Barry Richards, Iain MacRury, Heather Savigny, Darren Lilleker, Pawel Surowiec, Laura Bunt-MacRury, Shelley Thompson, Rebecca Jenkins and Janice Denegri-Knott, who have all been very supportive in this regard. I also want to thank Irene Eskanazi and John Biggs for their kindness in welcoming me to their home at Bournemouth.

I would also like to thank photographer and Bournemouth University colleague, Rutherford for kindly providing the image for this book. Thanks also to the editors at Palgrave Macmillan, Nicola Jones, Libby Forrest, Eleanor Christie and the project manager, Francis Arumugam, for their patience and kind support in helping me to complete and finalise the manuscript. Some parts of this book have been published elsewhere, and I want to acknowledge and thank those journals and their editors. Parts of Chapter 3 have been published previously in *Subjectivity*, 2010, Vol. 3, no. 3: 282–302; and parts of Chapter 5 have been published in *Psychoanalysis, Culture & Society*, 2012, Vol. 17, no. 2: 204–221. Parts of Chapter 4 have also been published in *Free Associations*, 2011, no. 62: 59–84.

Finally, I want to thank my family for their encouragement and support, including Dagan Wells and Elpida Fragouli; Lily and Alexander Wells; Julian Wells and Vicky Yanoula; Miranda, Dermot, Daisy and Oonagh Madden-Wells; Nikki, Ed and Woody Cima and Stella, Camilla and Clio Yates. I am very grateful to my uncle, David Gladstone (and my wonderful aunt, the late April Gladstone), who have encouraged me and listened enthusiastically to my ideas over the years. Huge thanks go to my sisters, Cary and Clare, and their partners Bee and Simon, and also to my brother, Christo, and my nephews Toby, Max, Harry and Michael. I also want to thank my father, Michael Yates, for his continual enthusiasm and encouragement and for being so proud of what I do!

Last, but not least, my thanks go to Lindsay Wells, who has now seen me through another book, and it is dedicated to him with much love.

1
Introducing Emotion, Identity and the Play of Political Culture

Developing a psycho-cultural approach to emotion and political culture

This book explores the relationships between emotion, identity and fantasy within the mediatised landscape of contemporary political culture. Focusing mainly on the UK context, the study of these relationships takes the form of an interdisciplinary 'psycho-cultural' approach that uses theories and methods taken from the fields of psychosocial studies, cultural and media studies. A starting place for this book is that politics – and our engagement with it – has become increasingly emotional (Lilleker, 2012; Richards, 2007). The emotionalisation of politics can be found in different aspects of political culture, which include the field of political representation, the content of political policy and the engagement with those representations and policies within and via different aspects of the media and popular culture.

One can cite numerous images of politicians performing emotively for the camera – from Tony Blair's speech following Princess Diana's death in 1997, to Hillary Clinton's tears on her 2008 election campaign, or the former Australian Prime Minister Kevin Rudd's tearful retirement speech in 2013. The UK government's focus on notions of 'emotional wellbeing' and 'happiness' also provides an example of the way in which the language and discourses of emotion have permeated the political discourses of public life (Lennon-Patience, 2013; Richards, 2007; Rustin, 2007; Yates, 2011). As I discuss, the study of emotions in this context needs to include a focus on notions of fantasy, affect and the unconscious and the psychological defences and anxieties that are stirred up, communicated and experienced within the day-to-day mediatised contexts of political culture.

1

Corner and Pels (2003: 3) usefully define political culture as that which includes 'political experience, imagination, values and dispositions', which shape both the environment for the 'political system' and the 'character of political processes and political behaviour'. The term 'political culture' refers not only to the official texts of government, (including, for example, public policy documents and political speeches) but also to the fluid, mediatised relationships that now exist between politics and popular culture. The latter includes the representation of politics in the press, broadcast news, television entertainment shows and social media, and also in fictional depictions of politics in films, novels and television programmes.

Political culture is also influenced by celebrity culture, the growth of social media and the marketisation of politics as a promotional activity. This book takes account of these factors shaping political culture and provides an analysis of the cultural politics of British political life by using methods of textual and contextual analysis, paying attention to both the popular and 'official' texts of political culture today. In focusing on the output of the UK press in print, broadcast and digital media formats in the period 1997–2015, I have identified a number of persistent themes that have emerged, and these can tell us something about the popular psycho-cultural imagination of that moment in recent history, which covers the shift from the rise of New Labour to the end of the Conservative/Liberal Coalition Government in 2015. It is interesting to think about the changing texture of politics in the period and the shifting metaphors used from 'the eradication of left/right polarity' (Giddens, 1998, p. 26), through to the 'clear blue water' differentiation of centrism politics (Addley and Woodward, 2007). More recently, in the UK as elsewhere in Europe, we have seen the emergence of a populist right-wing positioning. In the UK the UK Independence Party (UKIP) has attempted to differentiate itself from mainstream politicians who UKIP say 'are all the same' and as 'bad' as each other (Mardel, 2014).

This book, then, is about how media converges with politics and what that process signals about the public mood. Mediated examples of politics in this period can tell us something as they are symptomatic of a particular 'a structure of feeling' (Williams, 1977), where the (always) irrational social symbolic sphere of contemporary political culture is shaped by the practices and discourses of culture, history and politics and also by the forces of emotion and unconscious fantasy. Media coverage of politicians and political issues in real and fictional contexts can be read as being symptomatic of a public mood and that they are also linked to the fantasies that underpin shifting attitudes about culture and identity. As Braidotti (2002: 39) argues: 'Fantasies, desires and the pursuit of pleasure play an important and constructive role in subjectivity as rational judgement and standard political action'. In a period of change, flux and uncertainty, when it is often said that politics is in disarray, it is perhaps not surprising that such themes often focus on questions of identity, cultural belonging and the fate of the self at a time of crises and uncertainty.

The emotional tone of much political culture invites a mode of analysis that is able to accommodate the often irrational and contradictory nature of popular political discourse in an era of economic crisis, flux and change. Psychoanalysis offers a perspective on such issues that can take into account this set of contradictions in a way that opens up new ways of reflecting on and thinking them through. From Freud onwards, there has been a history of applying psychoanalytic concepts to socio-political themes and events (see Auestad, 2014; Adorno and Horkheimer, 1976; Clarke et al., 2006; Freud, 1921, 1930; Glynos and Stavrakas, 2010; Rustin, 2001; Samuels, 2001, 1993; Žižek, 2014). Yet as Bainbridge and Yates (2012, 2014) have discussed, albeit with some notable exceptions (see, for example, Layton, 2004, 2010, 2011; Richards, 2007; and Rustin, 1991), the application of object relations psychoanalysis has been used less within the field of politics, media and cultural studies, which is often sceptical of the 'universalising claims' of psychoanalytic thinking. However, I want to insist upon the usefulness of a psychoanalytic framework in helping us to understand the complexities of cultural experience and its ongoing role in shaping the psychological and affective processes of subjectivity. I apply an object relations approach because of its focus on the relational dimensions of subjectivity. From an object relations perspective, the experience of selfhood and identity is an ongoing, formative process that is bound up with relations to real and imagined objects of the mind and the social world (Bainbridge and Yates, 2014).

My approach is therefore one that uses psychoanalytic theories of the unconscious, affect, identification and play, to explore emotion and its symbolisation in culture at any one time. Alongside object relations theory, the book also deploys psychoanalytic theories of gender and sexual difference to acknowledge the significance of both oedipal and pre-oedipal fantasy in the shaping of images and processes of identification within political culture today. The discussions thus combine an understanding of unconscious processes – including the role of fantasy, desire and the mobilisation of unconscious defences, with an awareness of the historical and cultural context in which those processes take place. From this 'psycho-cultural' perspective then (Bainbridge and

Yates, 2014, 2012), the shaping of identity goes beyond the analysis of cultural and social factors, as instead, affective identities are mutually constituted and transformed by the ongoing interaction of psyche, culture and society.

As discussed elsewhere (Bainbridge and Yates, 2012, 2014), the psycho-cultural methodology deployed here has emerged partly from the field of British Psychosocial Studies and my work is influenced in particular by the psychosocial studies approach developed at the University of East London.[1] That work often deploys sociology and object relations psychoanalysis to explore questions of subjectivity, politics and society and it tends to focus on social, rather than cultural concerns. Whilst the approach taken in this book draws strongly on that psychosocial studies tradition – especially its insights regarding the inter-relationship between social and psychological experience, it also deploys a cultural focus that is shaped by media and cultural studies, thus combining aspects of both the humanities and the social sciences research traditions.

The aim of this opening chapter is to orientate the reader by defining some of the key concepts, themes and ideas which inform that psycho-cultural approach, to provide some theoretical and historical context for the analysis of the complex relationships between politics, emotion and the shaping of identities today.

Consuming politics as popular culture

There is now a vast body of scholarly research on the topic of 'political communication' and its influence in shaping voter preference and our engagement with politics (see, for example, Negrine and Stanyer, 2008; Sanders, 2009; Wolfsfeld, 2011). Yet as I have indicated, the term 'political culture' is preferred here to that of 'political communication', as the meaning of the latter is often too narrow to encompass the many areas within popular culture and the media, where political engagement now takes place (Corner and Pels, 2003; Couldry et al., 2010; Fielding, 2014; Richards, 2007; Savigny, 2016). From radio phone-ins to soap opera and comedy satires, the notion of what 'constitutes politics' now extends beyond the traditional communication channels of political engagement to the mediatised spaces of popular culture (Couldry et al., 2010). The term 'popular culture' is notoriously hard to define, and its use depends on the context in which it is being used (Storey, 2014). Following in the tradition of cultural studies scholars – and starting with Raymond Williams' well-known definition, 'culture' can be defined in its broadest sense to mean 'a way of life' (Williams, 1983).[2] In the past, popular culture has been defined in terms of its difference from 'high' culture, yet today, the distinction between high and low culture has become increasing blurred. The same can be said about the blurring of boundaries between 'official' versus 'popular culture' where, in the context of political culture, politicians market themselves or deride the opposition by using populist social networking techniques.

This process was evident in the 2010 UK general election digital poster campaign, in which playful references to popular culture were used to engage voters, and where the lines between the methods of 'official' political communication and those of popular culture were unclear (Dermody and Hanmer-Lloyd, 2011).[3] All the political parties used these posters in their campaigns and the 'Ashes to Ashes' poster campaign exemplifies this form of mediatised populist politics.[4] Following a competition organised by New Labour's advertising company, Saatchi and Saatchi, the winner created the 'Ashes to Ashes' poster, which depicted the Tory leader David Cameron as the television detective, 'Gene Hunt', sitting on his 1980s red Audi, wearing snakeskin boots, with the caption: 'Don't let him take Britain back to the 1980s' (Nikkaha, 2010).[5] However, during the 2010 election campaign, this technique was speedily appropriated by the Conservative party in a move, presented as a playful riposte, when they produced their own digital poster, which used the same image, but with the caption: 'Fire up the Quattro it's time for a change'.[6]

The seemly authentic, 'blokey' wit of this image and its message appropriated the playful, knowing meme-loving culture of the social networking generation, reflecting Castell's vision of the 'network society' (2009) with its horizontal structures of communication. The posters used a style, which in contrast to more traditional modes of political communication, appeared not to talk down *to* voters, but instead, seemed to share the joke *with* them; one which linked David Cameron to 1980s Thatcherite politics as a kind of nostalgic reference point. Political dialogue is presented here as 'banter', and as I discuss in this book, the laddish connotations of that particular campaign reflect the tone of the male dominated UK political scene more generally, where women are marginalised and where femininity continues to be represented mainly in middle class, domestic images of motherhood, as in the UK online network 'Mumsnet',[7] or as the wives of male politicians. The nostalgic aspects of the poster's message connotes a kind of 'back to the future' dimension to political life which not only captures reactionary sexual politics, but also looks back to an era in the 1980s, when in the UK, the entrepreneurial values of neoliberalism were established and reflected though comedy sitcom characters such as 'Del Boy', from the BBC television series *Only Fools and Horses* (1981–2003). Thus, in 2010, the poster not only looked back, but it also anticipated the culture of the present, which has since been reinforced by the material realities of austerity culture and the lived experience of loss and hardship that has occurred as a consequence.

The term 'austerity' has economic, ideological and cultural meanings that resonate within the contemporary political culture and its affective landscape.[8] The representation of emotions such as sadness and loss, occupy a key place in contemporary advertising imagery (Powell, 2011) and as a product of promotional culture, the poster campaign carries with it a desire to look back, as a means of managing the fears about the losses of the present. As I discuss in Chapter 6, the desire to stage a return to the past as a way of managing anxieties in the present is a recurrent theme of contemporary politics, and the current popularity of parties such as UKIP, which is largely premised upon a desire to return to the values of an earlier era, reflects that mood. UKIP does not employ sophisticated communication strategies, but instead has, at least in the period up until the UK 2015 General Election, relied upon the charismatic persona of its leader, Nigel Farage, to get its populist message of anti-immigration across on television, radio and social media. UKIP's reliance on the celebrity of Farage as its leader throughout that period, reflects the promotional turn in politics where the style and personality of politicians is now key to 'selling' the message of a particular political party and its brand.

Popular culture is closely bound up with consumer culture (Storey, 2014) and the consumption of politics is now big business (Lilleker et al., 2006; Powell, 2013). The marketing of politics takes place at a number of levels, and as with Farage, the marketing of politicians as brands provides an obvious example of this process at work. The promotion of political biographies, memoirs and diaries represents an extension of this phenomenon where, as in Tony Blair's (2011) biography, the 'journey' of the politicians is documented, reflecting the emotive narrative turn in political culture more widely. Indeed, as with the memoirs of ex-New Labour politicians Jack Straw (2013) or Alan Johnson (2014), it is the 'moving' and 'revealing' emotional content that is seen as being significant and interesting, rather than any political insights that they might hold.[9] The consumption of politics as entertainment through television shows such as *Have I Got News for You* (1990–, BBC1), or the weekly radio show *The News Quiz* (1977–, BBC Radio 4), or the television series *The Thick of It* (2005–2009, BBC4 and 2009–2012, BBC2), is also widespread and is indicative perhaps, of growing cynicism about political life.[10] Further examples of the consumption of politics as entertainment can be found in the television show and spoof documentary about Prime Minister David Cameron and London Mayor Boris Johnson, *When Boris Met Dave* (2009, Channel 4), and also in films that depict UK prime ministers, such as *Love Actually* (2003) or trade union battles (albeit in films from very different perspectives), including *Made in Dagenham* (2010), *Billy Elliott* (2000) and *Pride* (2014).

Politics now takes place in a consumer culture, where the values of advertising and promotion are brought to the fore (Banet-Weiser, 2012; Powell, 2013; Wernick, 1991). Consumerism is not governed by rational decision-making, but rather, it is shaped by the irrational vicissitudes of desire and identification – as in the development of celebrity politics, where like other forms of consumption, voters' responses are not always governed by rationality, but rather by the processes of fantasy, emotion and identification. This is not to say that voters are manipulated and brainwashed victims of false consciousness, but rather that the engagement with politics is also bound up with the emotional pleasures of what Colin Campbell (1989) calls 'illusory' hedonism.

The links between celebrity culture and politics have been explored at length by researchers in psychosocial and cultural studies (Evans, 2009; Evans and Hesmondhalgh, 2005; Farrell, 2012; Nunn and Biressi, 2010; Turner, 2004). At a time when the boundaries between political parties in Western democratic systems have become increasingly indistinct, the branding of politicians through the politics of 'personality' and celebrity has become significant as a means of marking out and promoting political parties to voters, whose loyalties and political identifications have also become more fluid than previously. Since 2005 there have been numerous world leaders, from Silvio Berlusconi to Sarah Palin and Barack Obama, who in different ways, exemplify the trend of celebrity politics. Using celebrities to enhance the reputation of politicians is an established practice and one can cite numerous examples of this in the 20th century, from J.F. Kennedy's association with Marilyn Monroe to Harold Wilson's courting of The Beatles. In the US, Arnold Schwarzenegger and, before him, Ronald Reagan used their prior film star celebrity status to enhance their performance as candidates standing for and entering political office. Today, in a neat reversal of fortune, UK politicians can perform in different entertainment settings because of their *existing* status as celebrity politicians. Examples of this development include walk-on cameos in television dramas, as in

Boris Johnson's performance as himself in *East Enders* (BBC1, 2010), or comedy sketch shows, such as Tony Blair's comedy performance as himself with comedienne Catherine Tate, as part of Red Nose Day (2007, BBC1), or reality shows, as in the UK Respect Party Member of Parliament, George Galloway's performance on *Celebrity Big Brother* (Channel 4, 2006); or Conservative Member of Parliament, Nadine Dorries's performance on *I'm a Celebrity Get Me Out of Here* (ITV, 2012) and more recently, ex-Conservative Member of Parliament, Edwina Curry (ITV, 2014). Boris Johnson, exemplifies the celebrity turn in politics. His day-to-day duties as mayor are continually turned into photo opportunities and his role as a broadcaster and television personality played a key role in the 2009 London mayoral election campaign (Yates, 2014a).

The UK New Labour government (1997–2010) was particularly adept in using celebrities and exploiting different media platforms to promote their image. It is pertinent to focus on the era of New Labour and its legacy today, where the processes of Public Relations (PR) and 'spin' have emerged as key in the struggle to attract voters. As I discuss, New Labour's emphasis on what I call the 'flirtatious' mechanisms of spin and PR in the 1990s and beyond, provided a model for the revamped UK Conservative Party in the early years of the 21st century. Like Tony Blair, Prime Minister David Cameron came to power by representing and promoting himself as the brand of the party. One aim of this book is to discuss the continuities between the New Labour and the Conservative Party in this regard, and also to explore the meanings of identity as they are constructed in their promotional material and in popular culture more generally.

Clearly, the image management of political leaders is not new, and in the UK context one can cite the example of Labour Prime Minister Harold Wilson, who used his pipe and altered his voice to sound like a man of the people (Pimlot, 1993), or Margaret Thatcher, whose image management has been documented and discussed at length (Nunn, 2002). And yet what is new is the mediatised context of celebrity culture, which provides a backdrop for the discussions that follow in this book.

The concept of 'mediatisation' is used here to denote the influence and dominance of different media in shaping subjectivity in all aspects of social and cultural life (Couldry et al., 2010). Today, this influence is defined increasingly in terms of the role of 'new' digital media and the engagement with political issues is often seen in that context (Livingstone, 2009). For some, the mediatisation or 'packaging' of political life has contributed to the 'dumbing down' of political culture and the quality of public debate (Franklin, 2004). The banality of much political coverage that focuses on seemingly trivial details of political personalities might seem to reinforce this view. Yet the distrust of 'celebrity politics' can also be seen as an extension of mass society critiques, which see popular culture as manipulative and appealing to the lowest form of common denominator.[11] Of course, one needs to maintain a critical scepticism about the processes of popular culture and its consumption, and not fall into the populist trap of only emphasising the opportunities it provides for radical protest and creative modes of symbolic subversion. As I discuss below, the huge media coverage given to the political antics of the celebrity and comedian Russell Brand exemplifies some these tensions.

The critical focus on processes of governmentality and the political costs of neoliberalism as a cultural ideology and economic system also reflect this scepticism (Fisher, 2009; Gilbert, 2013; Gill, 2008). The personalisation of politics involves the foregrounding of emotion as a reassuring signifier of authenticity in an age of uncertainty. In addition, there has for some time been a growing cynicism about the meaning of Western social democratic politics and the effectiveness of the parliamentary system within what some define as the 'post-political' or 'post-ideological' age (Fisher, 2009; Mouffe, 2005), in which the values and practices of neoliberalism have triumphed over all aspects of political debate.[12] Much has been written about neoliberalism as the dominant economic system of late capitalism (Harvey, 2007) with its accompanying managerial techniques and modes of governance (Gilbert, 2013) and also its development as a social, cultural and political hegemonic project (Hall et al., 2013).

The ideology of neoliberalism, which promotes competitive market values of individualism and self-reliance, has been discussed in terms of its emotional costs and its impact upon subjectivity and the unconscious defences and fantasies that are deployed as a consequence, both at individual and cultural levels of experience (Layton, 2010). Here, it is said that the vulnerable aspects of identity and the self are routinely projected onto the 'other' in the guise of the unemployed benefit claimant and so on, who must carry the shame of a system in which an ethos of success and self-promotion is all-pervading. As I discuss in this book, the management of anxiety in this context is now a constant theme of populist news journalism and also of the infamous genre of 'poverty porn', where the lives of 'the poor' are filmed, discussed and objectified, often in a voyeuristic and sensational manner (Jensen, 2014).[13]

Much has been written about neoliberalism and its history (Gilbert, 2013; Hall et al., 2013; Harvey, 2007; Wilson, 2015).[14] At the time of writing it is difficult to refute the dominance of neoliberalism as both an economic system and as the new 'common sense', influencing all areas of life. And yet politics has not gone away, and alongside the need to critique the powerful influence of neoliberalism in shaping political culture it is important to acknowledge the real and symbolic spaces of contestation that may emerge in the present historical conjuncture of neoliberalism, which is characterised by crisis, change and anxiety. Following in the cultural studies tradition of Stuart Hall and others, the methodology used in this book is informed by the ideas of Antonio Gramsci (Gramsci et al., 1971), who foregrounded the relationship between culture and politics and the notion of cultural contestation as an agent of change. Such an approach acknowledges hegemonic struggles of culture, along with the structural limits and potentials of identity as socially and culturally constructed in late modern societies.

Emotionality, history and crisis

At the moment of writing, a number of global economic, social, cultural and political shifts have come together to create what is now often called a 'crisis'. As elsewhere in Europe, when the Conservative-led coalition came to power in 2010, UK Chancellor George Osborne put in place the economic policy of 'austerity', which involved large cuts to welfare and public services as a response to a very large debt that was arguably caused by the financial crises of 2008. This response is a highly contested one, not only in terms of its economic efficacy, but on ethical grounds too, as the cuts target the poor rather than financial elite who set in motion the events that caused the crises in the first place (Harvey, 2007; Venn, 2012). The response to that crisis has often been articulated in intensely emotional terms, whether through the angry disillusionment of popular protest by those who have been referred to as the 'precariat' (Standing, 2011 a & b, 2014) or the angry and heated, if often empty, rhetoric of politicians in the UK, through parties such as UKIP or in the US, through the Tea Party Movement.[15] As Rustin (2010) argues, it is historically interesting to explore the ways in which emotions many be utilised at such moments of crisis, particularly when, as in the case of the UK Conservative–Liberal coalition (2010–2015), a form of government emerges to challenge more traditional forms of governmentality and political structures of authority. The term 'crisis' is not being used here as a concrete signifier of a specific moment, but rather to describe the ongoing processes of history, culture, society and the economy as being in flux and transition, and the different elements of this notion of crisis inform and provide a cultural backdrop for many of the discussions in this book.

As writers in the field of political and cultural studies have documented, the ongoing crisis as alluded to above, has been shaped largely by the financial 'credit crunch' and a loss of faith (for some) or at least, unease in the 'neoliberal project' begun in the UK by Margaret Thatcher and continued by New Labour and then by the Conservative–Liberal coalition (Biressi and Nunn, 2013; Fisher, 2009; Hall et al., 2013). Across Europe there has also been a sense of disillusionment in the political system and its accountability, and in the UK this is linked to the parliamentary expenses scandal, the Iraq war and the ongoing erosion of the welfare state, which in turn is linked to the collapse of the postwar welfare settlement (Hall et al., 2013). The crisis has been articulated in the news media and popular culture, and such coverage has often been intensely emotional, both reflecting and helping to shape what might be termed a 'political structure of feeling', in which loss, sadness, anger and anxiety are recurring themes in the cultural response to current cultural, political and social conjuncture.

Fictional representations of politics in novels and on television have captured the disappointments and anxieties about the political system at different moments in history. The social and political historian Steve Fielding (2014) has developed this theme in his discussion of 'dystopian' television dramas, which he links to a widespread cynicism about parliamentary democracy as a system of political representation. He says that today, there is often a tendency to look back in order to explore anxieties about the present through the lens of dystopian period dramas such as for example, in the depiction of political corruption during the Macmillan era in the *The Hour* (BBC, 2011–2012). Contemporary cynicism and disillusionment about politics can also be found in the ubiquity of satirical comedy dramas such as *The Thick of It* (2005–2012, BBC 4 and BBC2), or panel game shows such as *Have I Got News for You* (1990–, BBC2 and BBC1). The conspiratorial tone of contemporary political spy drama, such as the longing running television spy series *Spooks* (2002–2011), or the film *The Ghost Writer* (2010) or the fascination with spies such Kim Philby (Macintyre, 2014) are suggestive when thinking through the disillusionment with contemporary politics. Texts such as those just mentioned, arguably tap into a cultural tendency towards paranoid anxiety within political culture (Ortega Breton, 2014).[16] In psychoanalytic terms, paranoid feelings are associated with splitting objects into good and bad (Klein, 1946) and are symptomatic of defensive, paranoid schizoid anxieties, which in this context are prompted by cultural change and uncertainty.[17] One can apply these ideas to an apparent widespread preoccupation with conspiracy theories (Aaronovtich, 2010), and a shared concern that as members of the general public, we are somehow being 'played with' by the establishment, like pawns in a game over which we have little say. That is not to say that conspiracies do not exist and that the 'establishment' does not do 'bad things'. Yet the perception of plots and cover-ups connected to different aspects of the establishment, whether for example, that be the church, the banks or the Houses of Parliament, indicates a profound lack of trust in representative democracy and a sense of hopelessness in trying to bring about change.

Economists and cultural studies scholars have used the concept of 'casino capitalism' as a metaphor to explore financial mismanagement of banks and their investors, together with the addictive, short-term financial habits of late capitalism and the deleterious costs of that financial system for the structures of democracy and political accountability (Giroux, 2014; Sin, 2012). The language of the casino and the arbitrariness of being either an economic 'winner' or 'loser' are popular themes in UK political culture when talking about the 'reckless' behaviour of the banks.[18] A fascination with the capricious power of bankers as bad objects and as symbols of masculine hedonism can be found in Hollywood films such as *Wall Street, Money Never Sleeps* (2010) and *The Wolf of Wall Street* (2013), where the themes of masculinity, gambling, excess and addiction are foregrounded.

Despite the inevitable pessimism induced by the seeming impermeability of neoliberalism as a hegemonic cultural and economic system over which we have no control, it is still necessary and important in the context of political culture, to acknowledge the cultural spaces of contestation that are created and appropriated by the public. The latter can be found in direct action and in different forms of political activism, exemplified by the international Occupy movement that protests against social and political injustice and the concentration of wealth in the top 1% of the population (Hall et al., 2013).[19] Throughout 2011, protests against austerity were widespread and in the UK, students were active in challenging the cuts. Since 2014, the rise of European socialism and the success of the Greek Syriza party and in Spain, the Podemos party, illustrate the potential of such active political engagement to challenge the hegemony of austerity as the dominant common sense. As I discuss in Chapter 2, it is against this political backdrop that the social phenomenon, 'hashtag activism' has flourished and in a late modern, media – savvy context, the struggles over signification have become ever more salient. The satirical music and comic videos posted by the public on YouTube, spoofing the performance of political leaders also provide an example of this development.[20]

The UK comedian and celebrity political activist, Russell Brand, highlights the crossover between popular culture and politics and provides a useful case study to explore the tensions and crisis of meaning in contemporary political culture. In the UK, just as politicians such as Boris Johnson, or Nigel Farage use humour to appeal to the electorate and make them laugh, Brand, as a professional comedian, also uses his comic gifts to convey his message of *Revolution* (Brand, 2014) to the general public. As a renowned *Roué*, flirt and wit, Brand is skilled at using social media to promote himself and his populist, playful, anti-establishment communications about the need for 'a change of consciousness', and 'the way we think'. He regularly criticises the mainstream media and deconstructs the press, via his 'Trews' broadcasts on YouTube, where he presents his 'true' version of the news and challenges what he sees as 'the ignorance and lies' of regular media output.[21] Brand is feted by journalists, such as the *Guardian* political columnist Owen Jones, who admires his political stance (*Guardian*, 2014) and Brand was invited to edit a special edition of the current affairs journal the *New Statesman*, where he communicated his message about the need for a 'revolution' (Brand, 2013a). Brand has also appeared on BBC 'flagship' news programme *Newsnight* (BBC2, 2013) and on BBC Question Time (BBC1, 2013 and 2014), where in front of a studio audience, he competed for laughs alongside Boris Johnson and Nigel Farage respectively.

Yet, for some left-of-centre cultural commentators, Brand's foray into politics is a mixed blessing. For example, journalist Nick Cohen (2014) argues that, although Brand usefully deploys his celebrity charm to open up cultural spaces for political contestation and change, he merely flirts with the idea, as he is rather vague about how such change is meant to come about, and despite telling his fans to vote Labour in the final week leading up to the UK General Election in 2015, he had until that moment urged the public not to vote. As Brand (2014: 19) said, 'voting is pointless, democracy a façade' and that all politicians are as bad as each other. Cohen argues that Brand speaks from a position of wealth and economic privilege and comes across as 'smug', manipulative and 'cynical' and fails to recognise the political complexities of addressing material inequality. Despite criticisms about Brand's celebrity flirtation with politics, he has nonetheless wooed some critics over through his grass roots campaigning work, as with the tenants of the New Era Hoxton Estate in East London, whose homes were due to be sold off to US property developers (Withnail, 2014). Interestingly, Boris Johnson had also let it be known that he supported the campaign and was in negotiations with the company to ensure the rents charged would be affordable (Walker, 2014). Johnson is famed for his communication skills and yet it was the charismatic comedian, not the politician, whose face became linked with the success of the campaign and Brand's own relational narrative about his experience of getting to know the tenants on the estate was published on his own blog pages, describing it as contributing to the 'first stage of the revolution'.[22] That blog entry, which is entitled 'New Era for All', pictures Brand standing alongside the campaigning women and children of the estate, reinforcing his alignment with an image of an alternative, feminised politics that challenges the machismo of an older symbolic order.[23]

An important aspect of Brand's 'feminised' public persona is the emphasis that he places on feelings and how this taps into his own history of addiction and therapy.[24] Brand's reference to the emotional dimensions of his own identity as a man in the public eye is, as I discuss below, also symptomatic of a wider affective turn in public life, where as signal of authenticity, the feelings of celebrities and politicians are given greater attention. Yet, in cultural and political terms, the identification with the vulnerability of politicians in this context may evoke distrust on the part of those who wish to distance themselves from the infantile associations of addiction as a condition over which one may have little control. These dilemmas take on additional meaning when applied to questions of masculinity and the gendered dynamics of political leadership, which in the past has often been shaped by a desire for the containing good father. Brand's subversive qualities are arguably linked to his capacity to undermine the hierarchical structures that underpin such identifications, and for young men at least, he seems to align himself more with a fraternal fantasy of the transgressive and playful, naughty brother. In this respect, Brand's popularity with a youthful audience sits well with the horizontal structures of a networked society described by Castells (2012) and with the protest movements that have arisen as part of that development.

Thus, we can see in the example of Brand and also in the 'Ashes to Ashes' poster campaign, popular culture is not external to politics, but rather, is very much part of it, as the struggles over meaning and identity are symbolised, engaged with and experienced on a daily basis. The approach taken in this book thus reflects a growing body of research emphasising the cultural dimensions of politics, focusing critically, yet constructively, on the different aspects of contemporary mediatised political culture (Corner and Pels, 2003; Fielding, 2014; Richards, 2007 and 2015; Van Zoonen, 2005; Washbourne, 2010).

Political culture and the structures of feeling and irrationality

John Street (1997: 3) argues that the relationship between popular culture and politics is, amongst other things, linked by a shared 'intimacy', in which feelings and emotions play a key role. As he goes on to say:

> Popular culture's ability to produce and articulate feeling can become the basis of identity and that identity can be the source of political thought and action. We know who we are through the feelings and responses we have, and who we are shapes our expectation and our preferences.
>
> (Street, 1997: 10)

Following Street, one can argue that the structures of identity, popular culture and politics are closely linked and that the cultural 'glue' or cement which links them are the feelings and emotions that shape identity at any one time. We invest emotionally in political formations and also in the forms of common sense that emerge at different historical periods, and the latter is an idea that draws on Raymond Williams' (1977: 132) notion of a 'structure of feeling' as 'thought as felt and feeling as thought'. Thus, popular culture provides the spaces in which cultural, political and emotional aspects of experience come together, and are continually shaped and symbolised. The symbols and signs that are created in that domain become the focus in the struggle for power, meaning and identity. In this way, the affective structures of popular culture and identity are not external to the political sphere, but are very much part of it. Street does not elaborate on what he means by 'emotion' in this context, and he uses it in a fairly common sense way to discuss the 'passions', which motivate people. By contrast, the psycho-cultural approach used in this book pushes the boundaries of traditional sociological and cultural studies discussions of politics, popular culture and identity, by developing a psychoanalytically inflected approach that takes account of the irrationalities of political identification and the affective processes of culture and the unconscious that underpin those identifications.

The relationship between emotion, politics and identity can be analysed at a number of levels. Firstly, as indicated above, there is the emotional performance of politicians, who often use the display of feelings such as sorrow and tears to convey a sense of their authenticity and connection with the public. These emotional performances often draw on the codes, conventions and techniques of popular culture to connect with the electorate. Secondly, there is the cultural response to these emotions, which often employ the language and style of what has come to be known as 'therapy culture' (Furedi, 2004). The latter refers to the ways in which notions of emotion and therapy have come to play a key role in mediating psychosocial identities across public and private spheres (Furedi, 2004; Richards, 2007; Rose, 1999; Yates, 2011). As I have begun to discuss, political culture provides a key sphere of engagement in this respect. Yet, as explored in Chapter 4, there is a debate about the psychosocial and cultural dynamics of the therapeutic turn and its relationship to the shaping of identities, which, in turn, have implications for our engagement with political culture. The extent to which we can be viewed as passive objects of therapy culture, or as active subjects, will be a recurring theme of this book; and this debate forms an important backdrop for discussions regarding the nature of political culture today.

The play of political culture

As the title of this book suggests, the notion of 'play' can be put to work in order to explore the emotionalisation of contemporary politics, where politicians use a range of playful strategies to woo voters at every turn. On the one hand, 'play' suggests a form of manipulation where members of the public are seduced and positioned as passive 'dupes' of oppressive forces of ideological governance and Machiavellian political processes. Yet, on the other, it connotes a more interactive mode of political communication and engagement, where voters may identify, contest or flirt with political parties and politicians. As 'ideal types', these two modes of play and the roles they play in shaping different modes of political communication and engagement, partly reflect existing debates within political, cultural and media studies. These debates focus on the nature of political representation and the potential of the contemporary mediatised public field for active political participation (Craig, 2004; Thompson, 1995; Washbourne, 2010).

Yet, less has been said about the symbolic, playful spaces that are opened up for 'feeling-ful' modes of identification and fantasy as a consequence of the increasingly fluid boundaries between popular and political culture. This book applies the notion of 'play' and its symbolic potential as a metaphor for the processes of political culture, to explore the shaping of psycho-cultural identities, and the role of emotion within the postmodern mediatised landscape of UK political culture. Whilst object relations psychoanalysis can be applied usefully to the theme of play, omnipotence and the consumption of politics, feminist theories of sexual difference can also be used to examine discourses of mastery and power in political life (Yates, 2010). Today, the seductive context of mediatised political culture is increasingly fuelled by the playful strategies of flirtation. Political marketing strategists play a significant role in shaping the dynamics of political communication, applying a range of promotional techniques to woo the electorate and encourage them to identify with political leaders and their messages (Lillekar et al., 2006). At a wider level, the different dynamics of play are linked to a range of psycho-cultural dilemmas related to fantasies of cultural identity within the postmodern mediatised setting of contemporary politics – concerns that provide a focus for this book. As I discuss, the UK Conservative–Liberal coalition government (2010–2015) also forced its protagonists into a space that was markedly transitional and flirtatious in its attempts to transcend the limits of party-specific identities. The classed, masculine identities of the leaders are also pertinent when discussing the seductive presentation of the coalition and its appeal, symbolising the differences to images of ex-Labour party Leader and Prime Minister Gordon Brown, whose performance rested on his apparent authenticity as a man who refused to flirt and perform for the camera.

I explore these themes and issues by taking an approach that uses psychoanalytic ideas to argue that play can emerge as a metaphor either for interactive processes of communication and creative symbolic expression, or, in a more negative vein, for processes of mastery and political seduction. These negative and positive perspectives on the playful dynamics of contemporary politics are explored throughout the book, taking into account the contradictions of fantasy and feeling, which also shape the processes of political identification and desire. The potential of new spaces that have emerged within what has been defined as the 'mediatised political field' of political culture (Craig, 2004) can be linked to what the psychoanalyst D.W. Winnicott (1971) has defined as the transitional 'cultural field' of the psyche and imagination, where the ongoing engagement with transitional phenomena and fantasy take place. Winnicott provides a paradoxical model of subjectivity that challenges the traditional boundaries between the outer reality and the inner world. He argues that social, cultural and psychological worlds intersect to produce 'potential' or 'transitional' space, where meanings are continually created and where identity and a sense of self are also shaped (Yates and Day Sclater, 2000). Play, in all its different guises, is key to the kind of identity work described by Winnicott and this psycho-cultural model of play and identity will be applied and developed throughout the book in the context of politics and its representation in the public cultural field today.

Thus, as I have begun to discuss, this book examines issues of emotional identification and the cycles of seduction, desire and disappointment that are created by the emotive stylisation and the performative nature of contemporary politics. The performance of politicians involves the 'play' of emotion at a number of levels. The play of personality together with notions of charismatic leadership are linked to the desire for authenticity, truth and fantasies of 'the real thing', which in turn give rise to anxieties about being duped, 'played about' or 'let down'. Such anxieties are also linked to the broader social and cultural context of late modernity, where the fluidities of identity have given rise to anxieties about trust and 'risk' and new dilemmas about the experience of social, cultural and political belonging. The book applies these ideas to selected cases studies, which focus on both the cultural and unconscious dimensions of political life and the shaping of identities, interweaving relevant case study material and political images taken from the UK press and other documents and artefacts within popular culture. The themes of each chapter are outlined below.

In Chapter 2, 'Spinning the Unconscious and the Play of Political Flirtation in Political Culture', I introduce a number of key terms that will be discussed throughout the book. I provide a psycho-cultural analysis of the term 'play' by linking it to the notion of flirtation as a metaphor for the processes of 'spin' and the seductions of political culture. Psychoanalysis provides a useful language to explore the ambiguity of flirtation and the 'real/not real' quality of its interactions, especially within the political arena. Using examples taken from the popular media, the chapter explores examples of male and female politicians over the past ten years, and discusses their identities as flirtatious operators on the UK political scene and elsewhere.

Chapter 3, 'The Dilemmas of Postfeminism and the Fantasies of Political Culture', continues to explore the themes of play and flirtation by focusing on the 'play' of femininity through a discussion of the intersections between political culture, femininity and postfeminism. The latter is a contested term that is often aligned with neoliberalism and its influence upon political culture which can be found from the 1990s onwards. The chapter discusses the fantasies and affective investments that have shaped that relationship over the years since the New Labour government first came to power in 1997. The chapter develops the discussion by focusing on the symbolism of Margaret Thatcher and her enduring appeal for Conservative and right-of-centre women in politics today. The performative strategies that are used to 'play' with the electorate in the political sphere are always a risky process for women, who may evoke fantasies of dangerous femininity. As Jacqueline Rose (1988) argued in relation to Margaret Thatcher, images of women in politics often attract powerful, ambivalent identifications. This chapter revisits that work of Rose and also Heather Nunn (2002), which analysed the fantasies about Thatcher in the 1980s and in the 2000s respectively. I engage with that work within the contemporary context, where the neoliberal values and practices of so-called 'postfeminism' have contributed to revisionist images of Thatcher as a postfeminist icon and I link that discussion to popular conceptions of femininity in real and fictional contexts.

Chapter 4, 'Political Culture and the Desire for Emotional Wellbeing', takes up the book's themes of emotion, politics and identity by discussing the ubiquity of what is often called 'therapy culture' and its relationship to the promotion of 'wellbeing' within political culture. Here, I argue that a particular notion of therapy, which is linked to a desire for 'emotional wellbeing', has also become a signifier for anxieties about subjectivity, loss and cultural change. Tracing some of the key debates about notions of therapy culture within psychosocial and cultural studies, this chapter explores the relationship between therapy culture and political culture by focusing on examples taken from both popular culture and government policy since 1997, when in the UK, New Labour first formed a government. The chapter argues that displays of emotion have become important signifiers of authenticity for politicians and an emphasis on the value of 'emotional wellbeing' can also be found in UK government policy. Yet, more recently, there has been a shift in emphasis away from notions of 'wellbeing' to that of 'emotional resilience'. The latter is now often deployed by government, schools and businesses as a means of encouraging individuals to overcome their vulnerability, in order to adapt to the risks and uncertainties of late modernity.

Chapter 5, 'The Absent Parent in Political Culture', develops the discussion about the cultural politics of emotion and identity by turning to the fantasies that circulate about parenthood in contemporary political culture. Feminist studies of parenthood and austerity culture have tended to focus on relations of governance and motherhood. This chapter develops that work to include the place of fatherhood and its representation in political culture, which is promoted through images of male politicians and their families, thereby shoring up the identity of men and the forces of hegemonic masculinity. The chapter discusses the ways in which representations of 'new' fathers may be achieved at the cost of allowing new spaces for femininity and motherhood to emerge within the psycho-cultural imagination. I develop these themes by focusing on the trope of the 'absent parent', which occurs in the speeches, press reports and policy documents about parenthood today. As I discuss, the notion of the absent parent functions as a symbol of the lost, idealised object which is bound up with anxieties and defences related to patriarchal fantasies of gender and sexual difference. By focusing on the symbol of the absent, lost parent, and the *presence* of this fantasy within austerity culture, the chapter discusses the social and psycho-cultural dynamics of the relationship between constructions of parenthood and the play of political culture today.

The politics of nostalgia and the psycho-cultural desire to look back is also a theme of Chapter 5, 'Moving Forward to The Past: Fantasies of Nation within UK Political Culture', where the relationships between fantasies of nation as a lost object, and the processes of political culture are explored. Politics now takes place in a globalised, mediatised context and yet the construction of an imagined, national identity is highly seductive. The discourse of nation has played an increasingly significant role in popular political discourse in the UK, and the 2014 Scottish Referendum campaign and the ongoing debates about devolutionary powers of the Scottish Parliament provide examples of this process. This chapter explores shifts in the promotional discourses of nation, as over the past few years, sections of the UK electorate became disenchanted with the 'modernising' project of New Labour and instead embraced a vision of the past as promoted by UKIP. I argue that a key moment in this shift was arguably Joanna Lumley's 2008–2009 highly publicised campaign for the Gurkhas' right to settle in the UK. Alongside progressive discourses of social justice and nation, this campaign also signalled a change in mood towards what the late *Guardian* journalist Hugo Young once defined as 'an ideal of back-ness'. As I discuss, this nostalgia was reflected elsewhere through the right-of-centre populism of Farage and UKIP.

Chapter 7, 'Reflections on the Psycho-Cultural Dynamics of Political Culture', concludes by revisiting the merits of taking a psycho-cultural approach in the light of the themes explored in previous chapters.

It returns to the broader theoretical questions of the book, regarding the relationships between fantasy, identity and the cultural processes that shape political culture today. Is it the case that new transitional spaces have emerged for political dialogue, which can facilitate the psycho-cultural complexities of identity? Or have such spaces emerged only to be co-opted by the forces of consumption, narcissism and the least creative aspects of celebrity culture, thereby denying complexity and reinforcing discourses of mastery? At the time of writing, the cultural processes aligned with both those positions of creativity and mastery can be seen to be at work within British political culture. The chapter concludes by relating these themes of politics, play and the fantasies of sexual difference to the broader thesis of the book and the psycho-cultural processes at play within the dynamics of contemporary political culture.

2
Spinning the Unconscious
and the Play of Flirtation
in Political Culture

Introduction

This chapter deploys a psycho-cultural analysis of 'play' to examine the flirtatious cultures of spin and political communication by focusing on UK political culture since 1997.[1] The study of flirtation as a mode of communication, which operates as a cycle of seduction and desire, is highly suggestive in the contemporary context of late modern democratic party politics where, as in what was known as the UK 'New Labour Project', and then subsequently in the UK Conservative-led coalition government, political communication played a key role in 'wooing' voters at every turn (Chadwick and Heffernan, 2003). Given the current preoccupation with political 'spin' and public relations in the UK and elsewhere, images of flirtatious politicians alongside flirtatious mechanisms of communication have become commonplace as a means to communicate with the public in different mediatised contexts, including print and digital media.

Psychoanalysis provides a useful language to explore the power dynamics of flirtation and the tantalising, 'real not real' quality of its interactions, especially within the political arena. As psychoanalyst Adam Philips (1994) argues, flirtation is associated with coquetry, dalliance and play; it connotes a lack of seriousness or intention, as in the refusal to commit romantically, or as Georg Simmel (1909) reminds us, the desire to move between different opinions and ideas. One can apply these ideas to the sphere of political communication, where flirtation also involves the *play* of emotion and may be used as a strategy to manage difficult emotions evoked by desire for the other, and the pleasures aroused by it may also create an intense emotional response (Yates, 2009). Flirtation may also induce feelings of confusion and betrayal and there are clear analogies here with the public anger expressed towards politicians in Europe, such as the French 'Bling Bling President' Nicolas Sarkozy, who, following the financial crash in 2008, was seen to have 'over-promised and under-delivered' (Beaumont, 2012). In the UK, this sense of anger and betrayal is reflected in the electorate's 'fury' about the perceived duplicity of MPs (Clark and Mason, 2013).

As I discuss, the dynamics of political flirtation are also linked to fantasies of masculinity and sexual difference, and that dynamic is explored with reference to the wider hegemonic setting of patriarchal culture and the struggles that take place in that context. Flirtation has a number of gendered connotations – often associated with femininity, and historically, flirtatious women have exercised a power of sorts (Kaye, 2002; Yates, 2009). The term 'flirt' can be traced back to the French term *coquette*, and since the 18th century the nouns 'coquette' and 'flirt' have tended to be associated in Britain with French aristocratic women (Kaye, 2002: 21). The feminine associations of the term 'flirt' also have 19th-century Darwinian roots, linked to the notion of women as 'choosers', who must do all they can to attract a mate. As a consequence, flirtatious men have often been pathologised and feminised as effeminate and hysterical (Kaye, 2002: 27). Yet, when it comes to the performance and practice of flirtation on the political scene, men and women operate differently and have a different 'pact' with the electorate (Evans, 2009). Women need to be wary of using flirtatious behaviour in a way that projects weakness or reinforces stereotypes. Given these differences, the theme of flirtation can be used to explore the tensions of sexual difference within political culture and the undermining of hegemonic masculinity within contemporary political life.

The notion that the West is witnessing a 'crisis' of masculinity has received widespread attention by writers in the field of gender studies (Bainbridge and Yates, 2005). Some suggest that the undermining of hegemonic masculinity has created the potential for modes of masculinity that are less narcissistic and sit more easily with the complexities of change and relations of difference (Yates, 2007a). The idea of flirtation works well as a descriptive metaphor for the insecurities of contemporary masculinities, and in a feminist move, can be put to work to explore its potential as a signifier of plurality and a refusal to accept the hegemonic certainties of patriarchal masculinity and the impulse for mastery.

Rosa Braidotti's (2002) feminist analysis of sexual difference is pertinent here, as she evokes the language of flirtation when she argues for the importance of living with complexity and uncertainty in order to challenge the marginalisation of 'the feminine' within the rigid symbolic systems of Western patriarchal culture. Developing Braidotti's ideas, one can argue that flirtation opens up the possibility for something new, challenging the idea of sameness implied by the fidelity to the father and the hierarchical patriarchal order. On the one hand, flirtation, with all its connotations of playfulness, evokes, perhaps in its fluidity, the feminist potential of contemporary masculinities in its refusal of jealous patriarchal authority. Yet on the other hand, flirtation may also work in a defensive, retrograde way as a metaphor for the emptiness of masculinity as a defensive formation, mediated by narcissistic insecurities and an inability to cope with loss. Interrogating the image of the male flirt is pertinent when applied to representations of male politicians in the popular media, where the lightweight, feminised connotations of the term 'flirt' may sit uneasily with the electorate's desire for 'authentic' masculinity in the guise of paternal authority (Samuels, 2001). The different fantasies of flirtatious masculinity, which in various ways have coalesced around images of male politicians such as Tony Blair, Gordon Brown, Francois Hollande, Vladimir Putin or Barack Obama, represent a tension between a potential desire for what might be called defensive, 'retrosexual' fantasies of flirtatious masculinity on the one hand, and the wish for more progressive, playful and creative modes of masculinity on the other. The latter can be defined as 'metrosexual', and signifies perhaps, the potential for a 'feminised' mode of counter-hegemonic masculinity which, in its fluid and flirtatious ambiguity, refuses the certainties of mastery and fidelity to the idealised symbolic father.[2]

Having outlined the terms of the debate regarding the flirtatious turn in political culture, the chapter now turns to a discussion of the social and cultural context of flirtation and its links to the growth of 'spin' and public relations within political culture. It then turns to questions of fantasy and the unconscious by discussing psychoanalytic understandings of flirtation, play and sexual difference. Using examples taken from the media, the chapter then explores the flirtatious culture of spin and political communication and applies these ideas to examples in political culture in the UK since 1979. The aim here is to see how the emotional dynamics of flirtatious culture have in certain respects moved away from the potential of play as transformation, to one which is characterised by a defensive political structure of feeling and a reactionary relationship to change and the possibilities of transformation.

Setting the scene: Cultures of flirtation and political spin

The notion of a flirtatious culture is highly evocative in the late modern age, as it evokes well the fluid and often superficial, transitory nature of experience in the late 20th and early 21st centuries (Bauman, 2007; Elliott and Urry, 2010). Some researchers in psychosocial studies link what they perceive to be an inability to sustain emotional commitment and to cope with the disappointments of attachment and loss, with the prevailing emphasis on market values and consumer culture, together with the breakdown of traditional social structures such as the family (Craib, 1995; Lasch, 1991). Today, it is generally agreed that the language of emotion and therapy is all-pervading (Richards, 2007; Rose, 1999; Yates, 2011). Yet, despite the ubiquity of therapeutic discourse, some argue that both men and women seem to have lost the ability to actually feel in a meaningful way, or to live with the more difficult feelings, such as jealousy, that may cause shame and disappointment (Craib, 1995; Lasch, 1991).

These psychosocial and cultural developments can be viewed in the broader, historical context of the last hundred years and the emergence of what the sociologist Georg Simmel called a new flirtatious character type 'who does not take anything seriously' (Simmel, 1909: 147). Simmel linked this development to the changing social structures of modernity and the metropolitan life of the cities, where new opportunities for sociability and interaction in the form of brief, flirtatious encounters emerged. This emerging flirtatious sensibility evokes Baudelaire's (1965) description of the contingency of modernity and city life and also Benjamin's (1999) discussion of the *flâneur*, whose voyeuristic gaze allows him to live his life one step removed from the stresses of emotional engagement in a transitory context, where the culture of contingency and the flirtatious attitude 'what if?' is developed, perhaps, as a defence against the losses and insecurities of modern life (Kaye, 2002: 9). In the late 20th century, the cultural critic Lasch (1979) argued that in the US, late capitalist society had given rise to a narcissistic personality type, which is unable to experience emotions in a way that feels authentic. Lasch's work is still widely cited and his arguments are relevant for the contemporary age (see Day Sclater et al., 2009). Lasch argued that the latter has given rise to a narcissistic personality type that is unable to experience emotions in a way that feels authentic. The implication appears to be that we are all flirts now, darting from sensation to sensation, addicted to the image and the narcissistic pleasures of short-lived encounters. This image of the contemporary flirtatious sensibility is echoed by those who emphasise, if in less pessimistic tones, the mercurial quality of contemporary interaction and postmodern experience (Elliott and Urry, 2010). This line of thought implies that flirting has become a way of life and the practices of social networking often reflect this development (Braidotti, 2002; Castells, 2000; Lievrouw and Livingstone, 2006). The flirtatious pleasures of social networking also tap into developments within political communication and the promotion of politicians via different media platforms on the Internet.

The technologies of new media also create opportunities for collective activism and political protest and the emergence of 'digital democracy'. The radical potentials of this development, as exemplified through the use of social media in the early days of the Arab Spring in 2011 (Howard and Hussain, 2013) or the Wall Street Occupy movement (Castells, 2012), have also shifted and changed and have partly been undermined by governments that, as publicised through the Edward Snowden case, have deployed surveillance techniques to monitor and curtail the freedom of expression in those contexts. Yet as Howard and Hussain (2013) argue, the interest now taken by authoritarian regimes in Twitter and Facebook as technologies of political communication and protest, indicates the potential power of social networking to enable new forms of 'digital democracy' to emerge that can both tantalise and challenge the hegemony of state politics and their communication systems. In the UK, social media continues to be used in the service of a popular and often playful form of social activism, and the emergence of fourth-wave feminism, with its online campaigns, provides an example of this process in action (see Schuster, 2013).[3] Clearly, one cannot generalise, and this development needs to be explored in the different contexts of social activism. Yet the short term, and seeming flirtatious immediacy of so-called 'hashtag activism' has been critiqued (Carr, 2012) and the language and culture of digital campaigning is now often co-opted by advertising companies and the forces of promotional culture (Little, 2013). The 'leaderless', fragmented nature of such groups and their ability to actually affect change has also been critiqued (Little, 2013: 34). Yet as I discuss in Chapter 5, the horizontal structures of power in this context challenge a traditional, patriarchal model of leadership as underpinned by the fantasy of the strong father, and so perhaps it holds out the potential for a more feminised, flirtatious structure of communication.

Simmel applies the theme of flirtation as a mode of communication to politics and the practice of identifying with different 'political positions' (1909: 151). It is often the case that within the contemporary context of party politics and public relations (PR), both politicians and voters flirt with different political positions. Political candidates use their campaigns to flirt with 'floating voters' who, with their own flirtatious lack of commitment, resemble the Benjaminian figure of the *flâneur*, window shopping for political promises and consuming the spectacle of the political marketplace (Benjamin, 1992). Paradoxically, the flirtatious game between politicians and voters may have contributed to a loss of respect for politicians whose political pragmatism connotes a lack of seriousness and intention, producing an even greater sense of mistrust and uncertainty in relation to party political narratives (Classen, 2007). Floating voters provide the main target for such campaigns (Mattinson and Tyndal, 2013; Prior, 2007). PR teams direct their efforts towards wooing these groups of undecided voters who, given the loss of distinct ideological differences between parties in countries such as the UK, now have a greater influence on election outcomes (Corner and Pels, 2003).

The ways in which the public responds to the flirtation of politicians are linked to processes of 'spin' and PR, which have now become intrinsic to the promotion of party politics. The latter refers to the techniques of persuasion used by political parties and their press officers to lead the news agenda and present their policies and politicians in the best possible light (Barnett and Garber, 2001). This process of communication includes both the medium and the message. Whereas the 'message' may be overtly flirtatious in its attempts to 'woo' voters, the 'medium' also works flirtatiously as a process in the mediatised application of persuasive codes of communication and as discussed in Chapter 1, the fluid dynamics of social media are highly suggestive in this respect. Depending on where the form of political communication falls on the 'defensive' versus 'creative' spectrum of flirtation, the medium in this context has the potential to open up or close down spaces for meaningful engagement (Yates, 2009).

The flirtatious mechanisms of promotional culture

Andrew Wernick's (1991) ideas about the processes of 'promotional culture' can help us to understand the flirtatious mechanisms of spin and PR in the postmodern context. Wernick equates 'promotion' with 'advertising and its practices taken in the widest and most generic sense' and, like flirtation, he says that promotion is now a 'verb' and a 'rhetorical form diffused throughout our culture' (vii). In this way, 'promotion has come to shape not only culture's symbolic and ideological contents, but also its ethos, texture and constitution as a whole' (Wernick, 1991: vii). For Wernick, then, the 'ethos' of promotion now mediates all forms of personal and public communication and politics should also be seen in this context (132). In the US and in the UK, politicians use public relations teams – including 'special advisors' who communicate messages to the media and also directly to the public through various media platforms including the Internet. Examples of the latter range in scale and context – from Obama's 2008 and 2012 US presidential campaigns to the seeming intimacy of UK Conservative party leader David Cameron's 'Web Cameron' which began back in 2006. As Leader of the Opposition, he could be found, as in a Richard Curtis romantic comedy scene, throwing snowballs and joking with television presenter Carol Voderman,[4] or talking to voters while washing up at his kitchen sink.[5]

The close relationship between public relations and politics can be traced back to Sigmund Freud's nephew Edward Bernays, whose analysis of the relationship between propaganda and desire played a key role in cementing the links between consumerism, media and citizenship in Western democracies (Miller, 2005; Sanders, 2009). Bernays' distrust of mass society was clearly articulated in his desire to shape public opinion and 'regiment the mind' of the masses (Bernays, 1928). Following the success of marketing the merits of Western democracy and Allied propaganda drives of the First World War, Bernays developed those methods of propaganda in commercial advertising campaigns for companies such as General Motors and is credited with selling the pleasures of smoking cigarettes to American women through his campaigns for Chesterfield cigarettes (Sanders, 2009). As Ewen says, 'by the end of the Second World War, the systematic stylization of politicians, policies and political ideas had become commonplace' (1988: 266). In his 1947 essay, 'The Engineering of Consent', Bernays argued for the significance of radio and television in shaping hearts and minds and providing 'open doors to the public mind' (Ewen, 1988: 267).

The role of the media and public relations in shaping US political campaigns has been well documented (Cohen 2001; Hart, 1999; Wahl-Jorgensen, 2000; Yates, 2014a) and the personality-driven, PR-oriented, 'presidential' style of US politics has also influenced the practice and presentation of politics in the UK. A key moment in the history of the personalisation of politics was in 1978, when the Conservative Party opened their first full-time account with advertisers Saatchi and Saatchi, who, against the background of strikes and the 'Winter of Discontent', are credited with playing a key role in bringing the Conservatives to power in 1979, with their election poster 'Labour Isn't Working' (Davis, 2002: 19).[6] As I discuss in Chapter 3, it is reported that Saatchi and Saatchi worked closely with Thatcher to 'soften' her image for public consumption, a process that has since been re-represented in the film *The Iron Lady* (2011) as a necessary part in a revised feminist narrative of her transformation to power. It is perhaps significant that Thatcher's death in 2013 was announced by Tim Bell, a senior figure in Saatchi and Saatchi who was also said to be a close friend of Thatcher (Stone, 2013). Thatcher's reliance on the modern forces of political communication and PR was reinforced by her close relationship to her Chief Press Secretary, Bernard Ingham, whose tough style of setting the news agenda and dealing with journalists and Cabinet rebels anticipated the macho and uncompromising methods of Alistair Campbell, who worked for Tony Blair in the New Labour government (Davis, 2002).[7] Thus, this moment in the history of Thatcher's political ascendency, which was so closely bound up with the establishment of neoliberalism as both an economic system and as a new form of common sense, went hand in hand with the rise of promotional culture and the rise of PR politics in particular.

Stuart Hall (2011) has documented this moment or 'conjuncture' in British political history, when a number of social, political and economic events combined to create a crisis of faith in the Keynesian principles of the social democratic settlement that had been in place since after the Second World War.[8] The different elements of this conjuncture included high inflation, a 1976 crisis in sterling and, as a consequence, the need to borrow from the IMF, which at the time was widely perceived as a national and political humiliation (Hennessy, 2001). Throughout 1978–1979, the government imposed cuts and there was widespread industrial action as Britain was derided as the so-called 'the sick man of Europe' (*The Economist*, 2005; Sandbrook, 2012). As Hall (2011) argues, the forces of neoliberalism took advantage of the social and economic crisis of the late 1970s and a new common sense emerged, which supported the monetarist policies of the free market. The values of this new common sense promoted an ideology of individualism, together with the virtues of economic self-reliance and entrepreneurial activity and freedom from state interference (Harvey, 2007). The role of the state was to provide a good-enough environment for these activities to flourish, albeit with some help from the world of promotional culture. The neoliberal push towards the privatisation of publicly owned companies thus involved

[handwritten marginalia:] or at the same time nationalism

[handwritten note at bottom:] Why statism different from nationalism?

the use of advertising campaigns to sell the idea that this new turn in capitalist democracy was a good thing. Notions of citizenship and freedom were equated with consumerism and the opportunity to make a quick profit – as in the 1986 'Tell Sid' campaign, which used a populist, television promotional campaign to sell off British Gas shares 'at affordable prices'.[9]

Against a backdrop of social, cultural and economic change, the political structure of feeling in 1979 was one that was also fuelled by emotive political rhetoric that articulated a sense of fear, shame and the melancholy of a lost patriotism, linked perhaps, as Paul Gilroy (2004) has argued in another context, to the difficulties of mourning the end of empire. The message of the 'Labour Isn't Working' poster campaign seemed to articulate national anxieties about the loss of Britain's place in the world, as it pictures a long line of faceless unemployed people waiting in a dole queue.[10] These same fantasies have been galvanised in the present moment of austerity politics, where the language of national pride has been aligned once more with notions of economic prosperity and the virtue of work and 'hard-working families' in particular (Wheeler, 2005).

In 1978, the promotional turn in British politics was widely criticised as 'frivolous' by both Labour and Conservative politicians and even ridiculed by left-leaning papers such as the *Guardian*, which stressed the irony of hiring a state-of-the-art advertising company to promote a backward-looking Conservative party (BBC Home, 1978). Yet the promotional turn in British politics was set and in 1987, the Labour Party Opposition Leader Neal Kinnock launched a party political broadcast that has since been referred to as 'Kinnock the Movie'.[11] The broadcast was commissioned by Kinnock's director of communications, Peter Mandelson, and it was shot as a short US-style film by the film director Hugh Hudson, who made *Chariots of Fire* (1981), with Kinnock walking with his wife, Glenys, across the cliffs in Wales. The aim was to counter the associations of Labour with political extremism by emphasising Kinnock's personal qualities as a decent, family man with strong, high-minded principles. Music, combined with panoramic shots of Wales, was used to signify Kinnock's role as a man of destiny (Foley, 2000: 179). Although Kinnock's personal poll ratings improved, Labour still lost the 1987 election (Mandelson, 2010). Nevertheless, the film emphasising the personal 'journey' of the leader has been seen as very influential in the personalisation of subsequent political campaigning, as in John Major's (2002) election broadcast film, 'Major, the Journey' or Tony Blair's apparently 'unscripted' confession at a 1996 Labour Party conference about how his father's illness had 'traumatised' him as a child (Foley, 2000: 179).

The promotion of the New Labour brand

As I have begun to argue, the influence of US presidential campaigning practices (Foley, 2000) and the different elements associated with performative politics as developed through the modern practices of PR and promotional culture have contributed to the flirtatious turn in political life in the UK and elsewhere. These elements include a preoccupation with celebrity, personality and images of authenticity. As Richard Sennett (1976) anticipated in the 1970s, the growth of personality-orientated politics provides the context for what he called 'secular charisma', where the residual envy or *resentiment* of voters in relation to powerful politicians in social democratic societies is warded off by focusing on the personality and image of politicians rather than substantial political issues and policies.[12] As numerous cultural commentators have documented, when Tony Blair came to power in 1997 as Prime Minster, he was particularly skilled at courting voters and warding off their latent aggression (Foley, 2000; Rentoul, 2001). Potential envy aroused by the power of his presidential style was offset by his capacity to exude a likeable authentic persona, where, in flirting to camera, he became the face and personality of the New Labour 'brand' (Foley, 2000).

The themes of consumerism, charisma and personality all converge around the history of the New Labour Project, where news management played a key role in acquiring and exercising power (Chadwick and Heffernan, 2003). Communications Director Peter Mandelson and Press Officer Alastair Campbell were important players in managing the image of New Labour, and Campbell was initially liked by journalists who were somewhat seduced by his 'brutal charm' (Rentoul, 2001: 262). Indeed, it is reported that Campbell's relationship with the press was extremely flirtatious in his manner of tantalising journalists by having 'favourites' and by only giving stories to those newspapers who played 'the game' and reported what Labour wanted (Rentoul, 2001). Thus, flirtation operated at a number of levels in the promotion of New Labour, including the performance, the message and the flirtatious mechanisms of mediatised political culture.

The close, flirtatious relationship between the UK press and New Labour and Conservative party politicians was a recurring theme of the Leveson Enquiry.[13] The latter was set up by David Cameron in 2011 in order to investigate the ethics of the relationship between the press and the police, politicians and members of the public. The enquiry focused on the press's role in the 'phone hacking scandal' in which tabloid journalists were alleged to have listened to the voicemails of politicians, celebrities and members of the public for stories deemed by them to be newsworthy. The enquiry was filmed and its events relayed daily on radio, television and social media. The Leveson enquiry became the focus of huge media attention as the public tuned in to learn of the private details of prominent and lesser-known figures as revealed through the testimonies of those witnesses who were called to speak about the events that took place. The practice of hacking and the unscrupulous behaviour of some journalists caused humiliation and unhappiness for those whose private voicemails were hacked.[14] Yet for audiences watching on television and following the events on Twitter, the spectacle of the enquiry also worked as a form of entertainment, creating a form of voyeuristic fascination for the audiences who watched the events unfold from day to day.[15] The coverage often showed the intimate and often personal flirtatious networks and relationships that exist between politicians and journalists. For example, the press reported with great merriment the flirtatious rapport between the Counsel, Robert Jay and Alistair Campbell, with the former almost winking at him as he reminded him that in his 2010 memoir, *A Journey*, Tony Blair referred to Campbell's 'great clunking Balls' (Addley, 2012). The homoerotic connotations of the exchange between Jay and Campbell were echoed in the 'chummy' nature of the relationship between the then Culture Minister Jeremy Hunt's special advisor and his French counterpart from *News Corporation International* in the lead-up to its 'controversial £8bn takeover bid for BskyB' (O'Carroll, 2012). The flirtatious texts between *News of the World* editor Rebekah Brooks and Prime Minster David Cameron were also widely commented on, and Brooks' status as a kind of *femme fatale* with her 'flaming locks' reinforced old stereotypes and distracted, perhaps, from the serious nature of the power of the Murdoch press to influence government policy (see for example, Daily Mail Reporter, 2012).

The flirtatious and often erotic subtext surrounding the relationship between the press and politicians in this instance have a wider currency, and can be found in the highly compelling political television drama, *The House of Cards* (Netflix, 2013–). This programme was first made in the UK (1990, BBC1) and was set in the Houses of Parliament. The contemporary version was rewritten as a US White House political thriller, and focuses on the ruthless ambitions of a Machiavellian politician who has an affair with a young female journalist, thereby sexualising a number of contemporary concerns about the loss of faith in Western democracy as a political system and the integrity of journalists who are meant to hold it and its politicians to account. Against the slippery, flirtatious backdrop of a mediatised political culture, such dramas also illustrate the ways in which, as Phillips (1994: xiii) argues, flirtation eroticises uncertainty and contingency, 'making ambivalence into a game'. To understand the emotional power of such dramas, which, as we have seen with Leveson, seem to reflect the murky and tangled political romance of so-called 'real life', I now turn to psychoanalytic understandings of play and flirtation.

Flirtation and the play of the unconscious

Psychoanalysis provides a useful language to explore the seduction of flirtation and the fantasies that accompany the 'real not real' quality of its interactions, especially within the political arena. Yet in the past, classical psychoanalytic discourse has often viewed flirtation in a negative light. For instance, Freud (1915) links flirtation to regressive love and an inability to cope with mourning and separation. As Phillips (1994) argues, flirtation has a childish, playful quality to it, which has its roots in early Oedipal flirtations, where the imaginary possibilities for love are not yet closed down by the strictures of Oedipal law and the customs of monogamy. There is no place for flirtation in the classical Oedipal narrative of 'healthy development', where mature love is linked to mourning and accepting the loss of the mother and the femininity she represents.[16] The cultural distrust of flirtation as a mode of relating is reflected in psychoanalytic discourse where flirtation becomes a signifier of lightweight, superficial human relations and aligned with the image of the coquette as the seductive, if shallow, *feminine* other. In 1915, such misgivings are also inflected with national prejudice as Freud uses this negative image of flirtation as regressive, to signify his distrust of America and its difference from Europe and the seriousness of 'continental' romantic relations:

> It becomes as shallow and empty as, let us say, an American flirtation, in which it is understood from the first that nothing is to happen, as contrasted with a continental love affair in which both partners must constantly bear its serious consequences in mind.
>
> (Freud, 1915: 79)

Since Freud, psychoanalytic thinkers, such as Adam Phillips (1994), have debated the creative potential of flirtation and its malignant flip side.

In his 1994 study *On Flirtation*, Phillips provides a positive reading of flirtation and its ontological and creative potential as a form of playful object relations. Phillips applies the ideas of psychoanalyst D.W. Winnicott (1971) to flirtation, likening it to the interactive processes associated with 'transitional phenomena' and the 'transitional spaces' that shape subjectivity and which first emerge between mother and infant for play. Whilst acknowledging the sadistic pleasures which may underpin the flirtatious deferral and denial of commitment, Phillips defends flirtation on the grounds that:

> From a pragmatic point of view one could say that a space is being created in which aims or ends can be worked out; the assumed wish for the more or less obvious sexual combinations, or commitments, may be a way of pre-empting the elaboration of, making time for, less familiar possibilities. Flirtation, if it can be sustained, is a way of cultivating wishes, of playing for time. Deferral can make room.
>
> (1994: xix)

For Phillips, then, the flirtatious refusal of commitment connotes a radical sensibility, evoking (albeit drawing from a different philosophical tradition) poststructural conceptions of 'becoming', where certainty is refused and spaces are continually re-created in order to disrupt the old hierarchies and relations of difference, between self and other (Bainbridge, 2008; Braidotti, 2002). This disruptive process has important implications for relations of sexual difference in the field of popular political communication. However, before turning to the gendered implications of play and flirtation, it is necessary to take into account those views which see flirtation in a more negative light.

Messler Davies (1998) argues that the ambiguous, circular nature of flirtation may be used as a defence mechanism against the losses and disappointments of object relations and 'mature' object love. This view of flirtation as a regressive, defensive strategy used to ward off loss, can also be linked to Andre Green's (2005) critique of Winnicott's (1971) theory of play which, as we have seen, is key to Phillips' reading of flirtation. Green takes issue with what he sees as Winnicott's 'idealised' reading of play as being rooted solely in a 'benign' vision of the first mother/baby relationship. Instead he argues that play includes a sexual aspect to it that can be 'cruel' and 'narcissistic' and may be linked to destructive, sexual drives:

> I think the activity of play can sometimes become distorted, corrupted and perverted in society as well as in individuals. (11)

In particular, Green cites the 'distorted' forms of play that may take place in the clinical setting between the analyst and analysand:[17]

> Here, play requires the partner's submission and omnipotence based on the interplay of colluding narcissisms on the real desire to harm, debase and destroy the other. (12)

As Green says, destructive forms of play are 'not based on interchange, but on the will to dominate'. Green's discussion of 'perverted' play paints a very different picture to Winnicott, who links play to psychic health, a capacity for transformation and the development of 'trust' in the context of early object and then later group relations. By contrast, Green develops the ideas of Freud to explore the role of fantasy in play and its potential for the transformation of internal and external worlds. In particular, Green cites Freud's 1920 discussion of the 'Fort/Da' game in *Beyond the Pleasure Principle* to describe how play may be used in fantasy to obtain a sense of mastery in order to ward off loss. In that paper, Freud describes how his grandson, Ernst, used a cotton reel, which he repeatedly threw out of his cot, as a means of managing his mother's absence. This description of play is highly suggestive when applied to flirtation in both its benign and more manipulative guises as a form of mastery over the object. For example, as regards the latter, flirtation often involves the play of emotion, creating a powerful emotional response in the other, which may include desire, compliance or frustration. Green argues that to be caught up in someone else's play may mean that as an object of fantasy, the subject is used in a game where s/he is positioned as a substitute for the lost object (16). Green says that loss and substitution are always 'coupled' in the process of play; yet when the experience of loss is too great, the quality of play alters and becomes linked to the compulsion to repeat. Instead of using objects in a creative and transformative way, they merely become substitutes of 'reality' (a reality which is never objectively perceived), where wounded narcissism and loss are constantly denied.

Following on from Green then, we can begin to think about two forms of play, which can be applied to different models of flirtation on the political scene and which can be defined as either the 'creative' or the 'defensive'. The latter has a mindless, repetitive quality to it and can be used to ward off fears of mortality and in some contexts, the real or imagined traumas of the self and society. Defensive modes of flirtation invoke Luce Irigaray's (1993) feminist reading of the Fort/Da game as a way of using play to mask the potential losses of masculinity and also anxieties about femininity and sexual difference. In her discussion of Freud's 1920 paper, Irigaray discusses the relationship between play and the desire for mastery, relating it to Ernst's desire for unity with his mother, which she argues is a universal desire. Irigaray suggests that this longing for unity can be traced back to the first separation at birth, and its poignancy continues to resonate where femininity is repudiated culturally and fails to find symbolisation in the public sphere, unless as the other of male desire. This reading, which links play to the pleasures of mastery and the refusal of femininity and the other, negates the possibility of play and flirtation as a potentially radical intermediary space as offered in Phillips' account.

The distrust of male flirtation as a feminised activity is a recurring theme in psychoanalytic discourse. Freud (1914) reinforced the relationship between femininity and flirtation when he discussed women's narcissistic wish to 'attract' men, and the same distrust can also be seen by those who see a close relationship between flirtation and hidden primary sadistic aggression. For example, Ernest Jones (1929) links male flirtation to the narrative of *Don Juan* and his image as the cruel seducer. Jones argues that flirtatious behaviour works as a charming 'masquerade' to mask a more aggressive and (jealous) desire to defend a fragile narcissistic ego underneath.

For Jones, flirtatious men are emotionally immature and unconsciously remain overly attached to their mothers. This same distrust of male flirtation can be found in contemporary discussions where those such as Shengold (1982) echo the concerns of Jones. Messler Davies (1998: 808) also likens flirtation to a 'malignant form of seductiveness' in which the flirtatious subject defends an undeveloped ego by projecting unwanted feelings into the other. Thus, in contrast to Phillips, these negative readings of flirtation as a form of play imply that flirtation is used at the expense of the other to shore up a sense of self in the flirtatious subject and that this defensive strategy has wider implications for an understanding of the ontological possibilities of subjectivity as a psycho-cultural formation at different historical moments. As I now go on to discuss, these flirtatious strategies also have implications for relations of masculinity and sexual difference in political culture.

Flirtation and sexual difference in political culture

Van Zoonen (2006) argues that the language 'associated with masculinity' has tended to dominate politics, and that the stylised images and performance of male politicians flirting to camera have played a key role in selling messages to voters. For instance, here, one can cite the rugged masculinity of US President Theodore Roosevelt (1901–1909), the 'everyman' appeal of Richard Nixon (1969–1964), the 'folksy charm' of Ronald Reagan (1981–1989) or the warmth and openness of Bill Clinton (1993–2001) and, more recently, the cool, containing authority of Barack Obama, all of whom can be seen as examples of effective male political performers in action.[18]

As I discuss further in Chapter 4, it is often said that we live in a 'therapeutic culture' (Richards, 2007) where the boundaries between public and private spheres of experience and personal expression have become increasingly indistinct, and politicians are now required to provide signs of their authenticity through the display of intimacy and emotional self-disclosure. Lacan's vision of masculinity as a 'masquerade' takes on a new meaning in this light (Lacan, 1977; Mitchell and Rose, 1982). Emotions are now often paraded like trophies – especially in contexts such as party politics, where the performance of emotion is used to engage flirtatiously with the emotions of voters. This is well illustrated by UK politicians such as Tony Blair and David Cameron and also Barack Obama in the US, who constantly use their role as fathers, and their affection for their children in particular, as signifiers of authentic masculinity and as a means to empathise with women and appeal to what is often defined in stereotypical terms as the 'soft vote' (Spears et al., 2000). David Cameron and Gordon Brown's attempts to woo the women on the mothers' website Mumsnet[19] provide examples of this, where, like the male protagonist in Nick Hornby's novel *About a Boy* (1998), the fantasy of a paternal identity was used as a means to woo women and appeal to their so-called 'maternal instincts'.

As we have seen, in the past, flirtation has been associated with cultural constructions of femininity, and as a consequence, flirtatious men have often been pathologised and feminised as effeminate and hysterical (Kaye, 2002: 27). Yet interestingly, in the public sphere of political communication, it is often men, not women, who have colonised the playful space of flirtation for themselves. It may be that women in public life simply dare not adopt this position for fear of not being taken seriously or of being reduced to a flirtatious sexual stereotype. Women have more to lose and, ironically, cannot afford in the same way as men to utilise the ambiguities of flirtatious communication often associated with cultural constructions of femininity. On the one hand, if they flirt, they are seen as exploiting their femininity, yet on the other, if they don't, they are seen as hard and unfeminine, as the misogynist publicity surrounding Andrea Merkel as the all-powerful 'ball-breaking' *Über-Mutter* testifies (Treneman, 2014). At one level, the attacks on Merkel's image are of little consequence, especially given her status as the most powerful and influential politician in Europe. Yet, the gendered cultural attitudes towards such leaders are significant as they indicate the mood of a country and the imaginary spaces that are opened up for other women who wish to work as politicians and shape events in the public sphere. As I discuss in Chapter 3, Margaret Thatcher was highly skilled in the performative arts of political flirtation. Whilst her policies were not flirtatious, she was able to use a masquerade of femininity in order to woo male politicians and world leaders such as Ronald Reagan and Mikhail Gorbachev. As Heather Nunn has argued (2002), Joan Riviere's 1929 psychoanalytic analysis of 'Womanliness as Masquerade' can be applied to Thatcher's appeal in the public political arena, where the performance of femininity may be used by women in the public sphere to offset anxieties about their power and the castrating fantasies associated with that. Yet, as we have seen for women in the public eye, this strategy carries risks.

The risk of exhibiting flirtatious behaviour in the political arena was also illustrated by Barack Obama, whose success as a handsome politician nearly came to grief when he referred to a female journalist as 'Sweetie'. As a consequence of the 'sweetie' gaffe, Oprah Winfrey, Whoopi Goldberg and other high-profile women rushed to his defence and were given air time to neutralise the alleged sexism of the remark (Katz, 2008). Other US female journalists such as Diane Sawyer took a less politically correct line in choosing to interpret it as a playful mode of flirtatious communication, reinforcing the objectifying fantasy of Obama as an attractive politician and as the object of feminine desire (Traister, 2008). Obama's online status as a sex symbol was reinforced via the 'Obama Girl' MTV-style viral videos, which during the 2008 US election campaign claimed to tap into the pro-Obama youth vote.[20] The flirtatious strategy in this context affirms and shores up the certainties of patriarchal masculinity, as femininity in its postfeminist guise is commodified and exchanged between viewers on behalf of male politicians who are able to retain their dignity from a distance. Of course, the producers and viewers of 'Obama Girl' emphasised the playful, tongue-in-cheek nature of this emerging political genre and the subsequent release of the spoof video 'I got a crush on Hillary' would seem to reinforce this particular view, which exemplifies this turn in postmodern political culture.[21]

These videos can be identified as flirtatious, firstly because of their message or content, and secondly because of the inherent playful flirtatiousness of the *form* as a mode of social communication, which invites the kind of flirtatious engagement discussed above. The videos also generate additional free publicity for those involved and create a second wave of promotional cultural content that is more authentic, because it is created and owned by the electorate. As we have seen, the development of social media is linked to the idea that in the West, flirtation has emerged as a metaphor for many aspects of life in postmodern culture. The technology of social networking and dating sites are also harnessed for their flirtatious mechanisms by UK politicians to promote themselves and their policies.[22] As I discussed in Chapter 1, the public response to the e-campaigning of politicians on social networking sites demonstrates the playful and interactive nature of contemporary political culture and its capacity to facilitate the public resistance to a top-down model of spin and political campaigning (Harris, 2010a: 6).[23]

Such engagement on the part of the public with the flirtatious mechanisms of mediatised political culture also signals, perhaps, the cynicism of the electorate. The notion of 'spin' has become increasingly devalued in the minds of the public as manipulative and reinforcing the untrustworthiness of politicians generally (Barnett and Garber, 2001: 96; Corner and Pels, 2003: 11). Within newspaper reports, the language of flirtation, seduction and betrayal is a recurring theme in relation to discussions of politicians, even from journalists themselves who, for example, in relation to Tony Blair, asked how they could have fallen for him and been so 'taken in' (Parris, 2007: 15). The language of betrayal was also present in the public disillusionment with French President Francois Hollande following the entanglements of his love life and his publicised love affair with 'actress, Julie Gayet' (BBC News Europe, 2013). Journalist Andrew Rawnsley (2010b: 39) has commented on the tiresome nature of being continually courted by Obama through an email campaign asking for money and support: 'all these emails from Barack Obama make me feel cheap'. For Rawnsley, then, the overly aggressive nature of Obama's campaigning in this instance fails to work as a form of masculine flirtation. In contexts such as these, voters and journalists are positioned as dupes and are tarnished by association, or, to invoke the fantasy of Freud's Fort/Da game, 'reeled in' as the feminised objects of political flirtation. One can detect a similar mode of public resistance in relation to the much-publicised flirtatious 'poodle relationship' between Tony Blair and George Bush, where the British newspapers often watched in disbelief as Blair appeared desperate to maintain the illusion of a special relationship between the UK and US at all costs (Cannadine, 2006). Here, nationalist concerns were also aroused, as Blair's masculinity appeared threatened for supposedly operating from a feminised position of having to flirt with a more powerful ally.[24] There are analogies here between the reported charismatic charm of Blair and the depiction of Hugh Grant as the British Prime Minister in Richard Curtis's so-called 'feel-good' film (2003) *Love Actually* (Macnab, 2009). However, an important aspect of the popular appeal of Grant's character is that he doesn't flirt with the US president in the same way as his real-life counterpart, thus refusing the feminised connotations associated with the UK's perceived status as America's 'poodle' in the run-up to the Iraq war. Evoking Freud's anti-Americanism, it is reported that some UK cinema audiences even cheered when Grant's PM told the US president, played by Billy Bob Thornton, where to 'get off' (Sylvester, 2006). As I have discussed elsewhere, Boris Johnson played a similar game at the Olympic opening ceremony when he bonded with the crowd by taunting US Governor and Presidential candidate, Mitt Romney (Yates, 2014a).

The un-pleasures for voters identifying with male politicians in flirtatious contexts are linked to anxieties about masculinity in crisis. Some politicians on the international scene have been careful to promote themselves in a traditional masculine guise, closing down spaces of ambiguity and warding off potential anxiety. The now infamous image of Russian President Vladamir Putin, stripped to the waist on a fishing trip, projecting an image of himself as the handsome strong warrior and father of the nation (Anon, 2007), provides a case in point.[25] However, against a backdrop of masculinity in crisis, such images begin to look increasingly parodic, and as the negative coverage of former Italian Prime Minister Silvio Berlusconi's private and public flirtations indicated, often fail to convince.[26] What is more, in an era of crisis and austerity, the perceived lightweight, playful style of politicians such as Berlusconi appears not only frivolous but also unsafe when a stronger, more containing form of leadership may be desired. Politicians such as Tony Blair, whose alleged charm was still effective in certain circles even after the Iraq war, is now not only hated by large swathes of the Labour Party, but is increasingly viewed as a social and cultural 'embarrassment' (Lewis, 2015; White, 2013).

On not being able to flirt

The flirtation of senior male politicians such as Blair played a key role in the creation of New Labour. Yet when Gordon Brown replaced Blair as leader in 2007, his inability to 'connect' and communicate with the British public provides, in its own way, a cautionary tale regarding the

significance of flirtatious masculinity in the political arena. Brown's relationship to flirtation is interesting, as despite his non-flirtatious persona,
he does have a history of using the flirtatious mechanisms of political
spin and PR to promote his ideas and advance his career as a politician
(Gould, 1998: 260–261). Moreover, when Brown was Prime Minister,
he was not shy of flirting with members of the opposition, as in his
plan to invite them to join what he called 'the government of all the
talents', which bore the unfortunate acronym of 'GOAT'. In a bid to
out-manoeuvre his political rival, David Cameron, he also went on a
charm offensive and managed to lure the old Labour enemy Margaret
Thatcher round for tea at Number Ten Downing Street (Tran, 2007). Yet
when Gordon Brown took over from Tony Blair as the UK Prime Minister in 2007, his appeal lay in his apparent un-spun, solid, authentic
retrosexual style of masculinity.

Whereas Blair was a skilled flirt, who in his early days in office seemed
able to charm all in his wake, Brown was in a sense the 'anti-flirt',
representing a fantasy of the trustworthy 'good' father, an image that
was in stark contrast to Blair's playful guise as the frequent guest star
on UK TV breakfast show sofas and as the politician who initially, at
least, managed to woo middle England and the Murdoch press (Rentoul,
2001). However, following a series of PR blunders related to what the
press often referred to as Brown's 'dithering', his poll ratings began to
fall (BBC News Channel, 2007). The perception of his indecision on a
range of issues, including the 2007 election that never happened, undermined not only his image as the strong father but also his capacity to
promote and manage his own performance. Brown attempted to use
the flirtatious mechanisms of spin to convey a non-flirtatious, serious
image and when this strategy failed, the British public became increasingly disenchanted. As Wernick (1991: 140) argues, the electorate are
fairly sophisticated when interpreting the flirtatious messages of spin
and often know when the message is merely empty and superficial. Yet
the pleasures of flirtatious persuasion should not be underestimated and
the politician's ability to present his/her policies and image in the best
light may also signify a certain level of competency on the part of the
politician, and Brown's failure to do so, as in his awkward performance
on YouTube, resulted in public ridicule (Anon, 2009). Thus, despite his
strict, 'son of the manse' persona, it is Brown's gullible flirtation with
the banks that is often cited by journalists as the legacy of his time
in government (Rawnsley, 2010a). The latter also reflects a disillusionment with the objectives of 'third way politics', which relied on the
banks to fund its spending plans, a plan that failed once the crisis of

global capitalism took hold, despite Brown's promises to the contrary (Venn, 2012).[27] The dominant popular narrative as constructed about New Labour's time in office is that they mismanaged the economy, and the justification of the Coalition that took over was that austerity measures were needed to contain the crisis and put the UK's 'finances back on track' (Cameron and Clegg, 2010).

The 'political marriage' of the Conservative party and the Liberal Democrats represented the turn to flirtatious politics in terms of its style and content. The political culture during the period of coalition government also illustrates a shift towards a more overt form of authoritarian populism on the part of government and also sections of the media,[28] as the punitive message of austerity set in. David Cameron's career journey from spin doctor to media-friendly political leader is well documented. Initially, under the guidance of his policy advisor Steve Hilton, he set out to distance himself from the former leaders of his party who were perceived as being reactionary, unfeeling and unskilled in communicating with voters (Cockerell, 2007). Like Blair, Cameron became the brand for his party and he initially adopted a feminised, feeling-ful language to emphasise a need for 'hugging', 'yoga' and 'happiness'. Addressing issues known to be of concern to floating female voters, he regularly attended events where women reportedly gushed about his charm and integrity as a politician (Oliver, 2008). After becoming Prime Minister and leading an austerity drive of public sector cuts, which hit women hard (Jensen, 2012), coupled with some well-publicised sexism towards female colleagues, Cameron's popularity with women fell and his attempts to woo them remained unsuccessful (Kuenssberg, 2011).

UK Deputy Prime Minister Nick Clegg also experienced a dramatic fall from grace. When Leader of the Liberal Democrats in opposition, he came to prominence in the televised leadership debates, where, in the manner of the discovery of singer Susan Boyle's miraculous voice on the UK ITV show *Britain's Got Talent*, he performed particularly well, and the phrase that was used by Cameron and Brown throughout the debate, 'I agree with Nick', became a popular catchphrase. Clegg's apparent authenticity as the idealistic champion of a 'new politics' proved particularly seductive to young voters as he wooed the student vote for all it was worth, promising to cut tuition fees, which was a promise he later retracted. During Clegg's coalition negotiations with New Labour and the Tories, New Labour politician David Blunkett (2010) rather dramatically called him a 'harlot', as Clegg reportedly played the parties off against each other. Peter Mandelson also warned Labour voters: 'Flirt with Nick Clegg and you'll wake up married to David Cameron'

(Daily Mail Reporter, 2010). And that is what happened. Once the deal was done, there was the much-publicised performance in the Downing Street Rose Garden, where the leaders joshed around, coyly performing, again, in the manner of a Richard Curtis rom-com, their newfound togetherness.

Alongside their flirtatious performance in front of the cameras, there was also the necessary flirtation between their respective political *positions*, where, as it turned out, Clegg's 'Orange book' liberalism had more in common with Cameron's neoliberal conservativism than voters had previously thought.[29] Yet, once in government, Clegg and his party became most vulnerable as the objects of contempt, positioned as the partners with less power: Clegg was ridiculed as weak, and playing the subservient public school 'fag' to public school 'head boy' Cameron, who called the shots (Gibbon, 2010). All the flirtatious mechanisms of PR and spin could not seem to shift this contemptuous perception, and perhaps Cameron's communication officers, (first Andy Coulson and later, Lynton Crosby), had little interest in doing so. Throughout that period, the ire towards Osborne's policies was deflected in this way and Clegg's own policy pronouncements were often ignored and he was ridiculed and even feminised as the 'bride' who was desperate for a coalition husband (Bell, 2013).

From flirtation to mastery in an age of austerity

Richards (2000) has argued that the processes of 'spin' and news management can, in certain contexts, perform a function of emotional 'containment' in an age of fear, risk and anxiety. Yet, as he concedes, this is a difficult trick to pull off. Here, one could argue that any spaces that might have been created and opened up for play have increasingly been closed down. As we have seen, the language of fear, together with the message that emphasised the need for political stability in an age of financial uncertainty, was used by the UK coalition government when it came to power in 2010. As a number of researchers in the field have argued (Brammell, 2013; Jensen, 2012; Tyler, 2013), the message of austerity has been promoted at the expense of those groups such as immigrants or those on 'benefits', who have been marginalised and positioned as abject and split off as 'other'. This reactionary strategy was promoted by the Conservative Party communications director and 2015 General Election strategist Lynton Crosby. He is an Australian, known as 'The Wizard of Oz' because of his skill as a ruthless and effective political tactician, who has a reputation for employing 'dog whistle' methods of political communication to appeal to right-wing voters (Watt, 2013). In the lead up to the 2015 election, there was a move to woo right of centre voters who the Conservatives feared would be lost to fringe parties such as UKIP (Goodman, 2014). Here, against a backdrop of austerity politics, the play of political flirtation was arguably underpinned by fantasies of play as mastery, rather than as that which might open up potential spaces for creative engagement. This move also reflected the rigid practices of news management in the era of the Coalition government, which was reportedly more controlled than even in the previous era of the New Labour administration, when Alistair Campbell was the Communications Director (Deans and Plunkett, 2014).

The move towards a political culture of communication as characterised by a desire for mastery is also reflected in the hardened style and policy content of David Cameron's Conservative Party, which some political observers say contrasts with his earlier policy aspirations which were arguably more thoughtful and less macho in tone and represented an attempt to construct 'a less tribal politics' (Birrell, 2013). The potential closing down of new spaces for debate on the part of Cameron is symbolised by the removal of the online archives from 2000–2010 that contained Cameron's earlier speeches and broadcasts, thereby literally 'closing down history' and denying in 'Orwellian' fashion the spaces once opened up by Cameron for discussion (Hern, 2013). It is an irony that once Cameron actually 'reached out' across the tribal divide and went into coalition with the Liberal Democrats with a view to creating a new, more transparent and accountable 'new politics', he ended up doing the very opposite, while mimicking the behaviour of *News of the World* journalists who sought to cover their tracks by wiping their digital footprint by literally chucking that history in the bin (Hern, 2013).

Masculinity, flirtation and sexual difference

This chapter has explored flirtatious mechanisms of political culture in the mediatised context of politics and PR. As I have argued, flirtation works well as a metaphor for the fluid and transitory context of contemporary Western culture, where the old fidelities and attachments that previously structured the shaping of subjectivities are now often undermined and in flux. This process is linked to a loss of faith in the fictions of hegemonic masculinity, and new spaces have emerged within the mediatised spheres of politics and its promotion in mainstream culture, to challenge the old forms of patriarchal mastery and enable new forms of engagement, which allow us to imagine something new. Such spaces can be defined as 'flirtatious', as in the 'defensive' and 'creative' models of flirtation outlined earlier, which have the potential to either open up dialogue with the electorate or to close it down. The performance of masculinity is also used in that promotional context to engage with voters and shore up support.

The political modes of flirtation that take place are related to both the performance and content of the message and the fluidity of the medium. These processes of political flirtation are fuelled by the mediatisation of political culture, where the illusion of intimacy is promoted by an increasing focus on the personalities of politicians. Clearly, within the history of politics, the flirtatious charm of male politicians has always played a role in the promotion of political parties, and in the UK, one can cite figures from the past such as Benjamin Disraeli (Kuhn, 2006). Yet, what Benjamin (2008) once referred to as 'the mechanical reproduction of technology' now, in its present form, operates on a 24-hour basis, creating new modes of identification that are continual, mimicking the open-endedness of flirtatious encounters of the 'American' kind discussed by Freud. In the actual recent context of American political flirtation, Obama's use of technology to woo voters in the 2008 presidential campaign was highly effective as a creative model of political communication, which combined for the first time in the Western political sphere the promotion of black masculinity with power, seductive oratory and the promise of real policy change. The old cultural symbol of black masculinity as the 'other' to the hegemonic 'same' of white masculinity was transformed, providing an example of counter-hegemonic masculinity in that moment.

Yet against the backdrop of personality politics, the pleasures of identifying with particular political figures are also offset by more deep-rooted anxieties about trust and attachment, which, in the contemporary context of party politics, creates a number of dilemmas for the undecided voter who may, as UK journalists reported in relation to Tony Blair, end up identifying with a man who just 'led us on' (Parris, 2007). The contradictions surrounding Blair are interesting in this context, as in the early years of New Labour he appeared to exemplify the metrosexual flirtatious politician whose masculinity reflected a less patriarchal model of operating in the political scene. Even his affiliation with the New Labour Project as the 'third way' reflected, for some, a less split and rigid mode of political power (Richards, 2000). Yet his position regarding the Iraq war undermined that fluidity, suggesting a more defensive, retrosexual way of operating. Indeed, the way in which the decision to go to war was sold by him to Parliament and the country based on questionable evidence, illustrates his skill in political performance and playing the flirtatious game of mastery to his advantage. The willingness of many to suspend disbelief at that time may also be related to a desire for certainty in a post-9/11 context, and such scenarios are clearly linked to factors relating to the social and political specificities of the historical moment. At the level of unconscious fantasy, the wish to identify with narratives of mastery in this instance suggests an unmourned, melancholic structure of masculinity at play. In contexts such as these, femininity continues to be repudiated, as the authoritarian impulse to close down the space for creative flirtatious engagement with the other becomes dominant. Thus, despite the creative potential of political flirtation to challenge traditional forms of hegemonic masculinity, this seems increasingly unlikely in the current climate, where the desire to master the object through defensive modes of flirtation remains seductive.

3
The Dilemmas of Postfeminism and the Fantasies of Political Culture

Introduction

This chapter explores the intersections between political culture, the shaping of femininity in a postfeminist era and the fantasies that have underpinned that interrelationship since the New Labour government first came to power in 1997. The meaning of the term 'postfeminism' is contested and has been widely discussed by feminist researchers in the field of media and cultural studies (see, for example, Bainbridge, 2010; Gill, 2008; McRobbie, 2010, 2013; Tasker and Negra, 2007, 2014; Yates, 2007b). The emergence of postfeminism is often referred to as a 'stage' after second-wave feminism, in which a liberal, feminist language is used, yet is emptied of its progressive political feminist content (Bainbridge, 2010; McRobbie, 2010). Rosalind Gill (2008) argues that it is a 'sensibility' that influences all areas of life and is linked in particular to the growth of consumer culture and to the values and practices associated with reflexivity, neoliberalism and the promotional self. Thus, the meanings of postfeminism, with its links to neoliberalism and promotional culture, resonate strongly with the themes of political culture discussed in this book.

A central motif of postfeminism is the notion of 'having it all', whereby women are expected to successfully navigate the boundaries and contradictions of professional and personal life. The impossibility of that position resonates with different degrees of tension both at individual and cultural levels of experience. This chapter explores such tensions with reference to discourses of postfeminism and representations of femininity within UK political culture. The chapter applies psychoanalytic understandings of gender and sexual difference to explore the fantasies, identifications and anxieties that may be at play for both men and women with reference to the dilemmas of the postfeminist notions of femininity within political and cultural life. In order to contextualise the discussion, I begin by presenting a cultural and historical overview of the relationship between postfeminism and the social, cultural and political scene since the beginning of the New Labour era of British politics in the late 1990s. The chapter then focuses on the appeal of Margaret Thatcher past and present, using the shifting representations of her image as a way to explore the tensions that underpin the relationships between postfeminism, neoliberalism and fantasies of femininity within political culture today.

The flirtations of postfeminism and political culture

In 1997, and despite the infantilising sobriquet 'Blair's Babes', the incoming New Labour government, with its all-women shortlists, was meant to signal a new political era of equality for women and men in the UK.[1] This message chimed in with the postfeminist notion that the struggle for equal opportunity between men and women had been achieved, thereby rendering gender difference unimportant. In the early days of New Labour, the notion of a new, 'third way' politics connoted the potential for a progressively flirtatious mode of politics that could take account of different political positions, groups and positions to form new alliances, including a new feminist agenda.[2] As McRobbie (2004) argues, for New Labour, the links between the 'third way' political agenda and equal opportunities feminism were present in the intellectual ideas of sociologists such as Anthony Giddens, Ulrich Beck and Elizabeth Beck-Gernscheim,[3] who helped to shape the project of New Labour, foregrounding notions of 'reflexive modernisation' and 'individualisation', which sat well with the experience of Western neoliberal capitalism. Concepts of the 'reflexive self' and its relationship to new technological systems, which was said to enable new modes of agency, formed the backbone of the modernisation narrative for third-way sociologists throughout the 1990s, and women were seen to be at the forefront of such developments (McRobbie, 2004). Giddens (1992) says that men often struggle to adapt to the changing patterns of modernity – calling them 'cultural laggards' – and his reading of women as the progressive sex implied that women were more flexible and forward-thinking in every way. This notion of women's capacity to 'juggle their lives' has been a recurring theme in women's popular culture and especially in magazines such as the highly successful *Psychologies*, where the dilemmas of carrying emotional and financial responsibilities are regularly addressed.[4]

Throughout the 1990s and 2000s, the suffering of men as represented through the trope of 'masculinity in crisis' was a recurring theme in popular culture (Bainbridge and Yates, 2005; Yates, 2007a). However, in contrast to the cultural focus on male suffering, women were encouraged to 'have it all'. This mantra implied that women had both the capacity and also the emotional intelligence to multi-task – and for some men, it also reflected the notion that feminism had won its battles at the expense of men and boys who lagged behind their female counterparts. Minksy (1998) has discussed the envy of men who actually believed the hype regarding women who seemed to be able to combine a home life with a professional life in the public sphere and in fantasy at least, seemed to have it all their own way. This envy contributed to a 'backlash' against feminism in popular culture, giving rise to the idea that women had gained new status and opportunity at the expense of men (Faludi, 1991, 2000). This fantasy was reinforced by 'third way' sociologists who portrayed women as the emotionally intelligent sex, more able to manage their feelings within a changing landscape of promotional culture where material success is closely linked to the presentation of the self and the management of feeling both at home and in the workplace (Hochschild, 2012). With progressive state policies enabling financial support, the idea was that women could combine motherhood with a career and look 'good' at the same time (Gill, 2008). This upbeat reading of women and modernisation also echoes those studies that show (albeit from a critical standpoint) how well women are meant to adapt to the contemporary conditions of neoliberalism and its need for 'flexible workers' (Negra and Tasker, 2014; Power, 2009). From a Gramscian perspective, one can argue that the cultural and political alliance between neoliberalism and postfeminism, with its shared ethos of 'free choice' and self-determination, thus allowed the gains of feminism to be recuperated for patriarchal purposes – albeit unconsciously.

Feminist scholars have argued against that alliance and the neoliberal narrative of female empowerment, and also what they see as the spurious links between feminism and reflexive self-management (Adkins, 2002; McRobbie, 2009, 2004; Power, 2009). For example, McRobbie (2004: 46) argues that the philosophy of individual self-reliance that underpins reflexivity is also linked to the dismantling of welfare support and the Victorian values of self-help. She argues that 'third way' politics, as espoused by sociologists Giddens, Beck and Beck Gernsheim, has sacrificed feminism through the 're-traditionalisation' of the family, providing 'a rationale' for the rise of neoliberalism – and it is the latter which provides a touchstone for the continuities between the policies of New Labour and the UK Conservative-led coalition.

Postfeminism arguably emerged to manage the contradictions of femininity in the late 20th and early 21st centuries. Its philosophy of aspiration and reflexive self-management was, as we have seen, reflected in third-way politics and also in the style of female Conservative politicians in the UK coalition government and elsewhere. The history of second-wave feminism and its demise as an active cultural and political force in the UK and US have been discussed at length by feminist writers and scholars in the UK and the US (Bainbridge, 2010; Fraser, 2013; McRobbie, 2009; Power, 2009). In the UK, second-wave feminism emerged from a culture of class-based socialist struggle, which in the academies was rooted in historical materialism and an acknowledgement of the intersections between gender, class and 'race'. In the US, cultural issues such as the fight against pornography also attracted conservative women from the right to form an alliance with those on the left to fight against the values and practices of patriarchy. The transformation and subsequent fragmentation of feminism into what is often called 'third-wave' feminism, which took account of the differences between women, was both necessary and inevitable;[5] and the emergence of 'fourth-wave' feminism as an active campaigning force has already been discussed in Chapter 2. Yet the influences of second-wave feminism can still be found in a range of social, cultural and political institutions. The legislative achievements in the field of women's equal opportunities and equal pay, family law, access to contraception and abortion and so on, are often cited by governments as proof of the progressive nature of Western democracy. Yet as feminist commentators argue, these achievements have also contributed to a new consensus that in the West, the important feminist battles have been won and that feminism has been 'taken into account' and had its day (McRobbie, 2009).

As McRobbie (2009: 8) argues, the 'spectre' of feminism is constantly present in political culture and is also used as a promotional propaganda tool, as a reference point to signify progress and modernity within Western democracies. The use of the desire to export Western freedoms experienced by women in the West as a justification for sending troops to fight in Iraq and Afghanistan provides an obvious example here, and the law to ban the burqa in France because of its anti-feminist connotations provides another. As with the American involvement in the Vietnam War, in which the heroic language of chivalry was regularly evoked in public discourse in order to justify military intervention (Yates, 2007a), this same fantasy of what Freud (1910) named the 'rescue motif' is used by Western governments in the service of women, to rescue countries with non-Western values from their own sexism. This is a slippery issue, as many of the practices cited by Western governments, such as the violent curtailment of female education, are wrong and should be strongly opposed. Yet from a postcolonial perspective, such thinking sets up a false dichotomy between Western intervention and male violence and it should be possible to oppose, say, both the Taliban's violence against women and the harming of civilians in drone raids. Yet despite the appropriation of feminist language to justify military action, the idea of feminism as a movement that is rooted in the 'past' and which in the West has succeeded in its mission, is a recurring feature of the postfeminist landscape (Tasker and Negra, 2007: 1).

Fictional representations of feminism, history and politics

There are numerous examples of what Tasker and Negra call this 'pastness' in cultural representations of second-wave feminism on radio, film and television. For example, in the BBC Radio 4 programme *The Reunion*, women from the 1980s Greenham Common anti-cruise missile protest reunited to discuss that period in history,[6] while the 2010 UK film *Made in Dagenham* depicts the 1968 Ford women car workers' strike for equal pay that led to the Equal Pay Act in 1970. *Made in Dagenham* is unusual for its positive representation of strikers who actually succeeded in their aims and brought about improved pay and work conditions. This upbeat tone contrasts with other British films of that period, such as *The Full Monty* (1997) or *Billy Elliot* (2000), where there is a more fatalistic attitude to the role of the characters from the downtrodden and oppressed working classes (Bradshaw, 2010). A major difference between those two films and *Made in Dagenham* is the treatment of gender. Whereas the former focuses on male suffering, and are symptomatic of a wider 'masculinity in crisis', the latter reflects the turn to postfeminism in popular culture more generally. As the *Guardian* newspaper film critic Peter Bradshaw (2010) points out, there are similarities between *Made in Dagenham* and BBC4's 2010 television drama *The Long Walk to Finchley*, which follows the history of Margaret Thatcher's early struggle to be selected as a female Member of Parliament. The film does not offer a critique of the battles she faced as a lower middle class woman trying to gain access to an overwhelmingly white, upper middle class Tory establishment. Instead, a rather knowing, ironic tone is maintained throughout and, as with *Made in Dagenham*, *The Long Walk to Finchley* invites 'sympathy from audiences of all opinions, on the basis that fighting male chauvinism is an apolitical cause' (Bradshaw, 2010).

Made in Dagenham deploys a mode of retro-feminism writ large, and the celebration of its feminist 'pastness' is framed in heritage terms as the film references the music, clothes and style of the time. It conjures up an era when Britain had a car industry – albeit owned by an American company, when workers road bicycles to work in cotton frocks and supported each other in stoical British fashion through thick and thin. Even the Dagenham Ford plant and the surrounding flats are shot in a warm, sunny light. In this respect, the film contains elements of what constitutes heritage cinema (Hill, 1999: 77), using a celebration of feminist pastness to shore up a nostalgic sense of nation, even having its characters name check heritage brands such as Biba and Mary Quant to add a sense of faux historical authenticity and a feel-good postfeminist identification with the past. As the magazine *Grazia* puts it: 'inspiring and funny – think *The Full Monty* with Mary Quant dresses'.[7] As the film ends and the images of the strikers are transformed into black and white stills, the words, 'This led the way for equal rights for women to the rest of the world' appear, thereby reinforcing the symbolic equivalence between equal opportunities feminism and the civilising qualities of Britain to the rest of the world.

Today, feminist notions of 'personal choice' and 'the right to choose' have been appropriated by the market, and have become synonymous within an increasingly individualised neoliberal culture where the values and practices of consumerism and the market have become a way of life. As mentioned previously, the values and practices associated with postfeminism are also bound up with the aspirational ethos of neoliberalism that were promoted by New Labour and also by the UK Conservative-led coalition government that followed. The links between neoliberalism, postfeminism and affect have been discussed by Rosalind Gill (2008), whose extensive research into postfeminism and the media shows the ways in which women have become the target of advertising campaigns and makeover programmes in which the emotional work of self-surveillance is encouraged. As Gill (2008: 442) argues, the 'postfeminist sensibility' cannot exist without feminism, as 'feminist ideas are both repudiated and articulated, expressed and disavowed'. As she goes on to say:

> The patterned nature of the contradictions is what constitutes the sensibility, a sensibility in which notions of autonomy, choice and self-improvement sit side-by-side with surveillance, discipline and the vilification of those who make the 'wrong' 'choices'.
>
> (Gill, 2008: 442)

Tasker and Negra's (2007) research into postfeminism and popular culture suggests that the individualistic discourses of postfeminism are mainly to be found in popular culture, through rom-com genres, MTV, television makeover programmes and television series such as *Sex and the City* (HBO, 1998–2004, US), where shopping, female friendship and discourses of self-determination come together to provide – as it were – the perfect soup of postfeminism. Thus, postfeminism is contradictory, both in its celebration of gender equality on the one hand, and in the limited nature of its vision of femininity on the other, as articulated through the lens of consumer discourses of personal empowerment and lifestyle choice. This development is also reflected in the trivialisation of female politicians by focusing on what they wear and so on. The process of belittling women in the public sphere is something that was commented on by UK Labour MP Caroline Flint, who whilst performing in fashion shoots also complained that then Prime Minister Gordon Brown treated his female MPs like 'window dressing' (Flint, 2009). Flint resigned her post because she said that she was not taken seriously as a politician by her colleagues, and ironically, reporters continued to focus on her 'glamorous' appearance and reproduced images of her 'glossy photoshoot', with Flint lying back seductively in high heels and a 'glossy' red satin frock (Clarke, 2009; Day, 2009). Flint's decision to take part in a so-called 'glossy photoshoot' that reinforced her objectification in the press, as 'the flirtatious minister' who used Downing Street as 'a catwalk' (Letts, 2008a), provides another example of the contradictory pull of postfeminism and its allure for women, eliding the potential space of any model of politics around gender. As discussed in Chapter 2, the performative strategies used to 'play' with the electorate and the media in the political arena are always risky for women, and from a psychoanalytic perspective, they can evoke the spectre of dangerous femininity and fantasies of the transgressive, phallic woman. The psychoanalytic theory of the complex relationship between femininity, fantasy and 'the masquerade' is evocative in this context and it can be applied to the dilemmas of femininity in the postfeminist era of aspirational consumption.

Postfeminism, the masquerade and the return of Margaret Thatcher

The idea of the aspirational female consumer who playfully engages with notions of femininity through consumer practices associated with the masquerade has, over the years, been a perennial theme in feminist media and cultural studies. In the 1990s, the theoretical emphasis of that model, which stresses the 'pleasures of femininity' (Lury, 1996), reflected a wish at the time to escape the model of 'cultural dupes' that plagued mass society critiques of consumer culture.[8] Yet in her critique of postfeminism, Gill (2008: 434) has written persuasively about the problems of overemphasising the agency of the subject, and she cautions against losing sight of the psycho-cultural determinations that shape feminine subjectivities. The aspirational, postfeminist vision of identity is also linked to the 'long march of the neoliberal revolution' (Hall, 2011: 9). And yet, as I have argued in previous chapters, the identification with the hegemonic values of neoliberalism is not merely down to the processes of promotional culture, as it is also shaped by the processes of fantasy and the unconscious.

So what are the affective, psychical processes that underpin the cultural politics of gender and also shape identifications made by men and women in the sphere of political culture in particular? In her seminal article on the cultural fantasies about Margaret Thatcher, Jacqueline Rose (1988) argues that political culture is always gendered, constituting as it does the symbolic realm of fantasy shaped by patriarchal law and the father, which works as a form of 'psychic cohesion' to hold societies together (1–2). Nevertheless, as she says, this 'cohesion' is constantly undermined by the 'symbolic possibility' of femininity and the image of powerful women in the public sphere who push the boundaries of what is culturally permitted according to the psychical laws of patriarchal fantasy.

The postfeminist dilemmas of refusing the limits of subjectivity, of being all things to all people and trying 'to have it all', challenge the patriarchal 'limits of psychic fantasy' (Rose, 1988) in the contemporary context and a number of psychological defence mechanisms may be deployed as a consequence. These defensive strategies, which are used by the subject but which also resonate at the level of culture and society, have been discussed in terms of the 'masquerade'. The latter is a concept first discussed by the psychoanalyst Joan Riviere in her paper 'Womanliness as a Masquerade', published in the *International Journal of Psychoanalysis* in 1929, which has become an important text for writers within the field of psychoanalytic feminism (see Bainbridge, 2008; Butler, 1990; Doane, 1991). Riviere's paper can be used to discuss the public perceptions of femininity and also the fantasies that underpin it, together with the personal dilemmas of femininity as a cultural and psychological construction. Riviere's ideas have since been applied to political culture by feminist scholars Jacqueline Rose (1988) and Heather

Nunn (2002) to explore the ambivalent feelings stirred up by Margaret Thatcher and the fantasies of gender and sexual difference engendered by her image and her politics. The continued fascination with Thatcher in popular culture is evidenced by the publicity surrounding the film *The Iron Lady* (2012), and then her funeral in 2013, and also in the re-appropriation of her image by female politicians in the Conservative Party.[9] The fury that was expressed by some following the publication of Hilary Mantel's (2014) short story about the fantasy assassination of Margaret Thatcher also indicates her continued power to both fascinate and repel (Bentley and Duell, 2014; Sanai, 2014). In order to explore the fantasies that underpin such responses, it is worth returning to Riviere, to see if her analysis of femininity can still be applied to fantasies of Thatcher and her role as an icon of postfeminism in the contemporary era of neoliberal political culture.

In her paper on the masquerade, Riviere focuses on a female patient whose assertive professional identity as a successful intellectual who carries out professional public engagements, is equated with a 'desire to be masculine', thereby transgressing the cultural norms of the day that require her to identify with 'passive' femininity. The patient attempts to manage her anxiety about the 'retribution feared from men' by adopting a coquettish 'mask of womanliness' and by flirting with men in the audience (2009: 35). Riviere argues that the masquerade is symptomatic of the daughter's unconscious Oedipal rivalry with the father, who wants to possess the phallus for himself. She says that the woman's refusal to acknowledge her castration creates anxiety for her and other women in the public sphere and retribution is feared from the father. Yet as Nunn (2002: 19) argues in her analysis of Thatcher, anxieties about the vengeful father also co-exist with the pleasures of sexual flirtation and the power that comes with refusing the prescribed limits of her sex. As Nunn reminds us, there are pleasures to be gained from occupying an assertive role in the public sphere, whilst also exercising a flirtatious sexual power over the audience – a trick which, as Nunn argues, Thatcher often managed. The late Tory MP and political diarist Alan Clark illustrates this point in his rapturous 1980 diary entry about Thatcher, following her appearance on television when she spoke to interviewer Robin Day about withholding 'our EEC budget contributions'. He says: 'but goodness, she is *so* beautiful, made up to the nines of course, for the television programme, but still quite bewitching, as Eva Peron must have been' (2010: 82). This same adulation was expressed years later in a documentary film, *Margaret Thatcher: The Iron Lady* (2012), which includes former Conservative MPs and ITN interviewers waxing lyrical about Thatcher's capacity to charm her audiences. In 1976, following a tough speech she gave about the weakness of NATO's defences, the Soviet Union newspaper the *Red Star* first described her as 'the Iron Lady' and she responded in a speech to Finchley conservatives in the following flirtatious way:

> I stand before you tonight in my Red Star chiffon evening gown. (Laughter, Applause), my face softly made up and my fair hair gently waved (Laughter), the Iron Lady of the Western world. A cold war warrior, an amazon philistine, even a Peking plotter. Well, am I any of these things? (No!) Well yes, if that's how they ... (Laughter) ... Yes I am an iron lady, after all it wasn't a bad thing to be an iron duke.
>
> (Thatcher, 1976)[10]

The documentary represents her toughness as a leader and yet it is Thatcher's performance of womanliness that is foregrounded, as in the flirtatious example cited above. Elsewhere, Thatcher has also in retrospect been sexualised as an erotic figure of the imagination. For example, in the television drama of Thatcher's early life, *The Long Walk to Finchley* (BBC4, 2008), Thatcher – or 'Maggie the Minx', as she was represented in the review by the admiring *Daily Mail* columnist Quenten Letts, is a 'coy flirt' and 'the sex bomb who flirted with Ted Heath' (Letts, 2008b).

In Claire Berlinski's biography of Thatcher, *There Is No Alternative*, Thatcher is represented as both 'diva' and 'coy flirt', in the mould of 'Cleopatra'. Images that emphasise Thatcher's vulnerability as a woman can also be found in the television drama *Margaret* (BBC2, 2009), in which her last days as Prime Minister are represented, and also in the footage of the tears she shed during Michael Brunsdon's 1992 interview with her following the apparent humiliation of her forced resignation. The fantasy depiction of Thatcher's dementia in the 2012 film *The Iron Lady* also emphasises the representation of her frailty, working perhaps as a defence against the more castrating aspects of her persona as the ruthless, phallic leader.

Yet at the time of her premiership, it was the authoritarian nature of her persona and politics that often dominated (Hall, 1979). In her analysis of Thatcher, Rose (1988: 1) argues that Thatcher is a disturbing figure because of her contradictory identity as an aggressive anti-feminist female politician who appeared to embody the qualities of 'patriarchal society and the state'. Rose says that the re-election of Thatcher in 1987 was 'a crucial moment in the production of fantasy' within the symbolic realm of political cultural life. Thatcher's public persona as a woman in power pushed the boundaries of the masquerade and challenged the boundaries of the 'collective imaginary of British culture'. On the one hand, she invoked ambivalent fantasies of the mother, yet given her advocacy of violent confrontation,[11] fantasies of the heroic warrior father on the other. For feminists on the left, at least, Thatcher was especially disturbing, as instead of adopting what Julia Kristeva identifies as the terrorist position of refusing the socio-symbolic order and taking arms against it, she identified with the power of the state and sought to exercise power within it (Rose, 1988: 16).

Nonetheless, as Nunn (2002) argues, there is a strong cultural fascination with Thatcher's rise to power and as the publicity surrounding her state funeral in 2013 shows, her image continues to attract loathing and adoration in equal measure. Since Nunn's work, new biographies, documentaries and films on television and in cinema have emerged which signal the enduring nature of this fascination and the strong feelings that arise in relation to her and her performance of femininity. The authoritarian, military connotations of Thatcher's image and rhetoric are echoed today in the political language of US Republican female politicians such as Tea Party activists Suzanne Terrell or Michelle Bachmann, who like their UK counterparts cite Thatcher approvingly as a role model for their own careers. They quote her as a way to shore up their identity as strong women who refuse to be 'victims', using Thatcher's words as a slogan for their political action committee, 'ShePac': 'If you want something said, ask a man, if you want something done, ask a woman' (Freen, 2012). The language used by these women is often military in tone, referring to the way they have 'got the backs' of those such as Bachmann and Palin, who they say are regularly attacked in the press (ibid.).

It is important to acknowledge the historical and cultural dimensions of femininity as a masquerade – whether in 1929 when Riviere wrote her paper, or in the 1980s when Thatcher was in her heyday, or in the contemporary context of 'womanliness' in the 21st century. Although Riviere's paper is set in 1929, when women rarely occupied public positions of authority, the defensive strategy of the masquerade is still relevant when applied to the postfeminist dilemmas of femininity today and the cultural fantasies that underpin it. As we have seen, the ideology and practices of postfeminism – which exist both as mode of being and as a cultural system of representation – set up a contradictory and competing set of demands for women who are expected aspire to a neoliberal model of gendered subjectivity – to 'lean in' (see Sandberg, 2013) and combine a successful middle class career with a capacity to conform to non-threatening images of 'womanliness'.

This neoliberal model of femininity is easier said than done and as Lynne Layton argues, the aspiration to succeed in a neoliberal economy comes at a personal and cultural cost. Layton (2011: 111) has written about 'the violent effects of capitalism on psychic structure' and the narcissistic patterns of identification that emerge as a result. The internalisation of oppressive and 'unjust social norms' have implications for relations of class, 'race' and gender and the ongoing shaping of what Layton calls the 'normative unconscious' (Layton, 2007). The psychic cost of such processes are linked to what Layton (2013) describes as the 'defensive autonomy' of middle class white women who shore up their own narcissism by denying their own vulnerability and by experiencing a hatred of dependency and weakness in others. This narcissistic denial can manifest itself as an envy of working class men and women, who are stigmatised as abject and 'other' – as lazy and greedy benefit scroungers and so on (Tyler, 2013). Today, this sensibility is articulated in almost parodic form by right-wing public figures such as ex-reality television contestant and *Sun* newspaper columnist Katy Hopkins, who claims to be a fan of Margaret Thatcher and an aspirational Conservative politician, and who enjoys public notoriety for her cruel, so-called 'non-politically correct' comments (Hopkins, 2013). Ex-Conservative Minister Edwina Curry identifies herself in a similar mould, saying that food banks are wasteful and encourage a culture of dependency, freeing up cash for their users to spend on 'dog food and tattoos' (Alexander, 2014).

Clearly, such views are not gender specific, influenced as they are by the 'new right' philosophy of US political scientist Charles Murray's (1990) 'culture of poverty' thesis, who argues that there is a lazy 'underclass' who self-perpetuate their own conditions of economic poverty and social deprivation. However, in the context of the present discussion, they take on a particular emotional resonance when expressed by women in the public sphere, because of their authoritarian connotations. As Andrew Gamble (1994) argues, there was always a tension within the Thatcherite 'new right', between the philosophy of neoliberalism, which was underpinned by a belief in individualism and the free market, and the socially conservative belief in the need for a 'strong state' to ensure social cohesion through promoting the traditional nuclear family and so on. This tension, which was evident in John Major's 1993 'back to basics' campaign,[12] and which began to unravel through a series of sexual and financial scandals, played a key role in bringing down the Conservative Party in 1997 when New Labour came to power. Today, neoliberalism has won out over social conservatism, as women are encouraged to take up work and reject the once-idealised

model of the stay-at-home mother. In short, we are all neoliberal subjects now and motherhood offers no respite from the demands of the
workplace and the obligations of self-reliance, which, paradoxically,
more often than not, involves relying on another woman to care for the
children. However, the middle class fantasy of the stay-at-home mother
persists, albeit through nostalgic, 'make do and mend' television programmes where, like Samantha Cameron, one can escape to a world of
cupcakes or the recycling of vintage fabric to make curtains for the house
one stays away from in order to pay off the mortgage (Biressi and Nunn,
2013; Bramall, 2013).[13]

For many female MPs, Thatcher has become a symbol for the
neoliberal formation of femininity discussed above. For example, UK
Conservative Party MPs such as Claire Perry regularly cite Thatcher
approvingly, using her as a reference point for their own 'journey' into
politics (Isaaman, 2013),[14] while Priti Patel used her maiden speech in
Parliament to praise Margaret Thatcher (Isaby, 2010). Baroness Warsi
likened Thatcher's 'journey' 'from living above her family shop to number 10 Downing Street' to her own, as 'a young muslim girl growing up
in West Yorkshire', who later became a Minister in Government (Warsi,
2013). Like Perry, Patel and Warsi, ex-Conservative MP Louise Mensch
uses a postfeminist, self-reflexive style to emphasise her identification
with Thatcher as an inspiring role model. Mensch has carved out a name
for her self as an outspoken right-wing 'feminist', and says, 'Margaret
Thatcher shaped me as a girl, a woman, and a would-be politician'
(Cochcrane, 2012).

Given the identification between Thatcher and the fantasy of the
symbolic father, it is perhaps ironic that she is used by these female
politicians as an historical reference point for their own identities as
women in the public, political sphere. Her symbolic status as a matri-
arch also resonates for her opponents, who continue to express their
loathing of her in strong terms. For those who lived through the period
of Conservative rule in the 1980s, it is easy to recall the anger and
despair that was felt as a consequence of her policies. The strength of
feeling about Thatcher seems to carry a high degree of hatred, contempt
and even misogyny that suggest fantasies about her as the 'un-natural',
withholding and attacking, bad mother. For example, as the comedian
and cultural commentator Russell Brand (2013) wrote – albeit in playful
terms – shortly after her death:

> For a national matriarch she is oddly unmaternal. I always felt a bit
> sorry for her biological children Mark and Carol, wondering from
> whom they would get their cuddles.

The focus on Thatcher's image as a bad mother evokes the psychoanalytic ideas of Melanie Klein, which emphasise the significance of maternal 'phantasy' in shaping subjectivity and also emotions such as envy, love and hatred, which are all experienced in relation to the parental figures of the imagination (Klein, 1957). For Klein, a sign of emotional maturity is the capacity to tolerate and live with such emotional ambivalence towards the fantasy mother. These psychical dilemmas are often played out on the public stage and the emotional theatre of political life. As contemporary feminists argue (Bainbridge, 2010; Rose, 2014), Klein's ideas can be put to work in the current context in order to explore the ambivalence that men and women experience towards women in power and the envious projections that such women in the public eye attract as a consequence. These processes came to the fore during the period of Thatcher's funeral, when she returned to the forefront of people's minds once more.

US Republican 'feminists' who admire Thatcher are positioned in generational and ideological terms as 'daughters' of both Thatcher and Ronald Reagan's 'New Right' legacy. The fantasy of that legacy was also present in the media coverage of Thatcher's American granddaughter, who in 2013 performed a reading at her state funeral at St Paul's Cathedral in London. Thatcher's funeral provided an opportunity for the media and the public, through social media forums, to reflect once more on her legacy as a female politician. The highly ambivalent and emotionally charged responses to the funeral echoed the divisions of earlier years, as people lined the streets to either pay their respects or to celebrate her passing. The hatred and aggression towards Thatcher was evident in the symbolic violence that could be found in the representational practices that were active at that time, as in the alternative, mock funeral that was staged and also filmed in the mining village of Goldthorpe in South Yorkshire (Briddon, 2013; Vincent, 2013). The last pit had been closed down in 1994, and the fury towards Thatcher was symbolised in the celebratory burning of her in effigy as members of that community cheered and marched down the street with placards displaying irreverent and angry messages such as: 'The Devil has Come to Thatcher the Children's Milk Snatcher' (Briddon, 2013). In addition, the song 'Ding Dong the Witch Is Dead', originally sung by the 'Munchkins' in the film *The Wizard of Oz* (1939), became a popular refrain and despite being banned by the BBC, in April 2013, it rose to number two in the UK singles charts and number one in the Scottish singles charts. From a psychoanalytic perspective, the fairy tale villain connotations of the 'wicked witch' sits neatly with the

Kleinian reading of maternal phantasy and ambivalence as discussed above. One can extend Klein's (1940) ideas to the cultural level, and argue that phantasies about the dangerous, 'bad mother' are stirred up and experienced collectively at moments of loss, death and cultural upheaval and change, when paranoid schizoid defences come into play.

The affective process of mourning and working through Thatcher's legacy is ongoing, largely because at political, economic and cultural levels, the 'neoliberal revolution' (Hall, 2011) that she and her government set in place is not over. For British feminists on the left, who in generational terms at least, are positioned as (reluctant) daughters of Thatcher, she remains a difficult figure with which to come to terms. This ambivalence is represented in the film *The Iron Lady* (2011), where Thatcher's own ambivalence towards her daughter compared to, say, her adored son Mark, is depicted throughout. As mentioned earlier, the film is a biopic that focuses as much on the imagined private life of Thatcher as it does on her public role as politician and Prime Minister. In that film, the consoling narrative of 'pastness', as discussed earlier, is also to an extent present in its celebratory narrative of Thatcher's achievement in breaking down the barriers of the male political establishment. *The Iron Lady* has been subjected to criticism because of its historical inaccuracies and its lack of political substance (Bradshaw, 2012; Collin, 2012).[15] Instead, it deals with the personal life of Thatcher and the sphere of personal domestic relationships, most notably with her husband Dennis (Jim Broadbent) and her daughter Carol (Olivia Coleman). The representation of Thatcher's vulnerability as a sufferer of dementia, and also as a widow who is grieving for her husband, is present throughout, and as such, this allows for a more sympathetic identification with her and her losses than might otherwise be the case. Paradoxically, though, the character of Thatcher is shown to be scornful of being too emotional and she rails against the contemporary turn to emotion as somehow being more important that rational thought. Yet, the film does not operate at that register, because it works as a melodrama that invites us to empathise with the personal losses of Thatcher, which include her husband Dennis (played sympathetically by Jim Broadbent) and, of course, the loss of her job as Prime Minister.

The timing of the film is potentially symptomatic with regard to the wider socio-cultural losses of political certainty and leadership as discussed in this book. As I have discussed, such losses are contradictory in the context of Thatcher, who is mourned by some as a strong leader. Yet for others her resignation and subsequent death are linked to feelings of triumph at having killed off the woman who, according to commentators such as Brand, abandoned and hurt her own children. The film and its reviews illustrate the continued power of Thatcher and her ambivalent status as woman within the cultural imaginary of UK political culture. Nonetheless, what is being mourned in this film? Is it presenting Thatcher as someone to hate or admire?

The film's oscillation between these two positions echoes the dilemma of postfeminism, which as Bainbridge (2010) argues, seems to view feminism as an object that cannot be possessed, mourned or let go. This 'yes–no' pattern of repetition around the 'pastness' of feminism as an object from the past, which cannot be mourned or worked through, is also symptomatic of the repetitive fantasies that underpin the play of narcissism as a psycho-cultural formation within late capitalist culture. The ghost of Thatcher as an uncanny figure, who returns to haunt us through representations such as *The Iron Lady*, can be viewed as being symptomatic of these psycho-cultural dilemmas. It may be that the response to Thatcher and other women in the public political sphere, who are internalised as objects of fantasy at different levels of the cultural imagination, mirror back to ourselves an uncanny vision of our ambivalent relationship to women in power and the fantasies that are aroused as a consequence. In this respect, the notion of the masquerade still has purchase when applied to the dilemmas of women in the public, political sphere and also with regard to the construction of femininity in fictional representations of female politicians.

By focusing on Thatcher, I have chosen to explore a very particular example of right-wing femininity that I have linked to the discourses of postfeminism and the demands of neoliberalism. However, there are alternative models of femininity that could have been discussed that challenge the Thatcherite model and push at the 'limits' of what can be accommodated within the boundaries of patriarchal fantasy. For example, I could have explored the fictional political drama *Borgen* (2010–2013, BBC4) that follows the personal and political journey of a Danish female politician who becomes Prime Minister in a coalition government. The television series allows us to engage with femininity as an object of the imagination that is potentially transformational insofar as it opens up a space to imagine a more nuanced and reflexive model of women in public life and political culture. Such representations challenge the psycho-cultural myths of postfeminism and the masquerade, by allowing for the complexities of femininity across the boundaries of personal and professional life and convey the messy realities of politics in that context. In contrast to phantasies about Thatcher as the strong, visionary leader, one can perhaps begin to think about a more fluid, feminised model of political leadership that allows for the processes of compromise and negotiation.

4
Political Culture and the Desire for Emotional Wellbeing

The therapeutic turn in political culture

It is often said that in the West, the values and practices of psychological therapy have become dominant (Anderson et al., 2009; Furedi, 2004; Richards, 2007; Rose, 1999). The cultural preoccupation with therapy as a route to emotional wellbeing is regularly traced back to Freud (Rieff, 1966; Rose, 1999). And yet, Freud never promised a cure for his patients; rather, he said that the aim of psychoanalysis should be to help people live with normal unhappiness (1930). However, as I discuss, contemporary therapy culture appears to court a wider set of expectations than those set by Freud.

This chapter discusses the 'therapeutic turn' in political culture, where a focus on the self and 'emotional wellbeing' is often present in the promotion of politicians and also in the aims and language of policy-making in the UK.[1] A causal factor of this shift is said to be the loosening of traditional boundaries around public and private experience (Lasch, 1991; Sennett, 1976) and the emotionalisation of the public sphere has now become an increasing feature of modern life (Richards, 2007). Readers perhaps need no reminder of the death of Diana, Princess of Wales and its aftermath, which both symbolised and arguably helped to create a shift in public attitudes in the UK regarding the public expression of feelings hitherto kept private (Richards, 2007).[2] As I discussed in Chapter 3, the heightened emotional response to the death of Margaret Thatcher provides yet another example of public emotion, albeit of a qualitatively different kind, which included aspects of both love and hate.

The therapeutic turn has a number of implications for political culture, where it is represented in what I have called the 'flirtatious'

activities of politicians who foreground emotion as a means of conveying authenticity when trying to appeal to voters, and this development
is symptomatic of the personalisation of politics more generally. Public
displays of emotion by politicians are not new, and historically, political
leaders such as Winston Churchill are recorded as shedding tears in public, as on the occasion in 1940 when he wept in the House of Commons
following a declaration of fondness for him by David Lloyd George
(Nicolson, 2005). Yet, what is new is the mediatisation of political culture, and emoting to camera is symptomatic of that development, as it
provides new opportunities to woo voters. In the US, there are a number
of politicians, past and present, who have expressed emotion in public,
including Ronald Reagan, George Bush and Bill Clinton. Clinton's fake
tears at Ron Brown's memorial service in 2008 is emblematic of this kind
of political performance and it has been widely recorded on film, where
we see him laughing and joking one minute and then when he sees the
camera he begins to cry (YouTube, 2008). Journalists have grown cynical about this practice, as in the Clinton example, which was used by
the conservative press to attack the man and his politics.[3] Examples of
UK politicians emoting in public are also common, as when the ex-New
Labour Prime Minister Gordon Brown countered his stiff public image
by crying on prime time television about the death of his baby daughter.
That poignant episode may have been a genuine and heartfelt, but it was
met with scepticism by journalists, who penned articles such as: 'Brown
cries for votes' (Barkham, 2012). The ex-London Mayor Ken Livingstone,
was also derided as self-indulgent and even comic when he made a show
of sobbing at his own election campaign video (Anon, 2012).

The therapeutic turn in political culture is not only concerned with
the promotion of politicians who use emotion to convey their authenticity to the electorate.[4] It can also be found in the widespread use of
the term 'emotional wellbeing' in government policy documents, where
'emotional wellbeing' appears to have replaced the notion of 'mental
health', with all its potentially negative associations of mental illness,
and is therefore more consumer-friendly. The term often crops up in the
sphere of politics, in government seminars and policy documents on the
themes of education, happiness and mental health (Department for Education, 2010; David et al., 2003, Johnson, 2008; Layard, 2005, 2011). In
striving to achieve emotional wellbeing in these different contexts, the
goal is not to come to terms with the kind of emotional ambivalence
discussed in psychoanalytic discourses of the self, or the splits and
insecurities associated with the experience of late modernity. Instead,
there is a promise of 'happiness' and of a unified self, achieved through

instrumental strategies of self-management and personal development (Layard, 2005, 2011).

In this chapter, I argue that notions of therapy in contemporary Western culture have become linked to a desire for emotional 'wellbeing' and, more recently, to a capacity for 'resilience' in order to withstand the potential risks of modern life. The development of this phenomenon within political culture can be viewed as being linked to processes of governance and utilitarian attempts to manage the contradictions of neoliberalism by offsetting its effects by promoting cognitive behaviour therapy (CBT). The implicit narcissism that underpins the search for emotional wellbeing in this context also reflects the foregrounding of emotion in promotional politics. Yet, despite such reservations, one can also argue that the therapeutic turn does hold out the potential for a more compassionate and less schizoid mode of politics that acknowledges and respects the vulnerabilities of subjectivity in the late modern age. In taking into account these contradictions of therapy culture, I want to argue that at a broader level, the wish for emotional wellbeing can be read as a misplaced signifier for anxieties about subjectivity, loss and cultural change.

Much has been written in psychosocial and cultural studies about the therapeutic turn in contemporary culture and society, yet there are disagreements about the nature of its influence and whether or not it is a positive development, and this debate provides a wider context for the discussion that follows here. Richards (2007) asks, does the development of a 'therapeutic ethos' signal a positive development, where new spaces can emerge to facilitate self-understanding to help us live with the shifts and uncertainties of late modernity? Or does the growth of a therapy culture represent a form of emotional governance, where the desire to express oneself has, in the words of Frank Furedi (2004), become the 'opiate of the people'? Anxieties about the worrying rise of a so-called 'Oprah Winfrey tendency' within public life illustrate popular versions of this negative perspective. In the context of political culture one can, as I have begun to argue, link it to the narcissism of promotional politics and also the language of policy documents, where the negative associations of emotional vulnerability and mental illness are denied and projected onto those who are derided or pitied as lacking the necessary 'resilience' to 'cope' with the realities of austerity and the need to stand on their own two feet.

I want to revisit these discussions about the nature of therapy culture and contextualise some of this work by first tracing some key contributions to the debate about therapy culture over the past 50 years.

I then draw on those ideas to explore the language of therapy and emotional wellbeing in political culture. I then use representations of the therapist and self-named 'political campaigner' Derek Draper to explore the notion of 'charismatic therapy' and its implications for subjectivity and cultural change in a Western cultural context which is increasingly preoccupied by notions of therapy.

Theories of therapy culture and its discontents

The growth of therapy culture has many critics, and the debate about its development has taken different forms in the US and the UK. In the US, the debate has been linked negatively to the 'culture wars', where right-wing critics apply a (misguided) liberatory reading of Freud's secular world view to what they perceive to be a collapse of morality in US culture since the 1960s.[5] On the (US) left, it is argued that the politics of emotion and self-interest have replaced more traditional ideological modes of political debate (Imber, 2004; Nolan, 1996; Scialabba, 2007). In the UK, critiques of therapy culture have become aligned with concerns about the 'dumbing' down of society, particularly in relation to education and a lowering of academic standards, where there are concerns about the ways in which the emotional 'wellbeing' of children is now said to be more important than educational achievement (Ecclestone and Hayes, 2008). The link between therapy and educational standards also extends to debates about risk and concerns about the 'mollycoddling' of children in an overly risk-averse society.[6] A common theme amongst critics is that therapy culture creates passivity, constantly promoting the idea that 'we are in need of help' (Cummings, 2003). This image of the duped, passive subject of therapy has much in common with that of the 'duped' consumer subject of mass society critiques (e.g. Adorno, 1991). As Furedi (2004) and others argue, the alleged dumbing down is particularly present in relation to a particular kind of programme and media format, where it is argued that programmes are made to appeal to the lowest emotional common denominator. This viewpoint is exemplified in critiques of reality TV shows such as *Big Brother* (2000–2010, Channel 4), where it is argued that contestants, such as the late Jade Goody, are exploited for our enjoyment (Andrejevic, 2004; Biressi and Nunn, 2008).

Sociologist Frank Furedi is perhaps the best-known UK exponent of the pessimistic view regarding the encroachment of therapy upon all aspects of life today.[7] Indeed, following the publication of his 2004 book *Therapy Culture: Cultivating Vulnerability in an Uncertain Age*, he has become a popular spokesman on behalf of those who bemoan the loss of a particular British stoicism associated, say, with the Londoners who he says survived the horrors of the Blitz without any need for the kind of counselling that would no doubt be advocated today. The loss of political freedom is also mentioned in Furedi's account.[8] Echoing debates in the US about the relationship between therapy culture and the loss of a collective political sensibility, Furedi argues that therapy culture promotes a form of emotional correctness, which works as a form of social control, as political and social problems are individualised and reduced to the status of personal unhappiness. And perhaps he has a point. For example, in a neoliberal economy, where social and economic loss is often associated with being a 'loser', therapy is now advocated as a way to get people back to work (Leader, 2008).

In 2008, the then UK Health Minister, Alan Johnson talked about the significance of 'improving access to psychological therapies' through GP surgeries and so on. However, the kind of therapy he was advocating was not long-term psychotherapy, but rather the cheaper, short-term option of CBT, a move prompted by the utilitarian desire to get depressed people back to work.[9] The social and economic costs of mental illness had already been discussed by Richard Layard in 2005, and was linked to New Labour's wider 'welfare reform agenda', which emphasised the need to get people into work as a way of reducing poverty (Hirsch and Miller, 2004). The UK Conservative-led coalition government continued Johnson's policy initiative, and his Improving Access to Psychological Therapies programme (IAPT) is now embedded within the National Health Service (NHS), which, according to its web page, exists across Britain, to treat anxiety and depression.[10] This programme, which claims to advocate the use of the 'talking cure', often does this by getting psychotherapists to 'treat' distressed people over the phone from a call centre, using a questionnaire with a list of pre-set questions to assess the level of the person's distress. The mechanical nature of this experience, which is linked to the governance of 'audit culture' and 'evidence-based practice', has been defined as 'Therapy as Taylorism', in which the professional and subjective expertise of the therapist together with the experience of the client becomes standardised into a measurable outcome (Chapman, 2012).

Furedi's book does not set out to defend psychoanalytic psychotherapy against the encroachment of rationalisation and the promotion of CBT. Indeed, he is highly critical of psychodynamic approaches that argue in a stoical fashion (like him), that we need to learn to live with 'disappointment' (2004: 40–46). Furedi believes that rather than kowtowing to the 'colonising ambitions of the counselling profession', we should instead be turning to informal networks of friends and family for guidance and support (ibid.). The kinds of therapeutic values described pejoratively by Furedi and others are arguably a far cry from the boundaried codes and practices of psychoanalytic psychotherapy, where the principles of Freud's stoical philosophy of 'endurance' (Richards, 1989) continue to play a key role in UK psychoanalytic psychotherapy trainings (Leader, 2008). Yet Furedi tends to collapse all the different therapies under the same label as 'the authoritarian world view', and thus he fails to differentiate between the methods of CBT advocated by the government and those of psychoanalytic psychotherapy. As I discuss, this distinction is significant when discussing the potential merits, or not, of so-called 'therapy culture'.

Furedi isn't the first to talk about the influence of therapy in everyday life. Writers in the field of psychosocial studies have discussed it in various forms since the publication of Philip Rieff's 1966 book, *The Triumph of the Therapeutic*, which has been cited as a key text in this respect (see, for example, Elliott, 1996; Lasch, 1991; Richards, 1989). Rieff placed Freud and the growth of psychoanalysis at the centre of his narrative, arguing that psychoanalysis played a key role in shaping a new 'therapeutic ethos', which was linked to a growing cultural preoccupation with the self in Western societies. Rieff argued that the talking cure of psychoanalysis emerged as a response to the growing sense of disorientation within the secular, metropolitan context of modernity, where the old structures of authority were disappearing and where traditional modes of relating were dissolving. As Simmel (1903) had argued earlier in the century, the experience of modernity gave way to new short-lived encounters and a faster pace of life, creating new anxieties and pleasures in their wake.

Cultural historians and psychosocial studies scholars have also traced the 'therapeutic' preoccupation with the self in the early 20th century back to the development of mass consumer capitalism, and the growth of consumerism also contributed to this new metropolitan experience (Lears, 1995; Yates, 2009). Researchers have described the influence of psychoanalysis on advertising, and the 'harnessing' of the emotional loss experienced in the transition from the older societies to the new. Consumers were searching for an 'intense emotional experience' in order to compensate for the growing sense of alienation and homogeneity related to the anomie of mass society (Andrejevic, 2004: 144).[11] Against this backdrop, psychoanalysis provided a narrative through which the split subject might begin to explore the social and emotional dislocations of modern life (Elliott, 1996: 56).[12] Richards (1989) says that in a clinical context, the method of free association provided the means by which patients could begin to bring the psychological fragments of their lives back together. Yet as Rieff points out, the 'analytic attitude' employed by Freud was not one that invited the kind of consoling, 'transformative' self-narratives that can be found in contemporary therapeutic literature, where the emphasis is often on the promise of cure. Instead, the Freudian analytic attitude was 'informative', designed to help individuals live with the uncertainties and disappointments of modernity. In that respect, as Rieff argues, Freud refused the kind of authoritarian, positivist certainties associated with recent critical accounts of psychoanalysis as a regulatory, normalising practice (see Rose, 1999, as an example of such a critique).[13]

Whilst Rieff respected Freud and his work, he was less positive about the ways in which Freud's ideas were taken up and developed subsequently by his followers and society in general. Rieff agreed with Freud that a necessary tension between personal desire and a strong social order in a secular post-faith context is vital for creativity to flourish. Yet Rieff argued that this insight has been lost. Instead, he said that an emphasis on the 'virtue' of freedom from repression, individualism and narcissistic self-obsession had become dominant. Rieff was writing in the 1960s and as a social conservative, his critique was linked to the counter-cultural activity that was taking place at that time. For Rieff, 'psychological man' of the new 'post-faith' era had replaced the religious worship of gods with the 'worship of the self', driven on by an illusive desire for freedom (Scialabba, 2007). In his later work, *Charisma; The Gift of Grace and How It Has Been Taken Away from Us* (2008), Rieff articulates similar anxieties about the loss of social authority (and the necessary 'renunciations' which come from that), which he believes are necessary for human and social development. Applying the ideas of Max Weber and in particular, Weber's theory of 'charisma', he develops his critique of contemporary therapies and bemoans the loss of 'the sacred' in contemporary culture. Rieff argues that the charismatic figures of today are superficial and are of the 'spray-on' variety, are 'purely political' and have little to contribute except 'the doubt and scepticism they represent' (Frank and Manson, 2008: ix–x). For Rieff, then, 'therapeutic culture' has created an amoral political climate and an ethical vacuum associated with the loss of 'the sacred'.[14]

Rieff's arguments about therapy culture call to mind the confessional turn in political culture in which, as I discussed in Chapter 2, British political leaders adopted the values and practices of advertising and Hollywood cinema to promote themselves to voters. From party political broadcasts, such as 'Neil Kinnock The Movie' (1987) or 'Major, The Journey' (1992) onwards, a biopic formula was adopted, which took the audience back to the family roots of the politician and his emotional values. David Cameron's 'Web Cameron' promotional broadcast in 2006, which shows him at home in his kitchen with his sleeves rolled up washing the dishes, while batting off the attentions of his children, represents a more contemporary, naturalistic take on the genre, reflecting the informalisation of political culture and connoting a democratising sense of immediacy through the use of everyday technology. David Cameron has often relied on a personally inflected narrative to promote himself as the brand of his party. When his son Ivan died of cerebral palsy in 2009, the Houses of Parliament closed for the day as a mark of respect, thereby bringing a more compassionate tone to the business of politics. The Prime Minister of the day, Gordon Brown, led the tributes and newspapers reported that he was 'close to tears', as he had also 'recently lost a young child' (Chapman, 2009). One can argue that the latter reflects the positive influence of a more therapeutically aware culture of politics in the UK in which the emotional processes of mourning and loss are acknowledged and worked through. A year later, Cameron continued to draw on the history of his son's illness and, by association, the pain it must have caused him, with reference to the gratitude he felt towards the NHS during the televised election debates forming part of the campaign in 2010, when he gave his thanks to an NHS nurse. These thanks were then reproduced in press reports that covered the debates, as in this *Guardian* newspaper report:

> Cameron thanked a nurse who asked about the NHS. He described it as a 'wonderful, wonderful thing' as he spoke of the treatment for his eldest son who died last year. 'What it did for my family and my son I will never forget. I went from hospital to hospital, A&Es in the middle of the night, sleeping in different wards and different places – and the dedication and the vocation and the love that you get from people who work in the NHS, just I think makes me incredibly proud of this country'.
>
> (Watt, 2010)

As the above example suggests, the focus on the emotional lives of politicians such as Cameron can be read as being symptomatic of a more empathic, less macho and what some might call a more 'feminised culture'. Yet in offering up the loss of his son to the public as a way to signal his authenticity as a caring politician, one cannot deny that as with the example of Gordon Brown cited earlier, a transaction of some kind is

being made here in his bid for political power. In addition, the exploita-
tive connotations of that transaction need to be read with reference to
the feelings of the electorate and their imaginary identification with
Cameron's suffering as a therapeutic form (or not) of 'working through'
their own unhappy experiences. Here, one can apply the psychoanalytic
ideas of Heinz Kohut (1971) to argue that Cameron makes himself available as a narcissistic 'self object', that is, as someone who, on the one
hand, is a separate individual, yet who also merges in with the subject through the overlapping of emotional experience. As I discuss in
Chapter 5, Cameron often aligns himself with the image of the 'good
parent' and one can use Kohut's ideas to argue that this image allows
him to be experienced as the narcissistic, cathected, idealised father,
who instinctively knows and can share the emotional experiences of
the electorate. This therapeutic kind of self-experience, which Kohut
described as being of value in early development, might be seen as more
of a seduction when applied to the experience of political identification in adult life. Whilst Kohut sees the potential value of narcissistic
object choice as a necessary part of human development, others have
viewed the psychoanalytic concept of narcissism differently. In 1979,
Christopher Lasch wrote about the emergence of therapy culture, and
he used a more Kleinian framework to present that development in
negative terms, linking it to a widespread development of narcissistic
personalities.

In his book *The Culture of Narcissism* (which is still widely cited today),
Lasch argued that against a backdrop of Western consumerism and the
fragmentation of the nuclear family, people have lost the capacity for
attachment and meaningful object relations. Instead, they have become
insecure, anxious and narcissistic, and overly preoccupied with superficial appearance and the performance of self. He argued that the era
of Oedipal morality and guilt has been replaced by narcissistic insecurity and self-obsession, where short-term therapies and self-help books
are used as a means to rescue a fragile sense of self. Lasch was writing before the growth of celebrity culture and also the internet. The
proliferation of social media and its role as a tool of self-management
and self-promotion through social networking can perhaps be linked to
Lasch's particular vision of narcissistic culture. Lasch's ideas clearly resonate with Rieff's image of therapy culture as superficial, and from this
antipathetic perspective the therapeutic language of Cameron et al. can
be aligned with the phoney charisma of 'spray-on' politicians.

Nonetheless, Lasch's views have been contested on a number of
fronts, not least for the implied nostalgia in his account of a mode

of Oedipal morality associated with more traditional forms of paternal authority (Benjamin, 1990; Layton, 2007). Imogen Tyler (2007) has also critiqued Lasch's thesis in terms of its pathologisation of certain groups, such as 'career women' of the 1970s who had begun to reject what they saw as the drudgery of domestic family life. For Tyler, Lasch's thesis can thus be seen as part of a broader backlash in the 1970s against identity politics and those groups who challenged the hegemony of more traditional forms of ideological politics.[15]

Discussions about the short-term and self-interested, narcissistic orientation of individuals within the era of late modernity are also echoed in texts such as *The Importance of Disappointment* by the late UK therapist and sociologist Iain Craib. In that book, Craib (1995) examined the increasing influence of welfare professionals who tell us how to feel. He explored the cost of this form of emotional management in a culture where messy emotions, such as jealousy, are considered off limits and in need of quick-fix therapeutic solutions. Craib used a psychoanalytic Kleinian framework to argue that we have lost the capacity to live with disappointment and within the limits of a good enough life. Instead, certain therapies are consumed as a quick route to happiness, and as a short-term means to enhance the self. Like Rieff, Craib said that the practices and values of contemporary therapy culture have moved away from the insights of Freud and the philosophy of endurance he represented. Thus, Craib makes a plea for a return to a more stoical outlook and to resist the urge to respond to the uncertainties and 'disappointments' of late modernity by rationalising and managing emotional responses through the pathologisation of ordinary and messy emotions such as jealousy. The over-rationalised, machine-like structure of the NHS programme IAPT, as discussed above, illustrates Craib's views, which anticipated the rationalisation of therapy as a defence against the uncertainties of late modernity.

There are also those who have critiqued therapy culture from a Foucauldian perspective, who apply the ideas of Donzelot (1997), who discussed the emotional policing of the family, and Nikolas Rose (1999), who likens the 'therapeutic ethos' to a form of 'governance of the soul'. Rose provides a compelling account of the ways in which 'psy' discourses now 'saturate' a popular culture where 'public conduct' is increasingly scrutinised and judged in terms of psychological and emotional 'authenticity':

By the later twentieth century, public life and public actions become intelligible only to the extent that they can be converted into psychological terms, understood in terms of expressions of the personalities of the individuals concerned.

(1999: 267)

A particular theme that runs through Rose's analysis of therapy culture and subjectivity is, paradoxically, the loss of an autonomous self. Although he discusses the ways in which the desire for an autonomous unified free self is constructed as a cultural and psychological ideal, he says that the possibility for real autonomy is continually foreclosed through the impingement of therapeutic discourses that tell one how and what to think.[16] Rose's ideas are compelling in the contemporary era, where the standardised forms of therapy are deployed by the government and made available according to imperatives of neoliberalism. Yet the very things that alarm Rose are explored in a more positive light by Anthony Giddens (1991), who is optimistic about the possibilities of selfhood and its potential fate in late modernity. Giddens links the emergence of therapy culture (and in particular what he calls 'self therapy') to new opportunities for self-development. He takes issue with Lasch regarding the bureaucratisation of public life and the drive towards rationalisation that it represents in a late capitalist age. Whilst acknowledging the 'draining effect' it has on some individuals, Giddens argues that individuals 'never passively accept external conditions of action' and therefore resist the encroachment of therapy culture in the ways described by Lasch (Giddens, 1991: 72–73). There is little nostalgia in Giddens' account about the loss of old structures and public codes of behaviour associated with a previous era. Nonetheless, his optimism regarding reflexivity and the possibilities of selfhood in late modernity has been critiqued for ignoring the differences in the deployment of power in relation to new knowledge systems, which Giddens sees as key to the processes of self-therapy (Rustin, 1994, 2005).

Giddens makes use of D.W. Winnicott's object relations theory to explore the potential for subjectivity in the late modern age. Yet his application of a psychoanalytic framework has also been criticised for its ego-centredness, as the more contradictory, irrational aspects of subjectivity and the unconscious are not really addressed, and instead a narrative of 'mastery' is privileged (see, for example, Elliott, 1996: 73). Winnicott's vision of the 'self' is one that emphasises the potential splits and ambiguities of subjectivity and provides a more nuanced account of subjectivity than Giddens allows. Whilst Giddens escapes the problems of Rose's all-powerful vision of emotional governance, his account appears to fit well with the policies both of New Labour and the UK Conservative–led coalition government, where notions of 'mental health' and 'mental illness' caused by socio-economic circumstances were displaced by a fantasy of 'emotional wellbeing' (see, for example, Barstow, 2010; Johnson, 2008). Given Giddens' close links with the Blairite project of the 'third way' (Blair, 1998; Giddens, 1998), perhaps this is not surprising.

Giddens' notion that therapy culture might involve the facilitation of new reflexive spaces for identity work is reflected partly in the research of Richards (2007), who argues that so-called therapy culture is not just about the 'sentimental expression of feelings' as Furedi implies, but rather, it signifies a more complex set of ongoing psychosocial therapeutic processes, which include a new reflexivity and the creation of spaces for the development of a greater psychological awareness of self and others. He also argues that the media, and by extension political culture, has the potential to provide containing structures where people can work through anxiety and difficult feelings, and he cites the emotionalisation of broadcast entertainment as being significant in this respect.

Richards' analysis captures the psycho-cultural complexity of the processes of emotionalisation when he applies the psychoanalytic ideas of Melanie Klein to explore the therapeutic potential of popular culture. In Chapter 3, I applied Klein's ideas to explore the hatred of Thatcher and other female figures in political culture as objects of the cultural imagination. Yet as Richards' work reminds us, Klein (1937) argued that alongside fantasies of hate, there also exist love and the wish to 'make good' the experience of loss through the fantasy of reparation. As Richards (2007) argues, the cultural fascination with damaged figures and stories of redemption may well be linked to the kind of reparative impulses described by Klein. Indeed, as Richards suggests, some public figures such as the late Diana, Princess of Wales, are given authority and power because they appear to embody this struggle. The themes of loss, mourning and a desire to repair the splits of contemporary culture can also be found in academic, political and popular discourses about therapy culture today. The popular identification with suffering politicians, such as David Cameron and Gordon Brown, or the late Liberal Democrat MP, Charles Kennedy who struggled with alcoholism, or the former Northern Ireland Secretary Mo Mowlam, who suffered from a brain tumour, can also be seen in this light. I want to argue that discourses of therapy culture may be used productively or defensively in different instances to ward off anxieties that touch on ontological concerns about loss and separation and the survival of the self in an age of uncertainty and change.

Charismatic psychotherapy and emotional wellbeing

Iain Craib's (1995) argument regarding the 'importance of disappointment' and the ways in which we may seek to avoid it, is significant when discussing the meanings of therapy culture. Just as underlying concerns about therapy culture are linked to anxieties about the perceived losses of cultural change, so too can various aspects of therapy culture itself be seen as symptomatic of such avoidance strategies, seeking to avoid the pain of disappointment through a focus on issues of emotional wellbeing and the promotion of what I call 'charismatic' therapy in various media contexts. The term 'charisma' is being used here to connote the application of therapy in a post-Freudian era where the pursuit of happiness and the avoidance of pain are pursued through the consumption of short-term therapies and promoted by charismatic therapists as a quick route to emotional wellbeing. This perspective of charismatic therapy would seem to confirm in various ways the melancholic view taken by Rieff and Lasch regarding the superficial nature of therapy culture.

Today, the term 'emotional wellbeing' is often used interchangeably with those of 'happiness' and 'emotional intelligence' and this development is associated with the UK economist and former UK New Labour government 'happiness tsar' Richard Layard (2005). Layard's work also proved influential for UK Prime Minister David Cameron, who in 2010 set up the 'Happiness Index' as a means of measuring human happiness and the 'nation's wellbeing' (Lennon-Patience, 2013).[17] In continuing to develop this aspect of New Labour social policy, Cameron has been accused of de-politicising the debate about unhappiness and the potential links between unhappiness and the inequalities of wealth and social class. Instead, the experience of happiness becomes linked to other, non-material factors, where socio-cultural and economic circumstances are perceived as less important than 'emotional wellbeing' (Heathcote, 2010).

As a banal, catch-all phrase, the concept of 'emotional wellbeing' appears to refer to 'feeling good about one's self', thereby flattening out the messy complexities of subjectivity. The search for emotional wellbeing as articulated in political contemporary culture is linked to the growth of positive psychology, which argues in an instrumental fashion that there are positive steps that one can take in order to reach this particular goal (Seligman, 2004; Tal Ben Shahar, 2008).[18] Lennon-Patience (2013: 14) argues that the use of 'wellbeing measurement' is shaped by a 'culturally powerful therapeutic discourse', which emphasises 'self-help' and self-reliance that 'has an undercurrent of neoliberal pro-market values'. As Lennon-Patience argues (ibid.), the discourse of happiness and wellbeing has been 'strategically applied' by the coalition government 'as a means of situating the locus of responsibility for personal well-being firmly on the individual', contributing to a common sense of individual self-reliance, which has been central to the era of new liberalism.

In the UK, positive psychology is associated less with the clinic and more with the popular consumption of self-help books. Yet the self-help steps advocated by positive psychology, which focus on the 'here and now' and which aim to change negative ways of thinking and behaving, sit well with the methods and objectives of CBT, personal coaching and 'therapy' sites such as the one run by the UK celebrity psychotherapist, journalist and (former) political activist Derek Draper. His (twice) rise to fame and subsequent fall from grace became a *cause célèbre* in the UK press and on various Internet sites and political blogs, where he appears to attract a very powerful response from other bloggers and also members of the public. More recently, his blog and web pages show his move into coaching and company consultancy, a move that also echoes the relationship between aspects of therapy culture and neoliberalism today. Draper provides a useful case study to explore the development of charismatic psychotherapy and its links to political culture. The aim here is not to examine Draper the man, but rather to discuss representations of him and the textual implications of his image as a celebrity psychotherapist, political activist and company consultant and life coach.

From spin doctor to mind doctor; Derek Draper as the people's therapist

Derek Draper first acquired notoriety in 1998 as political advisor to UK MP Peter Mandelson and as a lobbyist whose boastful behaviour led to his downfall. At the time, Draper was recorded as saying that he could provide his clients with access to ministers for money and was subsequently sacked, ending up in the Priory Hospital with a nervous breakdown. Draper's own much-publicised tale about his fall from grace and, following that, his redemption, beginning with his exile in California, where he says he trained as a clinical psychologist, has all the key ingredients of 'therapeutic man' writ large, and indeed it is an inspiring story of reparation, change and redemption. His website tells us that when Draper returned to the UK, he set up a psychotherapy practice, married the *GMTV* presenter Kate Garraway, created a corporate video company and became a father for the first time.[19]

This transformation is documented in his many online sites and areas of self-promotion, which include his therapy, political and business websites, personal blogs, radio interviews, television presentations and also his columns as a journalist in the press and in *Psychologies* magazine, and he was even given the award of 'Mind journalist of the year'.[20] In 2009, he published his book *Life Support: A Survival Guide for the Modern Soul*, which at first received positive reviews as an intelligent and accessible self-help book, 'full of common sense' and containing 'a warm authorial tone of understanding' (Millard, 2009: 6). However, by early April 2009, Draper was in trouble once more over his involvement in 'Smeargate', an alleged plot to use a political gossip website to 'smear' members of the opposition party and their families through claims of mental illness and sexual scandal (Merick and Bell, 2009).

Draper's notoriety as a political blogger and 'campaigner' cannot be separated from the growth of celebrity politics and the growth of 'spin' in the marketing of politicians as 'personalities' (Evans, 2009; Yates, 2009). As I have argued, the marketing of political personalities has also been influenced by the growth of therapeutic culture. As we have seen, Richards (2007) takes a positive view of therapy culture and argues that a key aspect of the contemporary 'therapeutic ethos' is the management of anxiety. Richards (2000) also says that as a mode of political communication, spin can potentially contribute to this psychosocial process of containment. When New Labour first formed a government, it seemed to many that their policies and their friendly, informal mode of presentation played a role in reassuring the public, managing anxiety and promoting a more emotionally literate society. The Health Minister's desire to promote accessible therapy through CBT can also be read in this context (Johnson, 2008; Layard, 2006, 2004).[21] During the New Labour administration, Draper was active in promoting the policies of the government and their emotional wellbeing policies as his journalistic interventions indicate. For Draper, state regulation of therapists and greater access to CBT can be seen in a positive, democratic light (Draper, 2007). Yet, as we have seen, the New Labour government's plans were widely criticised by those who argue that CBT is being promoted at the expense of long-term psychodynamic therapy, which is now subject to greater regulation, thus undermining professionals and also the work being done which fore-grounds the workings of unconscious processes.[22] Here, Draper takes on the critics of government and defends government policy in the *Mail Online*:

> I won't have people undermining the Government's plans. I have seen CBT work. It was CBT therapy, in 1998 that first made me hope-ful that my depression could be cured. Like many, I needed deeper therapy, too, but many others don't want to dig deeper if they don't have to.... Therapists spend a lot of time trying to get patients to give up knee-jerk negativism and embrace the hope that things might turn out better than they expect. With all due respect, I would give the same advice to the critics of CBT (2009b).

A number of narratives and themes converge here, including the tale of his transformation and redemption through therapy, and the feel-good New Labour message that 'things can only get better' complements that other policy-driven slogan of 'emotional wellbeing'. The confes-sional tone of the first-person narrative is meant to convey perhaps a heightened sense of authenticity, which Richard Sennett (1976) iden-tifies as being key to the modern charismatic public persona, whose legitimacy in this context rests on what the person appears to reveal about him or herself in personal and emotional terms. As Sennett (1976) and Rose (1999) argue, charismatic public figures are defined by dis-plays of intimacy and a perception that they are revealing aspects of the 'true' authentic personality underneath.[23] For example, Derek Draper is recorded as saying that (now former) UK Prime Minister Gordon Brown would be more popular if he was more 'himself':

> I don't think that Gordon Brown needs therapy, but my hackneyed but genuine advice would be to be himself. What people want from their leaders more than anything is authenticity.
>
> (Draper, 2009a: 38)

There are also links to be made here between the display of emo-tional authenticity of male public figures and recent developments in the field of hegemonic masculinity (Yates, 2007a, 2009). In the West, the notion of a private sphere of intimacy, feelings and relationships has traditionally been associated with cultural constructions of femi-ninity. It is interesting that a particular kind of 'new' masculinity has emerged to define itself in these terms, as a means of shoring up a sense of emotional credibility in a therapeutic era. On his website, the construction of Draper as an accessible and sensitive therapist also represents such a move, challenging the machismo associated with the political sphere where he can also be seen to operate. Thus, as in the article cited above and also in others which can be found via links on Draper's personal website, pictures of his celebrity wife and himself are presented alongside links to his discussion about parenting on the mothers' website www.netmums.com, together with an article he wrote for the *Mail Online* about carrying out domestic chores at home with his wife (Draper, 2009b). The feminising characteristics of his public persona are reinforced further by a link to his contribution to a discussion about 'happiness' on BBC Radio 4's *Woman's Hour* with presenter Jenny Murray, where discourses of emotional wellbeing converge with those of feminism.

Yet Draper's public feminised persona as a therapist contrasts sharply with his performance as a political campaigner, which on television and in print is far more combative in tone and in keeping with the stereotypical macho culture of politics. The image of his face that is found on his book, as well as elsewhere on his business coaching and psychotherapy websites, reinforces the gentle qualities one might more readily associate with a healer or counsellor. In the picture, his face tips slightly to one side in a receptive pose, and in the iconic manner of Jesus, or a new age healer, his expression appears to exude the kind of calm serenity associated with a man at peace with himself and the world.[24]

I have argued that the charismatic aspects of Draper's persona as a therapist, lie in his consoling, 'feel-good' approach to therapy, which can be easily consumed, and he uses marketing techniques of promotional culture to enhance his appeal. That appeal is also reinforced by quasi-religious language, which he uses with reference to the experience of 'redemption' and so on. The third link one can make to his status as a charismatic therapist is his relationship to celebrity, and the glamour of celebrity is present for Draper in his publicised relationship with the TV presenter Kate Garraway and in the other celebrity endorsements of his work, including those of actor Stephen Fry and writer and ex-Labour spin doctor and political pundit Alistair Campbell, both of whom have spoken and written about their experience of depression.[25] Thus discourses of politics, celebrity, therapy, redemption and personal transformation all converge around Draper to create an aura which, given the contradictions of these different spheres, is hard to manage and sustain. The difficulty of containing these contradictions was made apparent by the actions of Draper himself during the latest phase of the

'Smeargate' scandal. The latter refers to the alleged role played by Draper in accepting an email from Gordon Brown's political advisor, Damian McBride, about smearing the family of a member of the (then) government opposition and also various members of the opposition. Draper is alleged to have replied: 'This is totally brilliant Damian' (The Guardian, 2009). The most damaging accusation for Draper was that he appeared to condone a plan to smear the wife of an opposition MP as mentally ill (BBC News, 2009). Whatever the rights and wrongs of his behaviour in that scandal, it is clear that he had attracted a great deal of hostility from members of the public and the press even before it occurred. For example, before the story broke, political journalist and presenter Andrew Neale said that following Draper's appearance on the UK *BBC2* television programme 'Politics Show', Draper received more 'hate mail' (via the show) than had any other guest since the series began (Neale, 2009: 37).

Such hostility can be explained on a number of levels. Firstly, Draper's political alignment with a crumbling New Labour project may be significant and the memories of his 'laddish' persona of the 1990s were still culturally present. For example, he is recorded as saying his greatest pleasure used to be to 'go to conference, pull the fittest girl from the labour students, then make a speech. My idea of heaven.' As the interviewer dryly observed, Draper hardly comes across as 'a neo Nye Bevan' (Millard, 2009: 6). His links to the macho and often misogynist culture of political blogging are indeed off-putting and one mustn't forget that 'Smeargate' came about after Draper condoned the smearing of a politician's wife as mentally ill, thereby using mental health as 'a weapon' rather than as an object of care and concern (Bennett, 2009: 27). Yet for many, the dislike of Draper appears to be connected to his feminised identity as a therapist and his sobriquet 'Dolly' continues to be used by journalists and macho political bloggers in a less than flattering way to undermine his masculinity.[26] The distrust of his links to the world of psychotherapy is apparent in the continual allegations about what some believed to be his bogus qualifications, which Draper continues to refute,[27] and many of the reviews of his book use the language of therapy and the chapter headings taken from his book to attack him.[28] Thus the language of transformation and redemption, which is a key theme of therapy culture and its narratives of wellbeing, are attacked in this particular context, and Draper as a symbol of New Labour and new therapy provides a target for this aggression.

One could argue, following Richards (2007), that this aggression provides a means of processing anxiety about political culture, where in the public imagination, mind doctors and spin doctors have become the bad objects with the power to manipulate and attack their victims in an unprincipled way. Yet, whilst the emotional work described by Richards may have operated in the early days of New Labour spin, the containment of anxiety is not evident here. Instead, the language of envy and projection appear to dominate the political blogs and also the popular cultural landscape where Draper has become a national 'hate figure' (Young, 2009), derided by those in the Labour Party and by newspaper readers as being 'pure poison' (Cecil, 2009). Yet, following a period of contrition, Draper once again employed the language of redemption in asking to be forgiven once more. For example, on Draper's latest psychotherapy website he tells us:

> First, I need to say that if you want a therapist who has never made mistakes in their own lives then I am not the therapist for you. I've messed up, suffered and (hopefully!) learnt my lessons. That's what life is about'.
>
> (Draper, 2014)[29]

According to his websites, Draper now combines a career as a psychotherapist with that of a business consultant, with the latter symbolising, perhaps, the complicated relationship that exists between therapy culture and neoliberalism, with Draper himself continuing to operate as a sign of the times.

Therapy culture as a symbol and symptom of return

One feature of the response to Draper's role in 'Smeargate' is that journalists used him to shore up support for increased state regulation and to attack the professionalism and autonomy of psychotherapists more generally. As the journalist Catherine Bennett put it: 'If you wonder why psychotherapy is in urgent need of regulation, just consider the actions of this practitioner' (Bennett, 2009: 27). Paradoxically, the debate in the press about regulation appears to reverse the argument used by Furedi and others about the ways in which people are rendered passive by the values and processes of therapy culture. Here, as in Bennett's article, the protection of 'vulnerable patients' by the state is juxtaposed against the danger of practicing psychotherapists who are opposed to the rationalisation of risk and the promotion of a 'safety first' culture.

Increasingly, we are witnessing the drive towards greater regulation of psychodynamic therapies alongside the promotion of therapies with so-called 'measurable outcomes'.[30] In their attempts to regulate the practice of psychoanalysis, the UK Health and Care Professions Council misunderstand the purpose and aims of psychoanalytic psychotherapy as a practice and even an 'art', which works with the unconscious and so cannot accommodate the kinds of safety checks associated with, say, nurses and health care professionals. In addition, the complex work of psychotherapist and patient cannot be reviewed via the kind of tick box methods associated with the market research of online shopping surveys (The Maresfield Report, 2012). Today, following a judicial review, and a sustained protest from psychotherapy organisations, the profession is self-regulated. Whilst the need for some form of regulatory process is necessary, the desire for standardisation of psychotherapy practice on the part of the government is also linked to a desire for order, a phenomenon, which, in psychoanalytic terms, illustrates a mode of concrete thinking associated with paranoid schizoid anxiety and a need to ward off bad objects. The concept of 'emotional resilience', which is now increasingly used in popular psychology in place of 'emotional wellbeing', reflects this way of thinking. Emotional resilience courses are now widely promoted by government and businesses to help individuals adapt to different forms of adversity in the uncertain and risky environment of contemporary culture.[31] Here, one could argue that whilst the concept of emotional wellbeing emerged in a pre-austerity era, the notion of 'emotional resilience', with all its connotations of 'Bear Grylls' survival tactics, seems more fitting in the contemporary age, where against a backdrop of paranoid uncertainty about the present, we are advised to take steps to protect ourselves against anything that might get thrown at us in the future (Rainy, 2014). Indeed, the ubiquitous phrase 'going forward', so beloved of politicians and go-ahead business leaders, has become a far more risky proposition of late. Part of its appeal may be that the notion of 'resilience' has more macho connotations than what some might see as the 'feminising' associations of therapy as nurturing.

The therapeutic values of caring for the emotionally vulnerable are culturally associated with traditional images of femininity, and Furedi's unease around the alleged infantilising aspects of therapy culture may well be linked to concerns about those feminising connotations.[32] As we have seen with Draper, a similar attitude can also be found in the press towards the practice of psychotherapy and also towards 'snivelling' male politicians who cry in public (Barkham, 2012). As the poet Blake Morrison (2003) argues, a central message throughout Furedi's book appears to be a dislike of enfeeblement and a plea to 'pull your self together'.[33] So perhaps Furedi has more in common with the former

New Labour governments (and also subsequent governments) than he thinks. As we have seen, similar anxieties can also be found in popular culture, where discussions about therapy and emotion often attract a similar form of derision. The emphasis on emotion, feelings and the self in therapy culture challenges older patriarchal certainties, disrupting the traditional gendered categories through which we have made sense of the world, including the duality of emotion versus rationality. The maternal connotations of caring and nurturance associated with therapeutic discourse may also provoke anxieties related to the vulnerabilities of regressive dependency and fantasies of maternal engulfment.

Our emotional engagement with mediatised images of therapy represent, perhaps, a desire to make sense of a range of questions related to identity and selfhood in a changing and uncertain world, and the processes of political culture reflect these dilemmas. A 2012 debate in the House of Commons, in which former Defence Minister Kevan Jones openly discussed his experience of depression, saying that MPs usually hid such unhappiness because they were worried in case they appeared 'weak' (Marsden, 2012), illustrates this process in action. Conservative Party MPs Sarah Wollaston and Andrea Leadsom also spoke about their post-natal depression and another MP, Charles Walker, spoke of his condition of obsessional compulsive disorder. Leadsom was recorded as saying: 'the Commons session had been "part debate and part group therapy" as she recounted her experience of post-natal depression' (Marsden, 2012). The sympathetic way in which this was recorded reflects a greater toleration of vulnerability in the politicians who represent us.

Given the centrality of emotion and therapy in contemporary culture, it is perhaps surprising that psychoanalysis has not been used more in media and cultural studies to explore that development. Indeed, the complexity of that relationship to culture and media is often lost where the Foucauldian principles of governance tend to be emphasised. The mistrust of psychoanalysis has a long history in media and cultural studies, stemming largely from the perception of psychoanalytic theory as a 'master discourse', blind to issues of cultural difference, history and political context. Rose's detailed analysis regarding the encroachment of therapeutic discourse has been influential in this respect. Yet, whilst holding on to Rose's scepticism, it is also necessary to acknowledge the contradictions of subjectivity, and the need to refuse the seductions of 'tight-fit' explanations of some applications of discourse analysis, where emotional responses are merely derived from the internalisation of 'psy' discourses where psychoanalysis is said to play a key role. As Cooper and Lousada (2009) argue, the 'slaves' both within and outside psychoanalytic institutions have long since rebelled. Moreover, the psychoanalytic emphasis upon the unconscious and the precarious nature of subjectivity continue to undercut the seductive, if arguably paranoid, view of the psychological subject propagated by Furedi and others, who bemoan the loss of mastery, something which psychoanalytic theory takes as given.

Anxieties about the nature of therapy culture can be linked to those debates about the nature of cultural and social change, and also work on the relationship between mourning and the transition from modernity to an increasingly narcissistic and nostalgic postmodern age (Radstone, 2007). The old structures and stories through which we have made sense of our world have shifted, resulting in a sense of disorientation, loss and confusion where it is feared that feelings are more readily accessed than those spaces occupied by thought. Against this backdrop of onto-logical uncertainty and doubt, the notion of 'therapy' becomes both the symptom and solution, where the promise of cure creates yet more uncertainty and dissatisfaction, yearning for something that cannot be returned to or fully grasped.

5
The Absent Parent in Political Culture

Introduction

The English riots of 2011 generated a wealth of political commentary that focused on the 'moral collapse of society', and the problem of 'absent parents' was cited by the UK Prime Minster, David Cameron as being the main cause (Sky News, 2011). As Cameron argued in a speech shortly afterwards: 'I don't doubt that many of the rioters out last week have no father at home' (Cameron, 2011a).[1] Today, parenting has become a key terrain of political culture both in terms of the politics of austerity and social policy and also in the presentation of politicians themselves, who try to appeal to the electorate by promoting themselves as parents. For example, concerns about absent fathers and the importance of paternal authority within family life have contributed to Cameron's political imago as a father himself, who is equipped to pick up the pieces of what he likes to call 'broken Britain' (Cameron, 2011b).

As Cameron's views on parenting illustrate, the vision of the good parent that is often presented is one where the neoliberal values of austerity culture dominate. This is evident in the emphasis on the virtues of the self-reliance of 'hard-working' families and also where getting people 'off benefits' and back to work is seen as a panacea for the so-called British 'social malaise', as the coalition government and media commentators like to see it (Wintour, 2011). The gendered dimensions of the UK government's address to parents are present in a number of ways. For example, in terms of promotional politics, there is Cameron's own identification with the reassuring image of the good, containing father and also his repeated performance in front of the cameras with his own wife and children. By contrast, UK female politicians are less likely to identify themselves publicly as mothers, as traditional cultural associations of motherhood have been seen as incompatible with the male-dominated career of politics in the public sphere (Campbell and Childs, 2014). In contemporary policy documents, and in contrast to the neo-conservative discourse of the family as articulated in the 1980s (Gamble, 1994), neoliberal language about the 'parent' tends, on the face of it, to assume a certain gender neutrality. Yet that neutrality masks the heavy load that mothers often carry as a result of the welfare policies and austerity cuts created by the UK male-dominated government Cabinet (Fawcett Society, 2013).[2] As feminist researchers argue, it still tends to be women who take responsibility for the 'caring roles' that sustain the daily business of parenting and family life (De Benedictis, 2012; Jensen, 2012). Rebecca Bramall (2013) has documented the ways in which contemporary 'austerity discourse' 're-inserts' a version of the British post-Second World War culture of austerity into the present era, and that this re-appropriation is widely disseminated in popular political culture through celebrities such as Kirstie Allsopp, who works for the Conservative Party and also as a lifestyle television presenter on shows such as *Kirstie's Homemade Home* (Channel 4, 2009–) and *Kirstie's Handmade Britain* (Channel 4, 2011–). As Bramall argues, 'austerity discourse often seems to interpellate a feminine or feminized subject position', drawing as it does on the virtuous image of the post-Second World War 'austerity housewife', who must 'make do and mend' and put herself second in order to support and raise her family (loc. 2271). As I discuss, the use of austerity discourse in the contemporary context has a number of implications for the neoliberal ideal of motherhood, which, as McRobbie argues (2013), is essentially a middle class one that combines older notions of the good housewife and mother with the second-wave feminist ideal of pursuing a professional career.

This chapter extends the research into austerity culture and neoliberalism by applying a psycho-cultural framework to explore what might be at stake in the fantasies that circulate about parenthood within political culture today. Alongside the analysis of unconscious processes, this framework takes into account the classed and gendered dimension of politics around parenting and its articulation more widely in popular culture. Feminist studies of parenthood and austerity culture have tended to focus on relations of governance and motherhood, and this chapter develops that work to include the place of fatherhood and its representation in political culture which is promoted through images of male politicians and their families, thereby shoring up the identity of men and hegemonic masculinity. This chapter discusses the ways in which these representations of 'new' fathers may be achieved at the cost of allowing new spaces for femininity and motherhood to emerge within the psycho-cultural imaginary.

These themes are explored by focusing on the trope of the 'absent parent', which occurs in the speeches, press reports and policy documents about parenthood today. As I discuss, the notion of the absent parent that is expressed in various contexts functions as a symbol of the lost, idealised object. This fantasy of the lost object is articulated differently in relation to mothers and fathers, and unsurprisingly perhaps, it is bound up with anxieties and defences related to patriarchal fantasies of gender and sexual difference. By focusing on the symbol of the absent, lost parent and the *presence* of this fantasy within austerity culture, the aim is to unpack the social, cultural and affective, fantasy dynamics of what that signifies for a psycho-cultural reading of the relationship between constructions of parenthood and the play of political culture today.

The chapter begins, however, with a discussion of the idea of the absent father and its links to wider political concerns regarding masculinity in crisis and anxieties about the loss of paternal authority in a post-familial era. The perceived threat posed by omnipotent mothers is then addressed by exploring the relationship between motherhood and attachment within parenting discourse today. The chapter concludes by discussing fantasies of inheritance and the gendered mourning of the symbolic parent in contemporary political culture.

A crisis of masculinity and fatherhood in a post-familial age

Since the late 1990s, the three main UK political parties have all deployed images of 'hands-on fatherhood' as a means of connoting a 'safe pair of hands' and of winning over floating voters (Rayner, 2010). The important familial events of pregnancy, disability and the loss of children have allowed the focus on fatherhood to be a key theme of their terms of office. The continuities between the neoliberal policies of New Labour and the Conservative-led coalition government, and also Tony Blair's influence on David Cameron and his party, have been well documented (Prabhakar, 2011; Seymour, 2010). The similarities between the two men are symbolised through their identities as modern 'new' fathers, and particular events in their private family lives have provided them with a justification for positioning themselves in this way. For example, it was during the period of the 2010 election that David Cameron became a father once more, an event that received enormous publicity, echoing the widespread coverage of the birth of Tony Blair's child, Leo, during his time in office as Prime Minister (BBC News, 2000, 2010). Nick Clegg, who at the time was the Liberal Party leader and Deputy Prime Minister in the UK Coalition government, also fore-grounded his identity as a father. Cameron and Clegg's early relationship as coalition partners was symbolically sealed when it was reported that they had together constructed an IKEA cupboard for Cameron's new baby at Downing Street (Daily Mail Reporter, 2010b).

This self-conscious move toward a new emphasis on the discourse of fatherhood has not occurred solely as a response to the individual cir-cumstances of the politicians involved. It has also emerged against the backdrop of a culture that is now widely held to be a particularly 'femi-nised' one, in which ideas about fatherhood focus on 'parenting ideals' grounded in the ideas of emotional literacy. The adoption of so-called 'feminised' values and a language of 'nurturing' is often evident in the personalised rhetoric of politicians such as Cameron and Clegg, a move which has emerged in public and popular discourse as a response to cul-tural and political changes associated with feminism, the emergence of 'therapy culture' and changes associated with the alleged 'crisis of mas-culinity' (Bainbridge and Yates, 2005; Layton, 2011). Nevertheless, such a move contradicts the more reactionary stance implied by the call of the same politicians for the reconstitution of 'traditional' family values and the restoration of paternal family authority.

Representations of fatherhood within political culture symbolise broader struggles over patriarchal masculinity and the experience of loss that has occurred for some as a result. Given the inherent insta-bilities of masculinity as a psychosocial and cultural construction, one can argue that masculinity is always 'in crisis' and that this was made particularly visible in the 1990s, when the old fictions and entitlements of masculinity appeared less credible than previously, and the notion of 'masculinity in crisis' became widespread in academic research and popular culture (Bainbridge and Yates, 2005; Layton, 2011). The loss of such entitlements has been a recurring theme in popular discourses of fatherhood within popular and political culture over the past 15 years. Thus, one can argue that the rise of fatherhood as a key trope of political culture is also linked to its status as a reassuring signifier of authenticity in an age of uncertainty, risk and a growing cynicism about the mean-ing of Western social democratic politics, where the personalisation of politicians often dominates.

While Cameron projects an image of himself as the strong containing father, his opposite can be found in the stereotype of the irresponsible, absent father who fails to support his children and allows them to liter-ally run riot. Concerns about the loss of paternal influence have emerged as a new form of common sense in which disquiet about the absent father has also been expressed by those on the centre-left of British politics, such as political researcher Marc Stears (2011) or Labour MP David Lammy (2011), who, like Cameron, argue that absent fathers play a key role in lawless behaviour of rioters and of black working class males in particular.

Political rhetoric in the UK about the need to 'shame' absent fathers, who leave 'wives and mothers unprotected', arguably betrays anxieties about the loss of containing structures associated with the patriarchal family (BBC News, 2011). Nonetheless, as psychosocial studies research indicates, today we live in a 'post-familial' age, in which new fluid and diverse models of the family have emerged that are less rooted in a fixed traditional heterosexual model of the nuclear family (Elliott and Urry, 2010; Roseneil and Budgeon, 2004). Elliott and Urry are optimistic about the 'constructive renewal' of the family in a post-traditional era, highlighting opportunities afforded by the blurring of the old gender boundaries within family life (89). Yet, this ambiguity has been less well received elsewhere, as it also threatens the patriarchal inheritance upon which a traditional model of masculinity and fatherhood has been based, evoking anxieties that find expression in the popular sphere of political culture (see Yates, 2007a). As Richard Collier argues (2009), discourses about the role of the husband often intersect with those that articulate a backlash against the gains made by feminism within popular culture, and thus underline the significance of 'father-rights' discourses and related representations regarding the loss of paternal control and possession for the preservation of hegemonic masculinity. The notion of 'father-rights' may sound extreme in its reactionary nostalgia for a lost patriarchal authority within the family, yet the anxieties that underpin its demands also resonate with a yearning for 'the good father' as symbolised in popular images of masculinity and fatherhood in the media and its representation in politics and popular culture in particular (Yates, 2007a).[3]

The mediatisation of fathers in political culture

Images of fatherhood have played an important role in signalling the authentic virtues of male politicians – whether as playful, active and caring 'dads', or as 'providers', conveying fantasies of reliability and a capacity to contain anxieties about leadership in an age of change and uncertainty. The performance of emotional authenticity through images of fatherhood has become a way for politicians to connect with voters, and David Cameron's promotional home video 'Web Cameron' provides a good example of this (Oliver, 2006). Discourses of paternal care and provision come together in this video as the reassuring fantasy of Cameron's authentic persona as a young, loving, affluent father is evoked.[4] As one contributor noted in the online 'comments' section, this film presents Cameron as a 'normal' – if 'upper class and twitish' – father, deflecting the envy of his privileged background by focusing on his persona as a regular dad.[5] Cameron's *presence* as a father in this and subsequent promotional material works in such a way as to stand in for the figure of the lost father, as articulated by him through his rhetoric about the *absence* of paternal authority more generally.

The highly emotional rhetoric about so-called 'feckless' absent fathers that has been a recurring theme of Conservative Party policy offers politicians from a privileged class background the chance to salvage their reputations by tapping into the reactionary commentary about the links between 'work-shy fathers' and 'broken Britain' (Travis and Stratton, 2011), appealing to a reactionary desire for paternal authority and the re-constitution of the traditional family. As the pro-family government Minister Ian Duncan Smith recently argued: 'We have been ambivalent about family structure in Britain for far too long' (Sparrow, 2011). In his 'fathers' day' broadcast, Cameron argued: 'It's high time runaway dads were stigmatized, and the full force of shame was heaped upon them. They should be looked at like drink drivers, people who are beyond the pale' (Hennessy, 2011). Such examples show how the figure of the father becomes the siphon through which the promotional tendencies of political culture tap into the emotive and personalised character of politics today. This is pertinent, because it reveals the extent of the investment in the father figure at the political and social level. It also shows the extent to which fantasies of encountering a paternalistic figure of authority can go some way toward shoring up the sense of crisis that characterises the contemporary socio-cultural scene.

The fantasy of the lost, idealised father in psychoanalytic discourse

The emotive rhetoric of Cameron and others raises a number questions about what is psychologically at stake in the desire to punish absent parents. It is perhaps not surprising that there should be a yearning for a good father as a symbol of stability amidst an era of social, political and economic crisis, and this desire has been explored more generally in the field of psychoanalytic studies. As I mentioned in Chapter 4, a well-known exponent of this view is Christopher Lasch (1991), who linked the growth of narcissism as a psychosocial and cultural phenomenon with the symbolic decline of the Oedipal father and the paternal authority he represents.[6] As Imogen Tyler and others have documented, Lasch has been subject to extensive criticism from feminists for his reactionary stance regarding the family in which he bemoans the loss of the father. Lasch argues that the family has been threatened by professional 'experts' who undermine the more traditional role of parents, thereby creating the conditions for narcissistic personality disorders. The rise of consumer culture and the influence of the media are also discussed by Lasch as causes of narcissism, in which the paternal influence of the superego is replaced by excessive, guilt-free narcissistic self-obsession. Lasch's descriptions of a narcissistic 'me' society can be linked to notions of a feminisation of society, providing as it does a cultural vision that sees a relationship between the siren call of consumption, regressed infantile appetites and selfish mothers who disrupt the normative parameters of psychosocial family structures by challenging the rights of patriarchal fathers. From the psychoanalytic perspective of Lasch, the role of the father should be to lead the child away from the all-engulfing irrational sphere of the pre-Oedipal mother, to enable the child to acquire a sense of third-ness and (for boys at least) to identify with him and develop a social conscience by internalising the patriarchal norms established by the father and generations of men before him.

Yet as Benjamin (1990: 138–146) and others have since noted, in mourning the loss of the father, Lasch uses a 'fatherless society' critique as deployed by the Frankfurt School in the late 1940s, and reproduces a particular selective reading of Freud that idealises the father and pathologises the pre-Oedipal relationship between mother and baby. The idealisation of the father can be found in Freudian psychoanalytic theory, which has tended to focus on the son's murderous rivalry towards the father rather than vice versa (Freud, 1913). As Benjamin argues, in Freud's later formulations of the Oedipus complex, he paid more attention to the ambivalence of Oedipus the son towards the father, Laius. Yet in 1900, Freud emphasises the inherent rivalrous aggression experienced by the father toward the son who he knows will eclipse him (Freud, 1900: 290). Freud explored the irrational, nostalgic longing for the primal father in the story of *Totem and Taboo* (1913). In that story, the hated primal father is murdered by his sons, who later experience a mixture of guilt, desire and aggression towards the father they collectively destroyed. The brothers respond to such feelings by idealising the primal father as a totem, and this idealisation is later transformed into the worshipping of gods. A 'gulf' is opened up between the 'unappeased longing' for the primal father and the patriarchal father of the family, who is later restored to his place in the family and wider society (1913: 149). As Susannah Radstone (1995: 153) argues: 'Totem and Taboo emerges ... as an account of patriarchal masculinity's psychic foundations in an impossible nostalgic identification with an idealized image of the father'.

This tale of collective (if deluded) longing for the lost father can be deployed to problematise the idealisation of the father within forma-tions of hegemonic masculinity and contemporary fantasies about the wish to restore the absent father in political life. As feminist readings of *Totem and Taboo* indicate, such a reading also highlights the irrational nature of fantasy associated with the patriarchal father, thereby blur-ring the boundaries within Lasch's split gendered reading of the rational father versus the irrational pre-Oedipal mother. Yet, as Benjamin argues, one can also counter the psychoanalytic narrative of idealisation of the father with a mode of parental identification that is less omnipotent and freer from authoritarian connotations as well as the ambivalent feelings that emerge from that configuration (1990: 14). This counter-narrative is necessary in order to challenge the dominant account of hegemonic masculinity and the accompanying fantasies that circulate within polit-ical culture, where as we have seen, discourses of fatherhood can be found and are used to woo voters.

Fantasies of the mother in the political culture

Yet, what of the role of the mother in government parenting discourse, and how might we explain the role of maternal fantasy within the polit-ical cultural imaginary? Anxieties about social, cultural and economic crises, together with the threat presented by the challenges to hege-monic masculinity within contemporary culture, provoke a number of defences and anxieties related to psycho-cultural shaping of femininity and the return of the repressed and repudiated mother within contem-porary cultural life. Luce Irigaray (1981: 36 [1991]) argues that in *Totem and Taboo*, Freud 'forgets a more archaic murder, that of the mother', and she cites the murder of Clytemnestra and her lover by her son Orestes, as portrayed in Aeschylus's trilogy *The Orestia*, as a foundation myth of Western culture. Irigaray argues that the cultural dominance of the Oedipus myth needs to be countered with a different story that is able to incorporate fantasies of the mother that are not premised on her matricide. Christina Wieland (1996) also takes up this theme, but from the psychoanalytic perspective of British object relations, when she argues that patriarchal culture is premised on the defensive splitting off and denial of 'the omnipotent bad mother', which takes place as a defence against the identification with her and the dangers that she represents in fantasy. As Wieland says, the mother is 'omnipotent because she is needed, omnipotent because she is desired, omnipotent because she is identified with, omnipotent because she is hated' (302). Wieland reminds us that following her murder, Clytemnestra returns to haunt and torment her son, who is later exonerated by the 'new paternal gods', which 'marks the beginning of Western culture and of the legal state'. For Wieland, the matricide and its consequences express 'both a psychical and a cultural problem – that of separating from the mother', where the superego and the law of the father is set up 'as a defence against bad internalized objects' that centre on the dread of the mother and where the father 'is used as a liberator, that is, as a defence' (302).

Wieland's discussion of matricide and the defences that are mobilised to cope with anxieties of separation can be applied to representations of the absent and unreliable mother in contemporary political culture. The contradictions of neoliberal policy around the role of the high-achieving mother, and the fantasy of her opposite in the guise of the bad, irresponsible mother from the 'underclass' who relies on 'benefits', are also bound up with anxieties about cultural crisis and social change. The potential losses evoked and actually experienced by such crises also create concerns in political culture in which the notion of the absent parent and the problem of attachment are recurring themes.

The absent mother and the politics of attachment in austerity culture

As we have seen, the problem of absent fathers has been cited as a cause of family breakdown. However, in the case of mothers from the so-called 'underclass', it is not so much that they are physically absent, but rather it is their lack of parenting skills that is emphasised, and the move towards greater government intervention for children under five is also linked to that concern (Jensen, 2012). The concept of the 'underclass' was popularised in the 1980s and 1990s by Charles Murray (1990), who used the term to refer to the poorest and what he saw as the most culturally dysfunctional group in society, characterised by 'illegitimacy, crime and unemployment' (Lister, 1996).[7] Today, the notion of the 'feckless underclass' is still used by the UK government (Allen and Duncan Smith, 2008) as well as the press and broadcast media (Biressi and Nunn, 2013) to explain the familial roots of antisocial behaviour.[8] Bev

Skeggs (2004: 44) argues that the discourse of the underclass in politics is awash with signifiers relating to 'familial disorder and dysfunction' and 'dependent, fecund and excessive femininities'. In the press, tales of 'welfare scroungers' and shameless 'benefits mums' (Riches, 2014), and of women 'getting pregnant – for an easy life on benefits' (Wilkes, 2014), are regular fare for readers of the tabloid press, and similar themes can be found in television programmes such as the Channel 4 'reality documentary' *Benefits Street* (Channel 4, 2013). The latter represents a growing voyeuristic genre known as 'poverty porn', where viewers are invited to consume images of people struggling to live and eat on very little money. Although *Benefits Street* attracted widespread criticism, it also acquired over 5 million viewers each week and was the most widely watched programme on Channel 4 since popular coverage of the 2012 Paralympics (Conlan, 2014). Its central character – 'self proclaimed mum of the street' Dierdre Kelly (or 'White Dee'), who receives social security and has two children, became a popular object of fascination and, for some, 'revulsion' as she was invited to appear on talk shows to talk about herself and also to justify her way of life (Wyatt, 2014).

The populist appeal of so-called 'poverty porn' and the excesses of what Tyler calls 'the grotesque' and 'comic figure' of the 'chav mum' (2008) are linked to the image of the irresponsible parent. The latter is also a recurring trope of the government's austerity discourse, which highlights the need for individual families to take up the caring and financial responsibilities formerly carried out by the state. In reality, mothers play a crucial role in this respect, managing the daily domestic, caring routines that such responsibilities bring (Jensen, 2012). As UK Chancellor George Osborne reminded the electorate in his 2010 spending review, this includes 'living within your means', which evokes the housekeeping skills of the British 1940s and 1950s austerity housewife (Bramall, 2013). Jensen (2012) argues that mothers are being asked to carry an especially strong domestic burden, as financial inequalities are not recognised as a barrier to what is now called 'class mobility', a notion which is linked to a 'fantasy of meritocracy' implying that everyone can move up the social scale and achieve prosperity, despite beginning from very different levels of material circumstance. Discourses of therapy culture and parenting converge here, as the early years of life are seen as essential when preparing children for the race up the social ladder. Parents are encouraged to equip their young offspring with the necessary social skills and 'emotional resilience' to withstand the pressures that the journey of upward mobility entails (Jensen, 2012). From the perspective of the government, poverty – or, 'worse' still, welfare dependency – becomes a 'lifestyle choice' that, with enough scrimping and saving, can be avoided or at least endured by mothers in the short term for the sake of the next generation. Given these many demands, it is perhaps not surprising that some mothers get depressed – a fact that politicians and journalists find alarming, especially when it comes to the 'troubled' mothers of children born into the 'riot generation'. As one newspaper reported:

> Neuroscientists and psychiatrists are joining children's campaigners to outline how a failure to help troubled mothers bond with their babies can stunt the development of the children's brains. In extreme cases it has created an underclass of young people more likely to be drawn into crime, unable to hold down a job or sustain a long-term relationship of their own, they will say.
>
> (Bingham, 2012)

The fantasies at play in the scenario of the neoliberal, self-reliant family hold a number of contradictions, as concerns about the social and emotional connotations of dependency and attachment become entwined. For example, on the one hand, both the media and the government appear to condemn the 'undeserving' poor, and also seem contemptuous about families being dependent on welfare, thereby pathologising the relations of attachment between state and family as unnatural and wrong.[9] Yet, at the same time, as policy documents (Leadsome, 2012) and press reports (Daily Mail Reporter, 2011) indicate, the early attachment bond between mother and child is also highly valued and encouraged. The degree of 'healthy' attachment is also a recurring theme in the press, as in cases when the mother either attaches *too much* (as when mothers sleep with the baby or breastfeed for 'too long' (Brady, 2014)), or when the mother fails to attach at all, which, as we have seen, is perceived as a precursor to delinquency and a tendency to riot in later life.[10] The preoccupation with dependency and attachment reflect Lasch's concerns about narcissistic mothers and also a wider psycho-cultural ambivalence about mothers and their place in the public sphere as being either cold and distant or omnipotent and over-engulfing. Such concerns are writ large in debates about breastfeeding, which is often simultaneously the cause of prurient fascination or disgust, especially in discussions about bringing babies into the Houses of Parliament, where, in effect, the real and symbolic merging of the maternal body with the body politic is widely resisted (Lindsay, 2014; Thorne, 2014).[11]

The dilemmas of neoliberal motherhood

The politics of attachment and dependency within austerity discourse is further complicated by the idea that despite emphasising the apparent emotional and biological benefits of early attachment, the UK Coalition government at the same time promotes the idea that mothers should take paid employment as early as possible. Of course the latter may involve paying large sums of money for childcare, often leaving babies in the care of other (poorer) mothers to look after them. Second-wave feminists have historically fought for the right to combine motherhood with paid employment. The image of the stay-at-home mother as parasite, who lives off a partner or – again, 'worse' still – off the state, arguably provides yet another aspect of the attack on mothers who must continually jump between these different subject positions in order to keep up with the reflexive 'project' of motherhood today, which emphasises ideas of maternal agency and free choice (Miller, 2005: 140).[12] As I discussed in Chapter 3, 'self-reflexivity' is a concept that was introduced by sociologists such as Beck and Giddens who were influential in the New Labour government (Chadwick and Heffernan, 2003), and whose ideas have also shaped the landscape of current government policy.[13] However, as Miller (2005: 18) argues, the social and cultural capacity for self-reflexivity is not shared equally as the agency of mothers is shaped by the 'material and structural circumstances' of life' (p. 18).

The social and financial pressures of what some describe as being 'pushed back to work' have been used to shore up the position of 'traditional' motherhood campaigns, such as 'Mothers at Home Matter',[14] whose members defend heterosexual marriage and the desirability of stay-at-home mothers (Perrins, 2013). As Bramall (2013) argues, the fantasy of domesticity may also be appealing as a kind of escapist 'fantasy' for some middle class, high achieving women who were never given the option of experiencing that lifestyle. And yet for many others, living out such a fantasy of domestic bliss is not even an option financially.[15] It may be that this same desire is projected onto those such as 'White Dee', whose 'undeserving' status in the popular imagination as a depressed, stay-at-home mother becomes symptomatic of an envious desire on the part of some to escape the relentless pressures of reflexive modernisation.

The feminist politics of 'stay-at-home mothers' are far from straightforward and are contested on a number of fronts.[16] As Littler (2008) argues, for some feminists, the 'return' to the home is linked to the eco-politics of anti-consumerism, of growing one's own food, recycling and living an ethically sustainable lifestyle. Others overcome the dilemmas of combining the care of young children with a career by becoming a 'mumpreneur' and setting up a business from home.[17] The so-called mumpreneur route is one that chimes in well with both the ideology of reflexive motherhood and neoliberal feminism, which celebrates women's agency and the capacity to combine mothering with an enterprising professional career. From a neoliberal perspective, women's labour power is too important a resource to waste on sitting about, finger painting with the kids at home, despite the promotion of such activities on television and in books by celebrities such as television presenter and former Conservative Party Housing advisor, Kirstie Allsopp (Bramall, 2013, loc. 522).[18]

As a media personality, Allsopp also has a very public media career, and as such, she appears to embody the neoliberal ideal of heterosexual motherhood, as does the much-publicised 'super mother' Nicola Horlicks, who for many years combined her role as a mother of six with running a bank (Kay and Arkell, 2014). Both women are highly articulate, white, upper class and affluent and from the perspective of intersectional feminism, it would probably take them some considerable time to finish checking their privileges. The public lifestyles and values of these women chime in with the kind of right-wing feminism discussed in Chapter 3, that combines neoliberalism with the feminist language of 'free choice' and also 'self-fulfilment', which is also so redolent of therapy culture. In the UK, this lifestyle is also espoused by successful entrepreneurial celebrities such as Louise Mensch, Karren Brady, Carol Vorderman and Katie Price, who have all aligned themselves publicly with the Conservative Party. These women combine motherhood with high-profile careers, and regularly appear on television and in the press to promote themselves and their ideas, thus feeding the aspirations of a 'free choice' feminist common sense.[19] Thus, as I discussed in Chapter 3, the dilemmas of combining one's domestic and professional identity are resolved for such women, who seem to live up to the postfeminist ideal of 'having it all'.

The contradictions of middle class parenting are regularly debated on the influential online self-help parenting website and campaigning group for mothers Mumsnet, created by mumpreneur Justine Roberts as 'a meeting place by parents for parents'.[20] Despite the website's stated wish to engage with 'parents' rather than mothers only, it is women who are seen to dominate the site (Ferguson, 2011).[21] Roberts and members of the website are regularly courted by the media for their political opinions in ways that female politicians in the UK are not. Alongside its tips and advice on coping with the experience of motherhood, it hosts web chats with celebrities and politicians and has discussion threads on familial lifestyle issues, and the names of celebrity mothers such as Louise Mensch crop up among their blog entries from time to time. Nonetheless, the maternal politics of Mumsnet is interesting because it refuses the dominant neoliberal feminist message about the virtues of high achievement in the workplace. The views of Roberts (Roberts, 2013) and its members also link in with the retro 'make do and mend' views of 'austere femininity', as discussed by Bramall (2013).[22] Yet others have criticised the site as 'smug', 'middleclass', judgemental and reifying of a particular 'worthy' image of motherhood as a lifestyle choice for women that is redolent of the promotional images of mothers in a *Boden* clothing catalogue (Street Porter, 2010) and which ignores both the potential pleasures and financial necessity of going out to work (Roch, 2013).[23] However, in terms of gender politics, it may be that the Mumsnet forum does hold the potential to challenge the structures of patriarchal masculinity by sidestepping the structures of the old established media and political networks, and creating potentially new, feminine spaces for political engagement. Indeed, the fathers' rights group Fathers4Justice has been unsettled by it, and responded competitively to the existence of Mumsnet by describing its members as 'barking mad harridans', arguing that it promotes 'gender hatred', and they bizarrely staged a naked protest against Mumsnet in the London branch of the store Marks and Spencer (Edmonson, 2012).[24]

The significance of Mumsnet for party politics was first highlighted in 2009, in the lead-up to the UK general election in 2010, when all three leaders from the main UK political parties were deployed to court the approval of Mumsnet members, who were seen as potential floating voters (Dowling, 2009). All three male leaders from the three main parties used it as a way to showcase their identities as 'new fathers', adopting a strategy that was in contrast to the aggressive, 'fathers' rights' stance of the naked Fathers4Justice protestors. However, the promotion of male politicians as Mumsnet-friendly fathers should also to be situated within the wider context of gender politics and the struggles of hegemonic masculinity, where as I have argued, the performance of new fatherhood is used by politicians to shore up the identity of men at a time when masculinity is in crisis. In addition, the promotion of male politicians as fathers takes place at a time when women remain underrepresented in the UK Parliament and where, for example, at the time of writing, there are no mothers at all in the British Cabinet. In 2009, when Brown, Clegg and Cameron were wooing the 'modern' mothers' vote via Mumsnet web chats (Dowling, 2009), female politicians did not join in or contribute and the strong female voices in this context were those of the Mumsnet mothers themselves, on a range of topics from questions about childcare and tax credits to favourite biscuit brands.

Throughout the period of the New Labour and the UK Coalition governments, mothers may have remained marginal within Parliament, but they have nonetheless impacted popular, political culture through a number of powerful and emotive, public campaigns that took place following the loss of a child, and each of these campaigns has been effective in changing laws and government policy in the areas of the press, criminal law and the police. These campaigning mothers include Sarah Pain, who, following the murder of her daughter Sarah, worked with former *News of the World* editor, Rebekah Brooks on a campaign to bring in 'Sarah's Law' (2011);[25] Kate McCann, who publicly campaigned to raise awareness about her missing daughter, Madeline McCann, and who spoke at the 2012 UK Leveson Enquiry about the need for Parliament to curb the powers of the press following the UK press hacking scandal; and Doreen Lawrence, who brought changes to the police service by challenging the institutional racism of the Metropolitan police following the racist murder of her son, Stephen Lawrence, in 1993. Doreen Lawrence was made a life peer in 2013, and so now exercises some institutional power and influence in that context.

In 2014, Baroness Lawrence was named as BBC Radio 4 *Woman's Hour* 'Number One Game Changer' on the programme's annual 'power list', and she received the award from the Home Secretary, Theresa May, who praised her for the way that she kept resolute and 'picked her self up' and fought to bring to book the murderers of her son. The language and tone used in May's address was very much in the neoliberal, stoical mould of austerity discourse in its appeal to, in effect, 'keep calm and carry on', despite the ongoing forces of institutionalised racism experienced by Lawrence and her family.[26] Doreen Lawrence's response to May's speech was indeed calm, but she refused to be interpellated by May's address and in rejecting that subject position, she also reminded radio listeners of the racism she experiences every day as a black mother, living in London, who is spied on by undercover policemen and who fears being accused of shoplifting every time she enters a shop. The encounter between Lawrence, May and the *Woman's Hour* presenters on that occasion was both powerful and poignant, partly because the grief for the loss of her son and the struggle for justice has, over the years, become a nationally shared experience. Yet the encounter also reinforced the tensions of sameness and difference between women, thereby limiting the possibilities for mourning because of the inherent denial that was present in May's address. Lawrence reminded us that despite being honoured officially by the state and the BBC, she is still looked on by policemen and ordinary store detectives with suspicion and treated as other because of her identity as a black woman.

The absent mother in Parliament

Whilst some women have publicly used their identity as mothers to campaign in extra-Parliamentary contexts, what of those who use their influence inside Parliament? The absence of mothers in this institution-alised and also mediatised setting reflects Irigaray's argument about the absence of the maternal and the threat that it represents to hegemonic masculinity and the symbolic gender order. As we have seen, whilst in the UK and elsewhere, male MPs are happy to promote themselves as new fathers, this is not the case with women MPs. The reticence of such women to talk about their children contrasts with politicians in the US, where evangelical Republican women such as the self-styled 'Mama Grizzly' Sarah Palin, highlighted her role as a 'regular mom' in the 2008 presidential campaign (Burrell, 2014: 234). There is a different culture in the UK Parliament, where the spheres of politics and motherhood are often perceived as incompatible. For example, feminist journalists have expressed concern about reducing women's identity as politicians to 'walking wombs' (Orr, 2014). The potential risks for women identi-fying themselves as mothers was seen when one of the very few black women MPs, Diane Abbott, talked of the fierce loyalty of West Indian mothers who would 'go to the wall' for their sons and was roundly attacked by the press as 'racist' (Walker, 2010).[27]

Campbell and Childs (2014) have carried out substantial research into the representation of women in the UK Westminster Parliament and say that it is not only that male MPs outnumber women by four to one; there are also many more fathers than mothers in the House of Commons.[28] As Campbell and Childs (2014) argue: 'without mothers in Parliament the soaring costs of childcare and the disproportionate effect of the economic crisis on women in low paid and part-time work (mostly mothers) will not reach the top of the political agenda'. The lack of diversity in this respect adds to the perception that the democratic pro-cess is unrepresentative and that political decision-making constitutes a sphere of power that excludes ordinary working mothers. Yet, some of those from the male political establishment do not see this as a problem, and take issue with those who challenge the gender imbalance within

Parliament. As Conservative Peer and ex-Home Secretary and Foreign Secretary Douglas Hurd recently argued in a public debate:

> I think, therefore, the danger of feminism, the danger of constantly putting near the top of agenda that there ought to be more women and more women in this and that sphere of our life, is that you balance over and you become slightly ludicrous.
>
> (Simons, 2014)

Hurd reportedly went on to say that 'all-women shortlists for parliamentary seats' are 'deeply undemocratic and will fail' (Simons, 2014).[29] Hurd's own educational background includes Eton and Cambridge, followed by a diplomatic career and two high ministerial posts in the Conservative government (Bedell, 1994).[30] For Hurd, there is nothing wrong with having a 'good looking chap from public school' as Prime Minister. He said that, if voters didn't like him, they would not have voted him in. Yet it is not voters who exclude mothers from becoming parliamentary candidates, but the selection panels (made up of men and women), who tend to pick men to represent them, and these men also tend to reflect their own social and cultural background (Campbell and Childs, 2014; Lewis and Pitel, 2014).[31] As journalist Deborah Orr (2014) reminds us: 'The typical MP is male, and always has been. That's a powerful subliminal expectation. A female MP is still an MP who contradicts the archetype, whose physical being announces: "I'm not what you expect".' The reproduction of gender, class and power through these selection practices also has a familial dimension to it, as when the sons of MPs go on to become politicians, thereby raising concerns about narrowing the 'political pool' of candidates (Addley, 2014).[32] For example, Douglas Hurd's son, Nick Hurd, who like his father was educated at Eton, and then, as a Bullingdon Club member, attended Oxford, also went on to become a fourth generation MP and Minister for Civil Society (Quin, 2013). It is fair to say, perhaps, that his views about the lack of 'grit' in the attitude of the unemployed who fail to find work reinforce such concerns about the reproduction and protection of male, class privilege in the parliamentary system (Quin, 2013).

A different kind of inheritance and the good enough parent

The notion of political dynasties foregrounds for us the themes of history and the generational inheritance of patriarchal authority that continue to shape discourses of the family within political culture today. Concerns about the absent parent are symptomatic of anxieties about the loss of containing structures that have maintained the familial patterns of inheritance (Cameron, 2011c). The notion of political dynasties also recalls my discussion earlier about the idealisation of the mythical father and the need for myths that foreground the symbols of maternal inheritance. A desire for a sense of heritage is not new, yet in the contemporary political age, which is beset by doubt, fear and crisis, the desire for certainty and knowledge takes on a new sense of urgency, and it is this which arguably lies behind the emotive images of parenthood discussed so far.

When focusing on the notion of patriarchal inheritance, questions of history and the difficulties of mourning have been recurring motifs in discussions about masculinity in crisis (Bainbridge and Yates, 2005), and these same motifs can be applied to the trope of fatherhood in the UK political scene and beyond. A widely reported theme of both Brown's and Cameron's terms in office has been the mourning of their children and their fathers. Cameron in particular was moved to say: 'My father is a huge hero figure for me ... he is an amazingly brave man' and he went on to cite his bravery in living with a 'disability' (Mulholland, 2010). Brown's decision to appear on Piers Morgan's television show in the UK to discuss, amongst other topics, the death of his child, was also used as a strategy to 'humanise' him in the face of negative personal publicity and reduce Cameron's lead in the opinion polls ahead of the 2010 general election (Channel 4 News, 2010). As discussed in Chapter 4, Brown was not the only minister to mourn the loss of his child whilst in office, and the death of David Cameron's son Ivan, who suffered from cerebral palsy, was also widely publicised before the 2010 election campaign and shortly before the birth of his daughter (Chapman, 2009).

The imaginary spaces that were opened for the public who were able to identify with the bereavements of Brown and Cameron as mediated news events, at once facilitated a potential space for mourning that might have allowed new forms of identification to emerge on the part of the electorate, whilst also allowing the leaders to appear as vulnerable and sad icons of fatherhood. Such examples show the potential for more flawed and less idealised modes of political identification to emerge in relation to hegemonic masculinity and the symbolic father. On a positive note, it may be that the current disillusionment with the political system potentially opens up new spaces for mourning, where less idealised notions of the father can emerge for public consumption. Such a move can perhaps precipitate the circulation of new modes of fantasy to underpin the formation of a political culture based less on narcissistic fantasy and the projection of envy and contempt.

Elsewhere, I have used the notion of a 'good enough masculinity' to imagine a more fallible and less idealised notion of masculinity and fatherhood that escapes the neat dualisms of the fatherless society critique, in which identifications with the sphere of the maternal are pathologised or barred, as in the Lacanian-inspired accounts of masculinity and sexual difference (Yates, 2007a). To be 'good enough' is to allow both spheres of masculine and feminine identification to exist and are not seen to 'dilute' 'real' masculinity' as more traditional phallic images of the strong father imply. This capacity to tolerate 'good enough' masculinity has implications for the kinds of fantasies and identifications that are invoked in relation to discourses of masculinity and fatherhood within political culture. Andrew Samuels (2001) reminds us of the analogies between the 'art of parenting' and the 'art of politics' and the similar processes of identification that occur in both contexts. Winnicott's original idea of the 'good enough mother' is one that acknowledges that as in the relationship between electorate and politicians, there is never a 'perfect fit' between parent and baby, but instead there is a kind of 'graduated let-down or disappointment of the baby carried out by her or his parents' (Samuels, 2001: 77). As Winnicott argued, this 'let-down' is equated with a perception of 'failure' on the part of parents, and it is this same sense of failure that the electorate may find hard to tolerate in their leaders (Samuels, 2001: 78).

It seems, however, that in the UK at least, this 'good enough', flawed perception of leadership and political influence is a particularly risky proposition for women politicians, and mothers in particular, who cannot afford to look vulnerable and fallible in the same way as men. The irony here, of course, is that the concept of being 'good enough' is one that was first applied by Winnicott to mothers. And yet, where is the space for the good enough mother of the political imagination? For women and mothers who work in the public sphere, a sense of a matriarchal generational consciousness is one that is often absent and that struggles to be heard and experienced beyond the parodic representations of mothers within austerity culture today.

6
Moving Forward to the Past: Fantasies of Nation within UK Political Culture

Throughout 2014 and in the lead up to the 2015 UK General election, much press coverage was given to the success of the UK Independence Party (UKIP) and its charismatic leader, Nigel Farage. Often pictured outside a traditional English pub, with a cigarette in one hand and a pint of beer in the other, Farage's 'blokey' image is awash with signifiers of a particular unreconstructed English masculinity, which, according to researchers, appeals to a constituency defined as 'left-behind voters' who feel alienated by mainstream politics (Ford and Goodwin, 2014, loc. 3001). Those sentiments are also fuelled by what UKIP voters see as high levels of immigration to Britain, which they say is caused by the imposition of laws by Brussels (Ford and Godwin, 2014). These fears, which signal a defensive, reactionary turn in political culture, also seem linked to wider anxieties about the pace of social and cultural change and the 'risks' (Beck, 1992) associated with the forces of globalisation and late modernity.

This chapter uses UKIP and other examples taken from political culture to discuss the role of nation and its meanings within the British political and psycho-cultural imagination. As with the charismatic London Mayor Boris Johnson (Yates, 2014a), Farage's larger-than-life public persona makes him attractive to some as a maverick, anti-political establishment figure whose brand of populist politics harks back to an imagined place and time when the boundaries of difference and cultural belonging were more clearly marked and less troubled by the dilemmas of identity and what it means to be British – or even English, within what is sometimes called the contemporary 'postnational' context (Habermas, 2001; Heller, 2010).[1] Politics now takes place in a globalised, mediatised context, and yet against a social and political backdrop of uncertainty and crises, the construction of an imagined local national identity is highly seductive for some voters. As with charismatic politicians such as the Scottish National Party Leader Nicola Sturgeon,[2] Farage is a skilled operator in an era of personality-driven politics, and he mobilises discourses of nation in order to promote himself as authentic to the electorate. In Farage's case, he is able to offer a consoling and often humorous narrative of an English-inflected Britishness in an era beset by uncertainty, crisis and change.

This chapter locates the current reactionary turn in sections of political culture and the appeal of UKIP as a popular political and cultural force within an historical context, by discussing the shifting and often contested field of cultural representation of nation within British political culture since the New Labour government in 1997. I draw on selected examples and case studies throughout, including Joanna Lumley's Gurkha campaign and the Scottish Referendum, and I conclude by returning to the case of Farage and UKIP and discuss their appeal in the contemporary context. I want to begin, however, by discussing the methodology adopted in this chapter, which includes the psycho-cultural meanings of nationalism and its relationship to the processes of political culture.

A psycho-cultural approach to nationalism and politics

The term 'nationalism' refers to 'a form of patriotism marked by a feeling of superiority over other countries'.[3] Yet it is also necessary to take account of the routine and ordinary character of nationalism when discussing its place in political culture. Michael Billig's (1995) thesis of 'Banal Nationalism' contrasts 'hot nationalist passion' with the 'banal' culture of its everyday expression through everyday symbols and rituals, and his analysis alerts us to the hidden significance of nationalism as a way of life (40–49). Obvious examples of such rituals might include national sporting events such as the football World Cup, or in a more ordinary, everyday fashion, the display of national flags and bunting at school sports days. Billig says that the ordinary symbols of nation reinforce the 'us versus them' dynamic that underpins nationalism and the acceptance of the nation state and its boundaries as natural. As Michael Skey (2009: 334) argues, 'our acceptance of nations as natural divisions of the global territory and population is essential to the maintenance of the existing geographical order'. Skey (2009) applies a Gramscian theoretical framework in order to explore the hidden political significance of banal nationalism as 'the ongoing production of a hegemonic discourse' and as a form of 'taken for granted, common sense' (333). One can extend Skey's thesis to argue that the contestation of the concept of nation within popular, political culture, together with the shifting psycho-cultural significance of its symbols, should also be seen in that light.[4] In Gramscian terms, one can argue that the way in which ideas of nation are deployed in order to cement alliances between different political parties is pertinent in the context of contemporary UK politics, where UKIP's distrust of immigration resonates with many voters.

The ways in which the British have engaged with the shifts in their national identity in the postcolonial era have been widely explored in history and cultural studies (see Gilroy, 2004; Nava, 2002; Yuval-Davis, 2011). Mica Nava (2002: 86) says that 'the legacy of nationalism and xenophobia at home' has been a recurring theme of such studies, whilst Gilroy (2004) argues that the attacks on multiculturalism have also been linked to a melancholic inability to let go of a white, colonial past. And yet today, as Nava argues, one can also present an alternative perspective on UK culture and its citizens that reflects a more cosmopolitan outlook 'in relation to popular, personal and cultural levels' and an openness to new experiences, difference and otherness (Nava, 2002: 88). Nava's perspective is influenced partly by Stuart Hall (1996) and it also chimes in with psychosocial theories of reflexivity, mobility and subjectivity that emphasise the fluid, open-ended contingency of contemporary global experience and the reflexive competence of the contemporary UK subject (Elliott and Urry, 2010; Urry, 1995).

The complexity of experience as presented in Nava's account of nation, subjectivity and desire is echoed in the work of Nira Yuval-Davis (2011), who explores 'the intersectional contestations' of contemporary experience and reminds us of the importance of the 'situatedness' of national belonging in time and place and history, in which the boundaries of belonging are shaped by a complex mixture of ethical, political and emotional factors. Yuval-Davis says that a nationalist politics of belonging is not the only form of belonging in the UK, as it is overlayered with other forms of attachment and identification such as religious identification, which, as a form of belonging, exceeds the boundaries of the nation state (2011: 1). Yuval-Davis develops this point by referring to the words of the British 7/7 London bomber, Mohammad Sidique Khan, who, in his Al Jazeera so-called 'martyrdom video', referred to 'my people'. As she says, Khan was not referring here to the British people, but rather, he was addressing Muslims 'all over the world' (Yuval-Davis, 2011: 9). In a post-9/11 context, the legacy of Khan's television address and actions provoked a nationalist response in sections of the British public, laying the seeds for further anti-Islamic prejudice and the reworking of an imagined divide between 'them and us'. Yet, as regards the latter, it is also significant that following the London bombings, many Londoners refused to align themselves with that split view and did not take up a knee-jerk nationalist position. Instead, the traumatic events were psychosocially and emotionally worked through via a number of collective rituals and gatherings, including, for example, the Trafalgar Square rally in London, led by then London Mayor Ken Livingstone, and the dance performed by Akram Khan's company at the 2012 London Olympics, which in psychoanalytic terms constituted a form of mourning and reparation (Yates, 2014b). Livingstone's speech at the Trafalgar Square rally that was held a week after the bombings exemplified a cosmopolitan ethical position in its appeal to a collective London sensibility of openness and a capacity of its citizens to embrace difference (Livingstone, 2005).

In this sense, the processes of identification and belonging are always mutually shaped and take place within relational contexts, and the mediatisation of contemporary experience is significant in this respect. Mohammad Sidique Khan's message was delivered on film and television, and the different responses to the events that were triggered by him and his fellow bombers were also shaped and communicated on different media platforms, including television, print and social media. On the one hand, the public reaction was countered by a desire for reparation. Yet at the same time, Khan's actions also triggered a defensive nationalist response that was linked to the wider so-called 'war on terror' as constructed and communicated on broadcast television and in national presses, which promotes the idea that cultures are highly vulnerable to the risk of terror (Ortega Breton, 2014). Since the 7/7 London bombings, this world view has hardened. For example, in the UK, the 2009 anti-war protests at Luton airport gave rise to the English Defence League (EDL), and the murder of the soldier Lee Rigby on the streets of Greenwich in 2013 was used by the EDL to justify the aims of their organisation.[5]

A further context of Khan's attack on the London public was (and is) the performative appeal of Hollywood machismo. Hollywood cinema has arguably responded to violent jihadists by returning to macho masculinity through Hollywood action heroes in films such as *Captain America: The First Avenger* (2011) and *Noah* (2014). Similarly, Khan's actions were shaped by the US television action hero 'Mr T' from the 1980s programme *The A-Team* (1983–1987). Khan and his conspirators were ardent fans of the programme and three days before the suicide bomb mission, they communicated with each other by text message using catchphrases from the show (Kahr, 2014: 31–32). The gendered dimensions of Khan's actions are telling, when set alongside his identification with the macho team spirit of the show's characters and the production values of NBC. Yet at a wider level, Khan's identity as a 'fan' of *The A-Team* also highlights for us questions of belonging, nation and identity in a mediatised world, where the production values of NBC may also shape the processes of politics, identification and belonging in postnational cultural contexts.

Psychoanalytic understandings of nation and the unconscious

Psychoanalytic ideas can help us to explore the emotional and irrational identifications at play in nationalist contexts. Using a psychoanalytic reading of the relationship between nationalism and unconscious fantasy, Lene Auestad (2014) has written persuasively about the rise of nationalism in European countries, both in terms of its expression in extreme far-right groups and in the context of everyday political language and policy. For example, in Europe, alongside the extremism of Greece's neo-fascist party, the Golden Dawn, Geert Wilders' Dutch anti-Islamic PVV Party or Marine Le Pen's Front National in France, Auestad (2014) reminds us that in recent years nationalist concerns have been foregrounded in mainstream political debates about immigration and multiculturalism in France, Germany and the UK (loc. 188). In his influential analysis of 'nation' as an 'imagined community', Benedict Anderson points to the irrational basis of 'nation' as an 'imagined community':

> It is imagined because members of even the smallest nation will never know most of their fellow-members, meet them, or even hear of them, yet in the minds of each lives the image of their communion.
> (1991: 7)

As I have discussed, what constitutes a nation in the minds of a community is always historically and culturally specific and has psychological and emotional dimensions that are shaped by the forces of unconscious fantasy and what Freud famously called the 'the narcissism of minor differences (1930: 305) and a desire, perhaps, for what Nava (2002: 21) calls 'the dull security of sameness'. Nava draws on the work of Julia Kristeva (1993) to argue that nationalism can be viewed as a kind of comforting 'transitional object' to 'hang on to' at times of uncertainty in which

'attachment to the safety of the local, the known, is interpreted as a narcissistic impediment to mature transition' (Nava, 2002: 21). This idea of
nation as a comforting object can be developed further in order to think
about the processes of object relating in socio-political contexts, and
the ways in which politicians and their policies that foreground the language of nation may be put to use as objects of either 'transformation' or
'conservation' within the psycho-cultural imagination. These two types
of object relating were first discussed by Christopher Bollas (1987), when
he developed Winnicott's ideas about selfhood and transitional phenomena to argue that 'the wide ranging collective search for an object'
is linked to the 'metamorphosis of the self' (Bollas, 1987: 15–16). Bollas
argues that we seek objects that may psychologically hold and contain
us, and that while these objects provide a continuity between inner and
outer worlds of experience, they also shape and change who we are on
an ongoing basis. Bollas describes this process in the following way:

> Each entry into an experience of an object is rather like being born
> again, as subjectivity is newly informed by the encounter, its history
> altered by a radically effective present that will change its structure.
>
> (Bollas, 1992: 59)

However, alongside the creative aspects of transformation, there are also
more reactive ways of relating in which objects may be shaped and
experienced defensively, in order to fend off anxieties associated with
change, difference and the fractured experience of late modernity (Yates,
2014a). Bollas's discussion of 'malignant' moods and their relationship
to the 'conservation' of objects can be applied in order to explore nationalist sentiment. Bollas (1987: 102) likens the 'special state of a mood' and
the emotional work that takes place within it to that of a dream, as the
mood works as an environment through which the emotional work of
object relating takes place:

> Moods are complex self-states that may establish a mnemic environ-
> ment in which the individual re-experiences and recreates former
> infant-child experiences and states of being.
>
> (1987: 102)

Bollas distinguishes between 'generative' and 'malignant' moods, and
in the case of the latter, the mood is used as a way to block object
relating and signifies an inability to work through the 'unthought
known', which is beyond representation and cannot be articulated
(1987: 100–101). Bollas's notion of 'living through of a mood' is highly

evocative when applied to a collective experience of nationalist senti-ment and a nostalgic desire to stage a return to the past as an object, where in fantasy at least, the psychosocial boundaries of subjectivity and belonging may seem more clearly defined and known. The latter is sug-gestive when applied to the vision projected by UKIP and even London Mayor Boris Johnson, whose public persona seems to evoke a particular nostalgic fantasy land of English 'jammy dodgers', Routemaster buses, boys-own comics and table tennis (Yates, 2014a).

However, the temporal dynamics of patriotism and imagined com-munities can take other forms, as when Tony Blair aligned himself and New Labour with the forces of modernity and the cultural aesthetics of 'Cool Britannia' and the 'Britpop' celebrities of popular culture (Harris, 2010b). To explore this further, and to provide an historical and cultural context for the emergence of UKIP as a popular political and cultural force, I now turn to the shifting and often contested field of cultural rep-resentation of nation in British political culture since the New Labour government in the1990s.

Shifting moods and images of nation and belonging: from Cool Britannia to Little England

When New Labour came to power in 1997, they liked to promote their image as a playful, youthful and progressive party, and the idea of the British 'Nation' was defined and promoted in modernising terms as 'rebirth' (Blair, 1995). The language of the 'new' and 'modernisation', so frequently employed in Blair's speeches, was used to mark the cultural difference of the New Labour era from the previous one that was associ-ated with a tired, old, backward Conservative government (Fairclough, 2000: 16). As Blair proclaimed, shortly before becoming Prime Minis-ter: 'a new Britain – a nation reborn, prosperous, secure, united – one Britain' (Blair, 1995). The cultural symbols and images of youth and pop-ular culture were appropriated by New Labour to enhance their brand, and the publicity that was given to the parties held at No. 10 Downing Street for celebrities and pop stars provides examples of this strategy. That moment of confidence in the early stages of the New Labour gov-ernment seemed to pick up on a wider cultural patriotic pride in the success of the British music industry, fashion and art world. Yet that same sense of assurance was also linked to the rise of a late capitalist performative aesthetic of advertising culture in which, perhaps, a less committed and more cynical, knowing postmodern irony was coupled with the playful re-appropriation of older patriotic symbols and images, including the Union flag.

The semiotics of national flags was famously explored in Roland Barthes' (1973: 109–159) short essay 'Myth Today', where he decon-structs the meaning of an image of a black soldier saluting the French flag in *Paris Match* and contrasts the contexts in which a flag is saluted and when it is not, as when Barthes came across the picture in the magazine in a French barber shop. As Michael Billig (1995) argues, the distinction between the two contexts of saluting the flag is significant because it alerts us to the 'banal' context of nationalism as an everyday experience. The shifting boundaries of when a national flag is consid-ered worthy of a salute can be used to explore the changing mores of nation and its patriotic structures of feeling for any country. The ironic reclaiming of the Union flag for purposes of promotion and fash-ion can be seen in this light, and in the 1990s, the Spice Girls singer Geri Halliwell's Union Jack dress and New Labour's promotion of 'Cool Britannia' provide examples of this practice. At one level, one can argue that the use of the flag in this context is an empty gesture that resonates more with the superficial aesthetic strategies of postmodern advertising. At another level, however, the semiotic charge of the flag imagery and New Labour's patriotism are linked to the affective traces of an earlier moment in the cultural and political history of Britain and the Labour Party when, in 1967, during a period of economic crisis, Labour Prime Minister Harold Wilson (1967) encouraged the British people to 'Buy British' in order to help shore up the economy.

That patriotic plea was accompanied by a wider popular campaign in which the words 'I'm backing Britain' were represented over a Union Jack background and reproduced on badges, mugs, clothing and car-rier bags. Nevertheless, this campaign was contested and it attracted criticism, mainly from the left, and the journalist Philip French (1968: 85) made a plea to 'put out less flags'. The contemporary stereotypi-cal upbeat images of 1968 and the 'I'm backing Britain' campaign thus mask the economic crisis of that period.[6] Trade unionists also protested because workers were encouraged to work longer hours without extra pay as a patriotic gesture – a message which resonates with the contem-porary context of austerity. At that time, there was even a patriotic song, 'I'm backing Britain', sung by the popular entertainer Bruce Forsyth, who encouraged British workers 'to lend a helping hand' and that 'an extra half an hour is all we need each day' (Forsyth, 1968).

Thus, in 1997, New Labour came to power claiming to 'look for-ward' whilst re-appropriating the patriotic pop iconography of an earlier period, which, despite its upbeat connotations, was shaped partly by the uncertainties of economic insecurity and political conflict.

As in 1968, albeit for different reasons, the theme of modernisation that underpinned New Labour's rhetoric about creating and celebrating a 'New Britain' also contained a number of contradictions that extended beyond the promotional imagery of British popular culture. New Labour's vision for the UK was meant to be about the rejection of old social hierarchies, and the introduction of the Race Relations (Amendment) Act in 2000, which set out to combat institutional racism, provides an example of this aim (Phillips, 2004). And yet the progressive, egalitarian connotations of New Labour's move in this area of social policy also contradicted some of its less progressive policies related to nation on immigration and asylum seekers.

When Ed Miliband became leader of the Labour Party in 2010, he was asked repeatedly to apologise for New Labour's stance on immigration when they were in power (ITV News, 2012). Indeed, Jack Straw, who was the British Home Secretary 1997–2001, is on record as saying that it was 'a spectacular mistake' (Hasan, 2014). Nevertheless, journalists and scholars have argued that while on the one hand, New Labour opened the borders to Eastern European immigrants in 2004, their attitude towards asylum seekers was anything but forward looking and was instead defensive and reactionary in its response (Hasan, 2014; Standing, 2011a). Throughout its first two terms in office, New Labour became increasingly concerned about the 'problems' of managing multiplicity and diversity 'thrown up' by multiculturalism and instead began to focus on a normative model of integration and 'community cohesion' (Worley, 2005: 492). Fears about the 'enemy within' and 'without' became widespread and were linked to the 'war on terror' following 9/11, and to concerns about the so-called 'race riots' in the North of England in 2001. The preoccupation with 'community cohesion' is one that implicitly includes a sense of 'them and us' and as such is powerfully bound up with the politics of nation and belonging (Yuval-Davis, 2011: 37). The notion of 'community' in this context, with its emphasis on homogeneity, also carries with it a number of racialised connotations that are more overtly expressed in the rhetoric that was and is deployed about the threat of asylum seekers to state sovereignty and national security. Maughan (2010: 6) says that 'British political elites have linked immigration policies to internal race relations' and that this 'indicates the existence of a specific understanding of national identity'. As she goes on to say:

> Labour and Conservative politicians have consistently argued that strict border controls are necessary for maintaining good race

relations ... By linking immigration and race relations ... politicians have consistently signalled that cultural or ethnic diversity is a threat to community stability' (7).

Negative images of asylum seekers are thus used as a means of shoring up national identity 'by providing a distinct "other"' (ibid.).

The contradictions of New Labour's policy about community cohesion and immigration were tackled by Gordon Brown (BBC News, 2006), when as the British Chancellor, following the 7/7 bombings in London in 2005, he spoke of his desire for 'a united shared sense of purpose' and of the need to be 'unashamedly patriotic'. Brown also talked about the Union flag as a symbol of British unification:

> Instead of the BNP using it as a symbol of racial division, the flag should be a symbol of unity and part of a modern expression of patriotism too.
>
> (BBC News, 2006)

Brown's efforts to present a unified and progressive reworking of what it might mean to be British need not be seen simply as a reactionary knee-jerk response to the threat of terrorism, even though it emerged in that context. Given the extremity of what had happened, one can argue that some kind of containing response was necessary. One could also argue that reclaiming the Union flag from its old negative right-wing associations and giving it a sense of meaning beyond the vacuous images of 'Britpop', signified the potential for a new progressive sense of identification with the notion of British citizenship, a stance that anticipated his views about the problems of Scottish nationalism in the lead up to the Scottish Referendum in 2014 (Brown, 2014). In psychoanalytic terms, one could, in a positive way, also link Brown's notion of the flag and a new patriotism to Christopher Bollas's notion of the transformational object, in which the subject engages with the objects related to the historical and cultural imaginary of the past, in order to create and relate to a new vision of the future.

And yet, Brown's speech was also set against the backdrop of the divisive legacy of the Iraq war, and his attempts to produce a unifying vision were made all the more difficult because of that foreign policy history, to which Brown was closely linked. As we have seen, the London response to the 7/7 bombings was effective at a more local level, when people came together and listened to Ken Livingstone in Trafalgar Square. Seven years later, the Olympic celebrations also demonstrated the power of cultural activity as a means of enabling a shared sense of identity and community spirit, as a means of bringing large numbers of people together to share in a mood of transformation and hope. However, Brown's attempts to create a new patriotism that unified the nation in a post-9/11 context was not successful and his actions, together with the policies of that time, have been widely criticised as divisive and authoritarian (see, for example, Yuval-Davis, 2011). Brown raised the theme of patriotism once more when he spoke about 'British jobs for British workers' in his first speech as Leader to the Labour Party in 2007 (Brown, 2007). In that speech, Brown referred to a number of imminent threats, including foot and mouth disease, floods and 'the resilience of the British people' in the face of the terrorist attacks and the need for British citizens to stand together, united in the face of such threats.

Brown's speech was initially well received by the press and the public, and yet his failure to follow through his rallying call to the British public is well documented.[7] What is more, Brown's refrain about 'British jobs for British workers' resonated with a defensive and fearful nationalist sentiment and a growing resentment about immigration, as alluded to earlier in this chapter. For example, two years later Nick Griffin, the leader of the far-right British Nationalist Party, said:

> What Mr Brown actually meant when he said British jobs for British workers is of course down to Mr Brown. But there's no doubt that it was perceived – and was intended to be perceived – by millions of ordinary Brits as meaning that they would be at the front of the queue in front of economic migrants from anywhere else in the world.
>
> (Griffin, 2009)

It is ironic, perhaps, that it was Brown's overheard remarks about what he perceived to be the 'bigoted' comments of Rochdale voter Gillian Duffey that seemed to finish off any hopes of him and his party being re-elected to government (Curtis, 2010). Duffey had questioned him about the national debt and the cost of immigration and Eastern Europeans claiming benefits, questions that have since been voiced more routinely in public by UKIP, the UK press and also by Prime Minister David Cameron, who in the summers of 2013 and 2014 following UKIP's success at the European elections, adopted a macho stance in promising to 'put Britain first', curb 'bogus students' and take 'tough action' on European migrants and to harden the rules about the length of time 'foreigners' can claim benefits (Dominiczac, 2014).[8] Cameron's attempts to assuage the jealousy and prejudice of those who fear the loss of jobs and resources to 'foreigners' chimes in with research that highlights the links between banal nationalism and the threat presented by a potential loss of economic and welfare provision (Skey, 2009). As Skey (ibid.: 340) argues, 'economic prosperity, wealth distribution and political stability' all play a role in 'cooling' the so-called 'hot' passions of nationalism, and at moments of economic crisis, the temperature of nationalist sentiment can rise once more.

A further response to the restrictions of austerity and the malignant mood to which it is linked is the impulse to look back and identify with what Bollas calls a fantasy of 'conservation'. The popularity of the retro-austerity slogan 'Keep Calm and Carry On', which was first used in Second World War Britain and was re-appropriated in 2000, appeared to symbolise – albeit in a parodic guise – a stoical attitude that British people were meant to adopt in the face of the Coalition austerity cuts. As Jeremy Gilbert (2011) argues, the humorous, postmodern irony of the slogan also contains a number of authoritarian connotations about the need for self-governance, and he links its appeal to a contemporary 'politics of pain', where in a masochistic fashion, one learns to enjoy the pain of deprivation and accept what one is given. In Chapter 5, I discussed the regressive sexual politics of austerity and its retro-popular cultural aesthetics of 'make do and mend' evoking the period of the Second World War and its aftermath in Britain. Joanna Lumley's 'Ghurkha Justice Campaign' that began in 2009, during the end period of the New Labour government, exemplifies some of the themes discussed so far, including a desire to look back that was also linked to fantasies of sexual politics and nation.[9]

Joanna Lumley and the 'Gurkha Justice Campaign'

Actor and television personality Joanna Lumley attracted widespread admiration when she fiercely took on the bureaucratic system of the Home Office in her campaign to allow former Gurkhas to remain in the UK. The New Labour government, who as we have seen were often in thrall to the celebrity system, thus found themselves in this instance a victim of it, as Lumley, who is regularly defined as 'a national treasure' (Aslet, 2010; Gold, 2013), was filmed 'confronting' then Home Office Minister Phil Wollas about his incompetence regarding the deportation of former Gurkhas (Wintour, 2009). Unsurprisingly perhaps, New Labour ministers resented her intervention and also the media that followed her around as she waylaid and challenged New Labour ministers on camera. In addition, the 'shaky authority' of the then unpopular Prime Minister Gordon Brown was reported as being undermined (even) further by Lumley's campaign (White, 2009). Labour Minister Paul Mullin complained about the hypocrisy of the 'immigrant-bashing Tory newspapers', who supported Lumley's wish to allow Gurkhas to settle in the UK (White, 2009). In his 2009 published diary entry, Mullin is recorded as saying:

> The whole thing has been got up by the tabloids and the Telegraph – which ironically, are rabidly opposed to entry for just about every other category of foreigner – and the dreadful Joanna Lumley, who all week has been emoting over our television screens.
>
> (Mullin, 2009: 324)

And yet, as one journalist put it, 'branding Joanna Lumley an irritant' was a huge PR mistake on the part of New Labour: 'Why didn't he moon at the Queen while he was about it?' (Aslet, 2009). References to notions of Britishness, femininity and a romantic vision of Britain's colonial history all coalesced in the UK press coverage around Lumley's public persona as a 'national treasure' and 'forces sweetheart' (White, 2009). Lumley's femininity was foregrounded in these accounts and she was likened to other idealised, iconic female figures of British history and the establishment, including Vera Lynne, Margaret Thatcher and the Queen. Such references seemed to position Lumley beyond the fray of masculine politics. Yet, of course, Lumley and her campaign were very much a part of it, as the history of Britain's relationship to the Gurkhas is linked to Britain's past as a colonial nation with ties that go back to the East India Tea Company (Aslet, 2009; Gimson, 2009).[10] The containing aspects of the fantasy of the Gurkha warrior as a noble symbol of Britain's colonial history was reinforced by Lumley, who as an upper middle class daughter of the British Empire, shored up a consoling sense of national identity as being rooted in its paternal links to the symbolic father of a British colonial past. Lumley was widely described as a 'daughter of the regiment', as her father, Major James Lumley, had been a member of the 6th Gurkha Rifles and had fought alongside the very men that Lumley was supporting in her campaign (Wanell, 2008). Analogies were made in the press between her father's heroic 'battle' and her own 'battle' for the right of the Nepalese Gurkha veteran soldiers to be granted settlement rights in the UK. Lumley's family was thereby aligned with a sense of national history that seemed to contrast with what many journalists saw as the shallowness of the New Labour project, which according to some critics had even disavowed its own radical history in its relentless march forward (Allen, 2008).

Lumley's campaign, with its insistence on fairness for war veterans, therefore represented a refusal of New Labour's message of 'modernisation' which, in its links to globalisation and neoliberalism, was opposed in different ways by an alliance of those on both the left and right, and the campaign exposed its lack of moral authority in this respect (O'Neill, 2009). Opposition politicians capitalised on this moment in order to oppose the government line and speak of a need to return to the values of an earlier era, including those of 'decency', 'morality' and grace', that had somehow been lost along the way (Aslet, 2010; BBC News, 2009b; Drury and Hickley, 2009).

At a moment when the Conservative Party was attempting to define itself in opposition to New Labour, whilst at the same time adopting some of their market-friendly policies (Seymour, 2010), David Cameron was able to use the plight of the Gurkhas in order to overcome these contradictions. His identification with the campaign appealed to the traditional members of the Conservative Party who were concerned about the liberalisation of the party and its values, whilst at the same time it appealed more widely to the voting public through the association with Lumley as a hugely popular celebrity. Thus, one can argue that just as the Gurkhas had once been used as warriors to support the British in colonial battles, they were now being used once more, albeit in a different context, to shore up the identity of British politicians and that of the British public more generally, as reassuring symbols of the past at a time of general uncertainty (O'Neill, 2009). Indeed, the appeal of Lumley's campaign also needs to be set against a wider backdrop of economic insecurity related to the 2008 banking crisis, and a growing disenchantment with the structures of authority that had once been seen as underpinning the forces of British democracy and national identity.[11]

The postmodern preoccupation with nostalgia as a defence against the losses and uncertainties of contemporary culture has been discussed at length within the field of Cultural Studies (Radstone, 2007) and the gendered dimensions of this process can be seen in Lumley's crusade for justice and the response it provoked. From a psychoanalytic perspective, it seemed to tap into a particular structure of feeling or 'mood' that sought out reassuring objects and symbols of national identity within the psycho-cultural imagination by staging a return to the stories and images of Britain's colonial past. Just as the boundaries of the old gender order were shored up by her campaign, defensive anxieties about national borders and immigration were reconciled in the press by reports of the Gurkhas being hired to 'guard' the Olympic Games site in order to protect it against any terrorist attacks (Jeory, 2009).

The Gurkha campaign is significant at a number of levels, as the events surrounding it seemed to signal the end of New Labour and its desire for modernisation, anticipating the widespread disillusionment with mainstream politics as articulated by UKIP voters. Indeed, the managerial and technocratic tone and style of the New Labour government and of the Coalition that followed, contrasted greatly with the righteous anger of Lumley, who answered her critics in a style that seemed refreshingly authentic and 'above politics' in its appeal to a particular common sense. Interestingly, in the spirit of earlier middle class feminist campaigners of the 19th century, who also emphasised their difference from men (Rendall, 1987), she used her femininity and her emotional sensibility to signal the authenticity of her motives, locating them above the symbolic masculine sphere of everyday politics:

> I know we have been accused of being emotional but that is because I am an actress and a woman, and we are always being accused of being emotional of which I am rather proud. I think that unless you can take judgments of right and wrong like an automaton, you must have emotions because that is our only way of moral guidance.
>
> (Lumley, cited in Wintour, 2009)

Thus, when the New Labour government lost the vote about the right of Gurkhas to stay in the UK and Lumley 'won',[12] it was widely reported that the old-fashioned values of 'moral decency' seemed to have won the day (BBC News, 2009b). Lumley's campaigning style was very much in tune with the emotionalisation of politics and the foregrounding of celebrity within political culture. Lumley's idiosyncratic charm and charisma also echoes the success of celebrity politicians such as Boris Johnson, who also deploys a non-managerial political style of rhetoric and charm to appeal to the general public (Yates, 2010).

The retro appeal of Lumley's 'doughty' style of campaigning femininity (Moore, 2008) was, in stylistic terms at least, in step with a wider shift away from the 'modernising' project of New Labour.[13] Although as I discussed in Chapter 2, many of the policies of New Labour were taken up by Cameron and the Coalition government, the promotional discourses of politics and nation now appeared to look back to the style and values of an earlier era, and aesthetically this shift could be found more widely in the popularity of clothing brands such as Boden and in the celebration of retro fabrics as in Cath Kidston products. Both brands have been publicly consumed by Tory politicians such as Boris Johnson and David Cameron, thereby highlighting the close links between promotional culture, nation, class and politics (Burrell, 2013).

The flag was used again. But in a different way than it had been in the modern Britpop New Labour era, and the popularity of the British Monarchy was also given a boost, following the public marriage of Prince William and Kate Middleton and then through the Queen's Diamond Jubilee celebrations in 2012. The Cath Kidston brand, which reclaimed the Union flag as part of its retro-austerity aesthetic, 'cooled' the nationalist connotations of its image as a symbol of the far right, and the flag could be seen planted in window boxes and waved at street parties by people without fear of being branded members of the British Nationalist Party. However, the acceptability of displaying the flag remains an area of contestation. For example, in 2014, the symbol of the flag became a flashpoint for the Labour Party when they found themselves out of step with current norms about the acceptability of flags. In this incident, Islington Labour MP Emily Thornberry was sacked from her shadow cabinet post for being an out-of-touch 'snob' for allegedly ridiculing an 'ordinary' 'white van man' on Twitter for ostentatiously displaying English St George flags over his house in the Rochester and Strood constituency, in which UKIP were set to win a by-election (Adams, 2014). The implication was that Thornberry had made a negative stereotypical link between class and nation and like Gordon Brown in 2010, she had alienated the very voters that Labour needed to attract, if they were to return to power. At one level, what this incident shows is the significance of social media for modern politics. Yet it also illustrates the nuanced, class-based significance of nationalism and its symbols for British identity. It also reflects, perhaps, a rejection by some sections of the electorate of the cosmopolitan elements of third-way politics as espoused by New Labour and David Cameron's Conservative Party (Gilbert, 2014). Third-way politics was linked to a globalised consumer culture, where, as with Cath Kidston bunting, identity and flag waving was linked less to a sense of national belonging and more to the identification with brands as an aesthetic lifestyle choice. Yet, as Thornberry's social media gaffe illustrates, the disillusionment with that system arguably opened up spaces for nationalism to return as a populist 'hot' concern, and this development has been expressed in different ways, both by UKIP in England and by voters in Scotland.

Brave hearts versus English coronets

The kind of Britishness that is linked to public figures such as Joanna Lumley and Nigel Farage is one that is associated with a white, upper middle class Englishness, evoking an earlier age of empire. Whilst

Scotland cannot be separated from the history of the British Empire, it is the cultural assumption that Englishness constitutes a sort of default Britishness that lies behind the wish of many Scottish people to separate from England and instead govern themselves. Discourses of nation took centre stage in UK political discourse during the 2014 Scottish Referendum, in which people living within the borders of Scotland voted on whether they wished to remain part of the UK. The Scottish nationalist sentiment of the 'Yes' campaign also needs to be seen against a backdrop of austerity culture and free market economics. For some of the electorate, the old and new myths of Scotland as a nation were embodied in the romantic and heroic spirit of the 1995 film *Braveheart*, and the stars of the film could be found promoting the message of independence on the Scottish National Party 'Yes' campaign website.[14] At one level, the nationalist appropriation of *Braveheart* evoked a sense of looking back and an engagement with a notion of Scotland as a sentimental object of conservation. Yet, this caricature of the *Braveheart* voter also emanated from the Westminster government and the British press, who resisted the emergence of a new kind of identity that was premised upon a rejection of traditional London-centred politics (see, for example, Jones, 2014). The 'Yes' campaign suggested the identification on the part of some with the hopeful politics of transformation and a rejection of free market austerity culture and the values of neoliberalism. At that time, the journalist Paul Mason (2014) argued that younger Scottish voters saw the independence referendum as an opportunity to challenge the hegemony of UK neoliberal culture and instead establish one in which statehood and a new cultural and national identity could be linked to the practices and values of social justice.[15] Bollas's theory of the 'transformational object' resonates when applied to the referendum politics as an object of the psycho-political imagination. It is especially pertinent when applied to the potential spaces that might open up as a consequence of taking a chance and making a 'leap in the dark', as David Cameron put it in his 'Stay with us' speech on the eve of the Scottish Referendum (Dominiczak et al., 2014), albeit in pejorative terms. Throughout the campaign, anxieties about loss and separation were also brought to the fore. Alongside the affective dynamics of transformation, Bollas's concept of 'conservation' as a defensive, regressive mood was also evoked through some of the campaigning on both sides. Thus, the referendum campaign reflected elements of both moods in the psycho-cultural spaces that it both opened up and closed down, in relation to the politics of nationalism, affect and identity.

The potential break-up of the United Kingdom provoked extensive discussion in the popular press and the painfulness of Scotland breaking away was described as an 'amputation' (Freedland, 2014). The potential wounds of separation, as expressed by the *Guardian* journalist Jonathan Freedland, remind us of the complex and even irrational emotions that exist in relation to the attachments and losses of nationhood and the psycho-cultural dynamics that shape them. Given those feelings, it is perhaps not surprising that the language of marital attachment and 'divorce' was often used when discussing the 'break-up of the UK', bringing into sharp relief the emotional theatre of politics and what is at stake when questions of nation and belonging are brought to the fore (see, for example, Memon, 2014).[16] In a last minute attempt to save the Union, David Cameron made a passionate 'plea' to the Scots to remain in the Union, and his tone was noticeably softer than that of his more combative opponent, Alex Salmond, as he tried to woo the Scottish voters, saying that he would be 'heartbroken' if they chose to separate (HeraldScotland, 2014). Cameron's speech, which was tantamount to a declaration of love for the Union of the United Kingdom, was made as he and the other two political leaders from Westminster travelled together to support the 'No' to independence campaign.

Alongside a Scottish nationalism, an English nationalism emerged, both from the left and the right wings of political life. British journalists and intellectuals have also discussed the problems and even desirability of so-called English citizens defining for themselves a sense of their own national identity. And yet some, including celebrity public figures such as Billy Bragg (2014), have argued that a new progressive Englishness can be developed (Painter, 2012). However, at the same time, as we have seen, discussions about the English nation can be found among populist far-right-wing groups such as the English Defence League, who define themselves in aggressive opposition to what they see as Islamic extremism.[17]

UKIP as the UK Home Guard

It is against the recent historical, political and cultural backdrop discussed so far that the popularity of the UK Independence Party and its values has grown. The appeal of the British National Party has waned, and yet UKIP has taken up some of their concerns and has given voice to a right-wing populism that in some ways evokes the ideological moment of 'Powellism' of the 1960s and 1970s. Powellism stirred up racist anxieties about immigration that were influential in shaping British political culture at that time (Hall et al., 1978). Those anxieties were articulated by the Unionist MP Enoch Powell, whose notorious 'Rivers of Blood' speech from 1968 has since been cited approvingly by Farage, who says that 'the principles' of the speech were 'basically right' (Huffington Post, 2014).[18] Following the 2015 UK General Election, UKIP returned one Member of Parliament, and yet it still attracted nearly 4 million votes (BBC, 2015) and as we have seen, its growing membership is linked to a number of complex forces that I have begun to map in this chapter. The Scottish Referendum was significant for UKIP, as it demonstrated disillusionment with what is often referred to as the old Westminster politics, and carried with it an affective energy that was driven by a desire for change. And yet, there are differences. Whereas the Scottish Independence campaign largely represented a desire for left-leaning progressive, radical change and a wish to create a closer relationship with the rest of Europe, UKIP seems to be driven by a desire to look back.

Research tells us that UKIP voters are largely made up of 'economically marginal and politically disaffected voters' who are also attracted by its 'anti immigration rhetoric and populist anti-establishment strategy' (Goodwin, 2010). The political sensibility of UKIP voters and their politicians are regularly defined in opposition to what Farage and others like to call the 'liberal metropolitan elite', whose cosmopolitan outlook is seen as synonymous with the forces of 'the establishment' and is viewed by UKIP voters and their politicians with distrust and contempt (Kirkup, 2014). This split between the so-called UKIP 'left behinds' and the 'liberal elite' is also influenced by social and economic factors related to class, in which there is a perception that the better off, affluent groups have benefited from cheap immigration labour. The 2011 British Social Attitudes survey on 'class' said that immigrant workers compete for jobs with British manual workers, who feel 'under siege', 'disenfranchised', 'squeezed between benefit claimants, immigrants and the expanding middle class' (Rentoul, 2011). These different factors shed some light on why those who fall outside the professional classes might turn to UKIP. Their status as a 'grass roots' party is attractive to those who feel angry and ignored by a government who, in the words of populist Conservative politician and UKIP sympathiser, Nadine Dorries (albeit with reference to the former UK Coalition government), is run by 'out of touch' 'posh boys who don't know the price of milk' (BBC News Politics, 2012).

The UK voter turnout at the 2014 European election was low, and yet those in England who did cast votes did so in Farage's favour, thereby confirming the anti-European mood of large sections of the English population. UKIP also did well at the English local council elections that were held on the same day, gaining 163 seats, making them the fourth party in English politics (BBC News, 2014).

Initially, UKIP voters were seen as a threat primarily to the Conservative Party, whose members were attracted by its anti-European stance and also its social conservatism on issues such as gay marriage. However, given the social demographic of its voters, and the high number of votes gained in the 2015 General election at the cost of Labour, UKIP is now also seen as a danger to the Labour Party (BBC News, 2015). Indeed, in the lead-up to that General Election, the Labour Leader, Ed Miliband, was perceived by UKIP voters as 'clueless', privileged and out of touch (Harris, 2014: 7). Following a 'slim' by-election win in Heywood and Middleton in the autumn of 2014, Miliband was put under pressure to foreground the 'problems' of immigration and 'harden his stance' in this regard as a response to the political agenda set by Farage (Wintour and Watt, 2014). As discussed earlier, the Rochester and Strood by-election also provides an example, perhaps, of Miliband's attempts to deflect charges of elitism in his own party and to accommodate the new right populism represented by Farage.

UKIP's appeal rests on a number of factors. At one level, the popularity of his anti-immigrant message is symptomatic of wider social, political and economic forces that are shared across Europe, where the popularity of far-right parties is linked to the experience of social and economic 'precarity' as a result of the banking crisis, the subsequent debt regimes and austerity programmes in the eurozone (Standing, 2014, 2011a, 2011b). Guy Standing (ibid.) argues that a social grouping that he defines as the 'Precariat' have the potential to create a new, progressive politics to challenge the reactionary messages of far-right parties and the complacency of Western democratic political parties such as the Labour party. Yet, the popularity of a party such as UKIP suggests a different kind of response to the precarity of the contemporary age. Led by the seemingly ever-genial Nigel Farage, UKIP with its MEPs and counsellors are happy to scapegoat immigrants and utilise fearful discourses of homophobia and misogyny to win over those who experience economic disadvantage and an existential sense of being 'left behind' (Ford and Goodwin, 2014). Discourses of contagion and crime are used to conjure up images of the dangerous other, and examples here include the Eastleigh by-election candidate, Diane James, who in 2013, spoke about the need to halt immigration because of opening 'the floodgates' to Romanian criminal gangs (Dominiczak, 2013), or Farage's comments in 2014 and 2015 about the need to stop migrants with HIV coming to the UK, who do so in order to receive free treatment (Watt, 2014; Butler, 2015).

As a charismatic personality and skilled communicator, Farage capitalises on the celebrity turn in politics through constant media appearances in which he regularly takes up his role as the main spokesperson for his party. Even BBC Radio 4 *Woman's Hour* presenter Jenni Murray (Woman's Hour, 2014) seemed to warm to him after he was invited onto the programme to discuss the misogyny of his party in general and the sexism of then UKIP MEP Godfrey Bloom in particular, who referred to women as 'sluts'. Farage's populist and playful public persona is one of an un-spun, genial host. He claims to speak from the position of an anti-establishment common sense and as an ordinary patriot and man of the people, who loves cricket, watching the BBC television sitcom *Dad's Army* and drinking English beer. As we have seen in previous chapters, the notion of authenticity is key to the appeal of celebrity politicians, and Farage shows how this quality can be exploited when harnessed to known, shared national symbols of the past. The numerous gaffes by UKIP members seem not to have harmed UKIP, and the hiring of the very experienced, BBC journalist Paul Lambert as director of their communications team was an attempt to professionalise the party in this respect (Siddique, 2014).[19]

It may be that UKIP has been able to shape a new common sense around immigration, and yet the hegemony of that position has been challenged on a number of fronts, as can be seen in the defensive rhetoric around the topic within the main Westminster parties. As I discuss in Chapter 7, one response to UKIP has been to mock its existence through different forms of satire and parody, thereby tapping into the comedic turn in postmodern politics, in which the views of comedians are often taken more seriously than the politicians they are satirising. The British comedians Russell Brand and Al Murray provide examples of this development; both have been highly critical – albeit in different ways – of Nigel Farage and the politics of UKIP. Al Murray's character, 'The Pub Landlord', stood as an MP against Farage, and he used the symbols of the pub and pints of beer to mimic and poke fun at Farage by calling himself the 'common sense' candidate.[20] Political activists on social media have also been energetic in opposing his views. The need to promote a different kind of populism to counter the right-wing populism of UKIP that highlights the positive, cosmopolitan experience of 'cultural multiplicity', has also been discussed (Gilbert, 2014).[21]

From a psychoanalytic perspective, the symbol of independence is key to UKIP's appeal, connoting as it does a fear of dependency and a narcissistic wish to defend against sameness and merging with the other. Infantile dependency is an historical fact of life for everyone, and the evocation of that early experience at times of uncertainty and loss can lead to considerable anxiety. The denial of relationality and an adherence to a false idea of independence as a defence mechanism is symptomatic of such anxiety, and UKIP's philosophy can be seen as one example of this process in action. At a time when, for some, identity seems threatened by precarious social forces and global processes beyond their control, the idea of independence and the denial of dependence can get carried into political thought so that a UK identity of splendid isolation may seem preferable to one in which there is a mutual dependency upon one in Europe. One needs to be wary of falling into a trap of pathologising voters and their voting preferences, and yet the emotive rhetoric of right-wing parties such as UKIP which foreground the notion of 'independence' in their name arguably call for such an analysis.

As I discussed earlier, it is often said that we live in a postnationalist era, in which the identification with nation may not be the central facet of one's sense of identity and belonging, as factors such as religion, generation and gender may also come into play. In order to build a sense of community in a global and mobile society, new fluid spaces of belonging and markers of identity need to somehow be held in tension together. However, as I have discussed with regard to UK discussions about Scottish Independence and devolution, one can see that the emotional attachment to the concept of nation as a marker of identity is still highly significant. Nationalist sentiment is not necessarily characterised by a defensive mood of conservation, but instead may signify a desire for community and meaningful relational politics at a more local level of engagement. In this respect, one can articulate different forms of nationalism that are not necessarily linked defensively to the fear of ethnic difference (Yuval-Davis, 2011). Yet for political parties such as UKIP, the idea of nation becomes caught up defensively as an object of conservation within the psycho-political imagination, and is used to shore up an identity based on a regressive fantasy of independence and a refusal to engage with the threat posed by the realities of interdependence and what it may be that we actually have in common.

7
Reflections on the Psycho-Cultural Dynamics of Political Culture

The current scene of politics and its discontents

In this chapter, I want to revisit some of the themes, concepts and ideas that I have raised in the preceding chapters and explore the broader theoretical questions regarding the relationships between identity, emotion and the play of contemporary political culture. Throughout this book I have used a psycho-cultural approach to explore the interactive relationships between UK politics, popular culture, emotion and fantasy and their symbolic influence in shaping subjectivity and cultural identity in the late 20th and early 21st centuries. More specifically, drawing on different case studies, the aim has been to provide a snapshot of a particular moment in UK political culture from 1997, when Tony Blair's New Labour government came to power, through to the end of the Conservative-Liberal Democrat coalition government in 2015. Today, small political parties such as UKIP and the Scottish National Party have emerged to challenge the old settlement of the two-party political system, and this is a development that also reflects the emergence of new modes of populism within the contemporary political scene.

That shift was illustrated on 10 October 2014, when the former Conservative Member of Parliament Douglas Carswell delivered a victory for UKIP as their first Member of Parliament for the constituency of Clacton, in Essex. The drama of the occasion was captured in the theatrical silence that met him as he entered the chamber of the House of Commons for the first time since being elected in order to take up his seat in his new party. That silence was linked to a sense of betrayal by those in the Conservative Party, and also perhaps to a concern by Labour MPs that given the appeal of UKIP for disillusioned voters, they could also suffer a loss of votes among those attracted by UKIP's populist message.

At a more general level, that silence could also be read as symptomatic of a wider fear that the old UK parliamentary system of two-party politics had ceased to work, or as Nigel Farage put it in rather dramatic terms, 'the tectonic plates of British politics are shifting' (McTague and Chorley, 2014).[1]

As I discussed in the previous chapter, UKIP is largely perceived as a 'protest party' who, like other protest parties in Europe, deploys a message that is centred upon reactionary anti-Europe and anti-immigration sentiment. The dissatisfaction of UKIP voters also taps into a wider disenchantment that views politics and politicians as objects of contempt and disappointment. One can trace the causes of that disillusionment with politics – and for some, even a hatred – back to a range of factors that centre upon a collective lack of trust in the structures and system of representative democracy. The public anger about the 'Cash for Access' scandal, which involved two senior UK politicians and ex-Foreign Secretaries offering their services as private consultants for large sums of money, provides an example of this process at work[2] (*The Guardian*, 2015; Ward and Walton, 2015). As I have discussed in earlier chapters, that distrust is also related to the current conjuncture of neoliberalism and the failure of the markets to deliver financial and welfare security (Ford and Godwin, 2010). Clearly, the negative attitudes, together with the anger and cynicism towards politicians, extend beyond the UK and that negativity has challenged the political complacency of Western governments who have hitherto relied on the aspirational, new middle classes to return them to power.

Since the economic crash of 2008, a growing divide between rich and poor has become apparent and as I have documented, that inequality has been examined in academic research, news journalism and in the Occupy protest movements in Europe and the US, where the '1 per cent' protest movement has been particularly vocal.[3] Standing's (2011a&b, 2014) discussion of 'the precariat' examines the ways in which stagnant wages, the loss of job security and the dismantling of welfare systems have resulted in the loss of the old social contract and created instead a new, rootless, global class of people, with little sense of purpose or belonging. And yet, Standing believes that the anger and dissatisfaction of the precariat class can potentially be harnessed for the good, in the service of a new progressive politics. The recent successes of European socialism and the left-of-centre political parties such as 'Syriza' in Greece and 'Podemos' in Spain also provide examples of the rise of a popular politics combined with a progressive ideology that challenges the hegemonic strategy of austerity that has dominated the UK and has been led by Germany in the rest of Europe. Such protest confirms the view that the lack of trust in what has been called the 'post-political' machine of party politics does not eradicate the material reality of political struggle, nor the desire for it (Žižek, 2009).[4]

The content and format of such struggles also reflect the mediatisation of political life, and there is now a large body of literature and research on the influence of the media in shaping democratic politics (Barnet and Gabor, 2001; Savigny, 2016; Thompson, 2000; Washbourne, 2010). Governments now use new media technologies in their election campaigns and similarly, social media has been harnessed as an empowering tool by political activists and citizen journalists who use different social media platforms to create or challenge the dominant news agenda and also in the context of political activism, to communicate their own message, through blogs, YouTube sites, Twitter or online petitions and so on. These developments reflect the mediatised dynamics of a networked society (Castells, 2000, 2012). The latter enables new horizontal modes of communication that challenge an older model of politics based on the vertical structures of political leadership and the symbols of patriarchal authority (Yates, 2014a). The horizontal dynamics of contemporary politics potentially creates new opportunities for political engagement. And yet, some, in a more negative vein, have identified the emergence of a new mediated sphere of politics as being linked to a narcissistic preoccupation with the self. Here, it is argued that such developments are linked to the fragmented nature of identity politics and single issue campaigns, which work against relatedness and the knowledge of what it is that citizens share and have in common (Fisher, 2013).[5]

The gendered dynamics of networked political culture and its relationship to fantasies of the father and a wish to preserve a hierarchical model of leadership and governance were explored in Chapter 5. Following the 2011 England riots, the notion that we are witnessing a crisis of paternal authority was often alluded to by politicians who used that moment to emphasise the significance of their own personal relationships with their fathers in order to align themselves with a particular kind of paternal inheritance. Given that context, it is perhaps significant that on one occasion when the UK opposition leader Ed Miliband was attacked in the press, it was phrased in relation to what was represented as the tarnished inheritance of his late father, the eminent left-wing sociologist Ralph Miliband. The attack on Ralph Miliband's reputation was carried out by the *Daily Mail* newspaper, which claimed that he 'hated Britain' because of his communist beliefs (Levy, 2013).

It is of note, for the purposes of the present discussion that the paper also claimed that Ralph Miliband expressed that hatred to the 'father' of socialism himself, Karl Marx, at his graveside in Highgate cemetery: 'The cemetery was utterly deserted... I remember standing in front of the grave, fists clenched, and swearing my own private oath that I would be faithful to the workers' cause' (Levy, 2013). The apparent 'dangers' of both Ralph and his son Ed Miliband are emphasised in the paper, which says that like his father, Ed's intention is to attack and destroy the elite institutions of Britain, including 'Eton and Harrow' and '*The Times* Newspaper'. At a broader, social symbolic level, one can link the preoccupation with the father as signifying a cultural yearning for a sense of paternal inheritance that is perceived as being under threat in some way. Yet, as I discussed earlier in this book, given the current context in which the UK government is both supported by and made up of large numbers of sons from those institutions, the *Daily Mail* has little to fear, as that inheritance appears resilient for the time being. The attacks by the tabloid press on Miliband and his father can thus be viewed as attempts to shore up the legitimacy of those institutions at a time when the 'elite' are regularly criticised as excluding 'ordinary' people. In addition, the perception of that inequality contributes to the disillusionment with politics as a system of representative democracy.

The loss of respect and trust in the processes of politics represents a form of disillusionment that also has implications for the weakening of the nation state as a source of emotional containment.[6] Richards (2015) argues that citizens often turn to popular culture as an alternative source of emotional comfort and identity. In the UK, as elsewhere, the boundaries between popular culture and political life have become increasingly porous and interactive, as the commercial and performative entertainment values of celebrity culture feed into and shape the culture of politics as a space for public engagement (Scullion et al., 2013; Van Zoonen, 2005). The emergence of a mediatised promotional politics presents a very different picture to what Habermas (1989) famously defined as the ideal model of the public sphere as a meeting place of 'real' people for rational, democratic debate. Van Zoonen (2005: 22) sees this development in positive terms, and she describes the personalisation of politics as a move away from what she sees as the modernist, patriarchal model of politics as a sphere for rational discussion, to one, which in its emotional tone and circular storyline format has much in common with the genre of soap opera. The battle between the two brothers, Ed and David Miliband, for the UK Labour leadership in 2010, provides an example of this particular narrative at work. The colourful depiction of the alleged sibling rivalry between the two brothers was widely covered in the press (Hall, 2014) and was also made into a satirical docudrama film, *Miliband of Brothers* (More4, 2010). The earlier, rivalrous battles between Gordon Brown and Tony Blair during their time together as Prime Minister and Chancellor of the Exchequer in the New Labour government provides another example of politics as soap opera. Their rivalry was even turned into a Channel 4 television drama, entitled *The Deal* (1994), where they were pictured in the Islington restaurant Granita, haggling over which one of them should take over as the Leader of their party.[7] More recently, the media coverage of the alleged rivalry between the UK Green Party Leader Natalie Bennett and her predecessor, Caroline Lucas, has also been the focus of attention and has been covered in relation to what has been satirically dubbed 'The Granola Pact' (Chakelian, 2015). In the case of the latter, the irrational, emotionalised dimensions of the so-called 'rivalry' are accentuated, thereby reinforcing older discourses of excessive femininity and its instabilities within the public sphere.

The representations of those personal conflicts between politicians emphasise the sibling quality of their rivalry, thereby reflecting the lateral dynamics of the fantasies that circulate within the context of a contemporary networked political culture. The latter evokes what is sometimes referred to as the 'sibling society' (Bly, 1996), which is a concept that is often used pejoratively to highlight the adolescent qualities of the baby boomer generation. The popularity of playful politicians, such as Boris Johnson, who mock the paternal figures of authority, is suggestive in the light of such discussions (Yates, 2014a). The sibling society critique also has much in common with Lasch's critical assessment of the shallow, self-regarding nature of narcissistic culture and the loss of the containing structures of paternal authority in that context. Unsurprisingly, perhaps, the soap opera-flavoured dimension of modern party politics has been derided by some critics as belittling political discourse, and like the promotional turn more generally, politics as entertainment asks us to believe in a 'false' set of images, adding to a climate of 'hyper-stimulation' and a 'debasement of the media of public communication' (Rustin, 2007: 76). Indeed, from that critical perspective, the disenchantment with politics and the lack of trust in its processes is connected to the lack of the 'real' in political life today.

Nonetheless, Van Zoonen (2005) argues that the soap opera-style narratives of contemporary political culture can, from a feminist perspective, be seen in more positive terms as a move towards what some have defined as a more 'feminised' mode of political engagement, which takes more seriously the private sphere of emotion, intimacy and domestic affairs culturally associated with women. In addition, the interactive relationship between popular culture and politics allows the public to deliberate on and engage with the issues of the day in ways that potentially draw new audiences and participants into the democratic process (Craig, 2004; Street et al., 2008).

The comedy of political culture

The popular, interactive dimensions of political culture are evident in the way that humour is deployed by politicians in order to appeal to the electorate. The Italian comedian-turned-politician Beppe Grillo, who co-founded the successful grassroots party, MoVimento 5 Stelle (Five-Star Movement) in Italy, provides an example of the crossover between politics and comedy today (Del Savio and Mameli, 2014).[8] Grillo's antagonistic stance toward the established system of representative democracy chimes in with the attitude of UKIP, and in 2014 he formed an alliance with Farage to 'bring down Brussels', with images of the two men laughing and joking together widely covered in the press. As we have seen, in the UK, Nigel Farage often uses humour to charm and 'play' with the electorate. Another example can be found in London Mayor Boris Johnson, who is well known for his humour and wit and whose comedic turn on the comedy television show *Have I Got News for You* (2003) is familiar to British audiences and added to his celebrity as a politician.[9] By contrast, Russell Brand, who is not a politician but in fact a professional comedian, regularly discusses politics and expresses his opinions on the cultural and political issues of the day on his 'Trews' YouTube broadcasts.[10] As I discussed in Chapter 6, the increasingly surreal nature of the blurred boundaries that exist between the spheres of politics and comedy was found in the Free the United Kingdom Party (FKUP) that was set up in Nigel Farage's constituency, West Thanet, by the comedian Al Murray, whose comedy character is called 'The Pub Landlord'.[11] Just as Farage portrays himself as a patriotic man of the people who likes to crack a joke whilst being pictured clutching a pint of beer, in or outside British pubs, Al Murray mocked Farage by standing in front of Big Ben, holding a pint of beer. The acronym FKUP satirises UKIP and its nationalist slogans by declaring: 'The Other Parties Offer a Moon on a Stick. We'll Do Better Than That: A British Moon on a British Stick'.[12]

One can read the popularity of such political satire as being linked to the emptiness of the late modern, 'post-political' moment, when the electorate might as well vote for a fictional joke character as vote for a 'regular' politician, who more often than not is perceived as a vacuous performer without any real principle or meaningful manifesto. The cynicism of that message was promoted by Brand who, while failing to stand as a politician himself, urged people not to vote, in the lead up to the 2015 UK General Election. After a much-publicised meeting with Labour Leader, Ed Miliband, who decided he needed to court Brand and his followers, Brand changed his mind and told his fans to vote Labour (Brand, 2015) However, by then it was too late for his followers to register to vote. The comedic turn in politics, perhaps represented in the UK by Brand, cannot be separated from the anxieties of the contemporary age, where alongside the social and economic instabilities of late modern life there are new others and threats to contend with, including, for example, at both global and local levels, the development of ISIS, widespread acts of misogyny and the growth of anti-Semitism. As Freud argued in his book *Jokes and Their Relation to the Unconscious* (1905), jokes provide a way to channel and communicate anxiety and manage aggression. In the same way as dreams, jokes are deeply symbolic and they can be used to learn more about the unconscious and the forbidden wishes and fantasies that shape human experience (MacRury, 2012).

Just as Farage's humorous and jovial demeanour is used to mask the aggression of his message about immigration, Al Murray also deployed humour in order to challenge the implicit aggression of UKIP, creating new spaces to engage with politics as an object of play. The emotional work involved in such contexts can be viewed not just as a form of escapism, but rather in a more progressive vein as constituting a potential space in which to challenge and work through the political dilemmas of the moment. Politics in this context functions symbolically as a psycho-cultural object that can be toyed with and played with, and as I discuss below, this notion of play and the work that it involves can be used to explore the shifting engagement with political culture at a time of uncertainty and change. It is also worth noting, perhaps, that alongside the pleasures of being tickled – so to speak – by the likes of clowning politicians such as Boris Johnson, there is also the experience of being the butt of a joke, and being teased can carry with it the sadistic and humiliating connotations of being played *with*. That perception of injury, albeit magnified on a psychotic, murderous scale, may have partly contributed to the massacre of the Charlie Hebdo cartoonists by ISIS terrorists in Paris on 7 February 2015.

The psychodynamics of play: from creativity to mastery

Throughout this book, I have used the notion of 'play' as a metaphor to explore the psycho-cultural processes of political culture, which is now also bound up with the values and practices of promotional culture. That examination has included the discussion of emotional identification and the cycles of seduction, desire and disappointment, as created by the emotive stylisation and performative nature of the contemporary political scene.[13] A recurring theme has been what Richards (2007) calls 'the emotionalisation' of public life, and I have developed this idea to discuss the ways in which the 'play' of emotion is often used as a marker of identity for politicians who weave it into their performances on the public stage within the mediatised arena of political culture. The performance of politicians involves the 'play' of emotion at a number of levels. The play of personality, with its links to fantasies of charismatic leadership, are related to a desire for authenticity, truth and fantasies of 'the real thing'. Such desires may also give rise to anxieties about being duped, 'played about' or 'let down' – anxieties that are also linked to the broader social and cultural context of late modernity, where the fluidities of identity are bound up with the experience of trust and risk and new dilemmas about social, cultural and political belonging. The loss of faith in the systems of governance following the economic crash of 2008 have also contributed to such dilemmas.

I have explored the wider social, cultural and economic context in relation to other cultural factors, including the marketisation of modern politics, where, as is now well known, the significance of consumption in shaping political identities has been key (Lilleker et al., 2007). The growing role of 'therapy culture' and the debates about 'emotional governance' were also discussed, and I applied those ideas to the analysis of various case studies. Moreover, psychoanalytic theories were used in order to explore the irrational pleasures, longings and fears that mediate identifications with political figures and their parties and policies.

The psychoanalytic theories and concepts of D.W. Winnicott (1971) are useful in this context, because he is able to capture the dialectic relationship between self and society that underpins the identification with politics as a relational process. Winnicott describes the interplay of the social and psychic processes in shaping everyday experience and refers to what he calls the 'third' area of experience: a 'potential' or 'transitional space', between the subject and m/other,[14] where meanings are shaped and reshaped and where subjectivities are 'bound into the matrices of cultural experience' (Yates and Day Sclater, 2000: 137). Winnicott describes this process in the following way:

We experience life in the area of transitional phenomena, in the exciting interweave of subjectivity and objective observation, and in an area that is intermediate between the inner reality of an individual and the shared reality of the world that is external to individuals.

(1971: 64)

When applying Winnicott's theory of transitional phenomena to the different coordinates of the political scene that I have identified throughout this book, is it the case that new transitional spaces have emerged for political engagement that facilitate and reflect the psycho-cultural complexities of identity and contemporary culture? Or have such spaces emerged only to be co-opted by the instrumental structures of neoliberalism, narcissism and the commercial forces of celebrity culture? One can recognise both scenarios at play in different contexts. Winnicott emphasised that a 'facilitating environment' was essential for the processes of transitional phenomena to work effectively. Following the uncertainties and crisis-laden context of contemporary culture, together with the rhetoric and experience of austerity, it appears that a more defensive response seems to characterise the present era of political life, in which the processes of disillusionment and conflict are hard to bear and are defended against through the mechanisms of fantasy and object relating described earlier in this book.

For example, as I discussed in Chapter 6, with regard to the potentially regressive politics of Nation, one can apply the ideas of Christopher Bollas (1987) to think about the engagement with objects of 'conservation' as a way to manage the losses that the culture of crisis and uncertainty can bring. As I also explored in relation to the contemporary politics of parenting, one can see such psycho-cultural processes in action in relation to UK political discourses of parenting, where class prejudice against so-called 'benefits scroungers' has been a recurring theme in recent years. Persecutory fears about the 'abject' other become located in the scapegoat of 'bad' parents who are represented as depleting 'the nation' by 'draining' the public purse. Such fears are indicative of an explicit turn on the part of the government and the press to discourses of mastery during the period of austerity, where the language of dangerous appetites is a recurring theme. David Cameron's call for 'fat people' to go on diets or 'lose benefits' (McTague, 2015) exemplifies the tone of this shift in rhetoric which attempts to exploit the symbols of excess as a means of communicating with voters.[15]

From a psychoanalytic perspective, the focus on bodies is significant because it evokes destructive modes of fantasy and archaic structures of feeling and development described by psychoanalyst Melanie Klein in

association with the first stages of life (1957). The underpinning philosophy of psychoanalysis is that the biological fact of infantile dependency
leaves a mark that shapes us forever after and from which we never fully
recover. The defences against the memory of that early infantile vulnerability continue to shape the relationship between the individual and
society, and the notion of the autonomous subject can be viewed as a
defence against dependency and the early relational context of subjectivity. Klein's ideas are pertinent when discussing the paranoid fears that
underpin the culture of austerity and the uncertainties of the contemporary era, where a politics of 'othering' (see Tyler, 2013) is deployed as
a means of managing primary anxieties and shame about dependency
and loss, and the attacks on publicly funded institutions within what is
known as the welfare state can also be seen in this light.

The play of maternal ambivalence and political culture

The anxieties that I have just described may also be linked to fantasies of maternal ambivalence and such scenarios are bound up with
the gendered dynamics and symbols of political culture and images of
women in public life. Today, on the world stage, there are a number
of women who occupy powerful political roles, and German Chancellor Angela Merkel provides an obvious example of this phenomenon.
In the UK, the three opposition parties have women leaders, including
Natalie Bennett for the Green Party, Leanne Wood for Plaid Cymru and
Nicola Sturgeon for the Scottish National Party. Nonetheless, it remains
the case that women continue to be under-represented in the UK Parliament more generally (Fawcett Society, 2014). The shortage of women in
UK politics, which is reportedly linked to the poor conditions of life in
that field of work, may also be linked to the difficulties of negotiating
the masquerade of public and private identities as discussed in Chapter
3, as well as the ambivalent projections that women face when taking
up a public, political role. When women do enter the public sphere as
politicians or as journalists who cover political issues, they often engen-
der a powerful emotional response from the public and are subject to
misogynistic abuse in the press and broadcast media. As we have seen,
the news coverage of the two leading women in the UK Green Party,
who are represented as being in conflict with one another, reproduces
old stereotypes of rivalrous femininity.

The development of social networking provides new opportunities
for this misogyny to take place and facilitates the quick discharge of
destructive emotion that is often aimed at women who voice opinions

in the public sphere (Beard, 2014). This online aggression is found in the comments made about female politicians on Twitter and social networking blogs and in the online comments that can be found under the bylines of female journalists. The UK MP for Walthamstow, Stella Creasy, former MP Louise Mensch and campaigner Caroline Criado-Perez have all been subject to cyber-bullying, and Criado-Perez received rape threats for having the temerity to campaign for a woman's face to be put on UK banknotes (BBC News, 2013). As Bainbridge (2010) has noted in relation to female journalists, such attacks are not confined to men about women, but also include women attacking other women.[16] Some women even appropriate the language of old masculinity in order to reprimand themselves, as with the former UK Government Minister with Responsibility for Equality Lynne Featherstone's description of herself as a self-confessed 'nag' within government (Martinson, 2012). In this respect, the cultural analysis of women in political culture and the fantasies that those representations stir up, and which shape our identifications with women in public life, need further attention.

A theme of this book is the flirtatious nature of late modern political culture and given this context, I applied Joan Riviere's reading of femininity as a form of masquerade to explore the unconscious dynamics that shape the fantasies of gender and political culture today. Riviere's analysis is useful to understand the powerful emotions and cultural anxieties aroused when encountering images of women in power as well as the strategies used by women in the public sphere to ward off aggression. And yet, despite being in a culture that values certain forms of emotional expression as a means of signalling authenticity, women have a different relationship with the electorate than do their male colleagues, and they must be wary of how they use the flirtatious methods of political communication to their advantage, in case they attract stereotypical associations of being 'lightweight' or 'over-emotional'. During the time period that I have discussed in this book, certain men have been skilled at wooing the electorate, and this was particularly the case in 1997, when Tony Blair first came to power as the New Labour Prime Minister. I want to now return to Blair and his legacy as a flirtatious politician.

Blairite dressing and the masquerade of political flirtation

When I began my research into the play of political culture, I decided to foreground the notion of flirtation as a metaphor to explore the personalisation of politics in Western democracies, where the integrity of political ideology had been replaced by a focus on the seductions of personality and the mechanisms of a media-driven celebrity culture. As I have discussed, Tony Blair seemed to exemplify this flirtatious turn, both in terms of what seemed at one time to be his likeable and charming persona, and also in the 'third-way' political agenda, which replaced the tribal antagonisms of what came to be called 'Old Labour' with the more consumer-friendly 'New Labour'. The third-way politics of New Labour was about taking a version of the 'centre ground' which, aided by the market research methods of focus groups and so on, flirted with marginal floating voters (rather than the committed ones), attempting in a sense to be all things to all people. As is well documented, the fall of the New Labour government coincided with and was also largely caused by a series of social and economic crises in 2008, and in 2010 it was replaced by the Conservative–led coalition government. As I discussed in Chapter 2, the disillusionment with New Labour often focused on Blair and his role in the Iraq war, and the public were painted as victims of his charm and false methods of persuasion. Yet the 'downfall' of New Labour was also linked to the inability of Tony Blair's successor, Gordon Brown, to perform and flirt to camera in the same skilful manner as his predecessor, instead becoming the object of ridicule every time he attempted to smile in public.

When David Cameron took over as the UK Prime Minister in 2010, the theme of flirtation continued in relation to the coalition partnership between Cameron and his deputy, Nick Clegg, whose initial press meeting and photo-call in the Downing Street garden appeared to signal the beginning of a new 'bromance' between the two men and their political parties. That relationship also took on homoerotic connotations in press reports of the 'Brokeback coalition', an image, which reportedly caused 'unease' amongst the more traditional male Conservative MPs (Watt, 2010). Yet, the term was said to have been coined by the macho Conservative MP David Davis, who used it pejoratively in the context of 'lampooning' the coalition, which at that early stage seemed in danger perhaps of eschewing hard-core Tory values. The symbolism of Clegg and Cameron's seeming intimacy and their political alliance caused anxiety for those such as Davis, who wanted to re-insert some difference between them (Watt, 2010). The sneering, homophobic connotations of the 'Brokeback' label carries traces of anxiety about the instabilities of masculinity and the sameness of the two men. Yet that anxiety also masks problems about a different kind of sameness, both in relation to the similarity of the cultural capital and class background of the two men, but also more importantly, perhaps, with regard to the sameness of their political positions and the shared advocacy of neoliberal free market economics.

From 2010, during the period of the Conservative–Liberal coalition government, the flirtatious cycle of desire and disappointment that characterised the New Labour era continued. It became apparent that the coalition was unable to deliver what it had promised and so feelings of disillusionment, anger and contempt returned to the electorate. In 2010, Cameron let it be known that rather than being likened to a protagonist in the 'gay cowboy film *Brokeback Mountain*', he wanted instead to be identified with the film *True Grit*, which originally starred John Wayne (Daily Mail OnLine Reporter, 2010). At the same time, Cameron was also encouraged to drop his 'big idea' about the 'Big Society' (Norman, 2010), because as a concept it was too 'vague', 'cosy' and unclear (Watt, 2010).[17] Cameron (Cabinet Office, 2010) said that the Big Society was about instilling a sense of civic engagement in communities that would bring people together to build a better society.[18] Yet, as the senior Conservative politician David Davis pointed out, the Big Society was really 'a Blairite dressing' for plans by the coalition... to trim the state' (Watt, 2010). As the cuts were implemented, the Blairite style of address fell away and the notion of the Big Society also disappeared from public discourse. As I have discussed, the consent for the programme of austerity was achieved partly by targeting those groups who could be scapegoated as wasteful and dysfunctional and who could carry the 'shame' for 'the regime of debt' built up over many years (Venn, 2012). Instead of 'us' 'all being in it together', the message shifted to one of individual 'resilience' and self-sufficiency. Such a strategy is symptomatic of a defensive structure of feeling as identified above, in which vulnerability is repudiated and where the common ground is denied, thus affirming well-entrenched public opinion about the cynicism of the political class and its failure to represent them.

In this sense, one can argue that while pockets of political culture have, in a positive way, the potential to create new transitional spaces for object relations and the political imagination, the contemporary psycho-cultural dynamics of 'play' within the political scene often appear to be shaped defensively by the processes of repetition and mastery. The latter connotes, perhaps, an addiction to a system that does not function effectively and yet cannot change or move on. The 'stuck-ness' of that position evokes the term 'interregnum' that was used by Gramsci to refer to a state of 'crisis' in which 'the old is dying and the new cannot be born' (1971: 276).[19] The repetitions at play within such a scenario are analogous to the circular rhythms of gambling, with its emotional dips and euphoric highs, where in an age of late market capitalism the language and practices of the 'Casino' with its culture of illusion and risk are now widespread (Giroux, 2014; Strange, 1997).[20]

It is against this backdrop that the popular perception has taken hold that politicians are empty performers who fail to communicate with and represent the lives of ordinary people. The appeal of politicians such as the UKIP Member of Parliament Douglas Carswell can also be seen in this context. When he defected from the Conservative party to UKIP in 2014, he was recorded as saying that Prime Minister David Cameron is a 'Love Actually Prime Minister' who is similar to the fictional Prime Minster as played by Hugh Grant in the 2003 film of the same title (Hattenstone, 2014).[21] Yet, Carswell himself has not evaded the 'as if' space of performative politics inhabited by Cameron or even Blair before him. Indeed, Carswell's alliance with Nigel Farage and the populist politics of UKIP suggests that he has not escaped the fictional dimensions of political culture today.

This book has explored such phenomena by discussing the continual interweaving of social, cultural and psychological processes that shape the contemporary political scene. Whilst focusing mainly on the UK and on a particular time period, many of the concepts, themes and concerns that have been discussed are ongoing and retain their pertinence. The psycho-cultural approach developed here can also be applied elsewhere to political contexts in Europe and the US for example, where the dilemmas of late capitalism continue and where the ethos of promotional culture interacts with the emotional theatre of politics and the struggles of identity and popular culture.

Notes

1 Introducing Emotion, Identity and the Play of Political Culture

1. Psychosocial Studies at UEL was first developed by Michael Rustin, Barry Richards, Mike Smee and Amal Treacher alongside colleagues at the Tavistock and Portman NHS Trust in North London. For a discussion of the Psychosocial Studies field, its history and its differences: see, Day Sclater, Jones, Price, and Yates (2009), and the Special Issue of the journal, *Psychoanalysis, Culture and Society*, 2008, Volume 13, Issue 4, 2008: 339–385.
2. John Street has defined popular culture 'as a form of entertainment that is mass produced or is made available to large numbers of people' (1997: 7).
3. An advantage of using digital posters to promote a political party is that they are cheap to produce, and can respond quickly to issues and themes raised on the campaign (Nikkaha, 2010).
4. For this and other posters of the UK 2010 National Election Campaign, see Guardian.co.uk (2010) 'Election Campaign: General Election Campaign 2010 in Pictures', 15 April 2010, http://www.guardian.co.uk/politics/gallery/ 2010/mar/30/general-election-2010-labour#/?picture=361777434&index, date accessed 18 January 2014.
5. "Gene Hunt" was a detective in the popular BBC 1 television drama *Ashes to Ashes* (2008–2010).
6. To view this image, click on the link http://newsimg.bbc.co.uk/media/images/ 47582000/jpg/_47582724_cameronhunt466.jpg, accessed 23 July, 2015.
7. See: www.mumsnet.com, date accessed 12 February 2015.
8. The discourse of austerity, which is underpinned by the message of non-state intervention and the so-called 'hidden hand' of the market, has a strong ideological dimension to it that chimes in with the values of neoliberal 'revolution' that is traced back to the monetarist policies which began to take shape in the 1970s (Harvey, 2007) and to its cultural formation as a hegemonic project (Hall, 2011).
9. Here, I am referring to the promotional review comments on the back of Johnson's (2014) book. See also Peter Mandelson (2011) *The Third Man; Life at the Heart of New Labour*, or the political diaries of the self-effacing Chris Mullen (2010) *Decline and Fall; Diaries 2005–2010*, or the emotive diaries of 'spin doctor' Alistair Campbell (2008).
10. See also: *Bremner, Bird and Fortune* (1999–2010, Channel 4), *10 O'Clock Live* (Channel 4, 2011–) and quiz shows on television such as, *Have I Got News for You* (BBC2, 1990–2000; BBC1, 2000–); comedy drama series *The Thick of It* (BBC4, 2005–2007; BBC2 2007–2012) adapted as a feature film: *In the Loop* (2009) and the television comedy series *Yes Minister* (1980–1984) and *Yes, Prime Minister* (1986–1987), which, for the timeframe under discussion in this book, was also staged as a play in London theatres in 2010–2011. *Yes, Prime Minister* was later revived in 2013 on the 'Gold' television channel.

11. This is a tradition that has been critically documented by cultural studies scholars from Raymond Williams (1983) onwards. See Street (1997: 162–166) for further discussion of this critique.

12. The notion of the 'post political moment' is a contested term within the field of philosophy and cultural studies. It broadly refers to decline of progressive social democratic politics in the West and the triumph of neoliberalism in all aspects contemporary life (Fisher, 2009; Mouffe, 2005).

13. See, for example, Tracey Jensen's (2014) analysis of this genre at work, through programmes such as *We Pay Your Benefits* (BBC1 2013).

14. Foucault (2008) traces the origins of the term, back to a meeting attended by German economist Friedrich Hayek and economist and philosopher Ludwig von Mises. He discusses its use in the German economic texts of the 1930s and 1940s, through to the monetarist economics of Milton Friedman and the Chicago School in the 1950s and 1960s, which advocated the need for governments to create the necessary conditions for the market driven neoliberal values and practices to flourish (Wilson, 2014). Gilbert (2013) reminds us that the Chicago School provided the model for Pinochet's Chillian government, which is widely recognised to be the first government to combine neoliberal economics with a system of neoliberal governance. It was against this backdrop that the emergence of neoliberalism really took hold in the 1980s, when Thatcher and Reagan promoted neoliberal economics and social policy.

15. As cultural studies scholars have argued, against the backdrop of the credit crunch, a new politics of austerity has emerged, where the Second World War slogan 'Keep Calm and Carry On' has been co-opted once more in the context of consumer culture – albeit in a 'post ironic' mode in order to reinforce a masochistic message that following on the from the economic deficit, we should take our medicine and accept the pain of austerity as 'we' brought it on ourselves and thus somehow deserve it (Gilbert, 2011).

16. In her discussion of paranoia on television, Woodhouse Hart (2014: 137–138) says that, 'paranoia can be recognised clinically as featuring anxiety states that are delusional, persecutory, aggressive and threatening. "Something (or someone) is out to get me", would be a typical example of its presentation'.

17. See Woodhouse Hart's (2014) elaboration of this psychoanalytic analysis of paranoia and its links to television entertainment.

18. See, for example, Russell Brand on the BBC 1 political discussion panel show *Question Time*, 21 June 2013.

19. The movement is also linked to the Spanish *Indignago* movement in 2011 and before that, to the Arab Spring uprising in 2010.

20. Well-known parodies of UK politicians include, on YouTube:
    'Cassette Boy – Cameron's Conference Rap', 1 October 2014, https://www.youtube.com/watch?v=0YBumQHPAeU; 'The Nick Clegg Apology Song', 19 September, 2012, https://www.youtube.com/watch?v=KUDjRZ30SNo&list=RDKUDjRZ30SNo; 'Gordon's Smile', 26 April 2009, http://www.youtube.com/watch?v=Vor03-uUeuM&feature=fvwrel; all the above links accessed 12 December, 2014.

21. See Russell Brand's 'The Trews', https://www.youtube.com/playlist?list=PL5BY9veyhGt46KMmgAJYi1LF0EUkpqcrX, date accessed 27 December 2014.

22. See Brand's (2014) entry entitled: 'New Era For All', http://www.russellbrand.com/tag/new-era-estate/, date accessed 28 December 2014.
23. The working class women on that estate have publically praised Brand for his support (Withnail, 2014).
24. See, for example, the 2014 YouTube video, 'Listen You, Let Me Talk', broadcast on 13 February, that contains Russell Brand's interview with Channel 4 television broadcaster, Jon Snow: https://www.youtube.com/watch?v=VrVe7jJE__M, date accessed 27 December 2014.

2 Spinning the Unconscious and the Play of Flirtation in Political Culture

1. Parts of this chapter have been published as an article in the journal *Subjectivity*, 2010, Vol. 3, 3: 282–302.
2. These terms, as used here, are very loosely based on Mansfield's (2006) discussion of metrosexual and sexual masculinities, which he discusses in terms of new and old masculinities respectively.
3. Fourth-wave feminism is a contested term, but it is associated with the current generation of young feminists who use social networks to promote feminist campaigns, often focusing on issues of intersectionality and the marginalisation of ordinary women from mainstream political debate (Munro, 2014).
4. Who, at the time, was his advisor on teaching mathematics.
5. See: 'David Cameron: Webcameron Highlights', YouTube, http://www.youtube.com/watch?v=qxh1YhHytDk, date accessed 21 February 2014.
6. For further details of the poster campaign, see the BBC web page 'On this day, 1950–2004', http://news.bbc.co.uk/onthisday/hi/dates/stories/march/30/newsid_2530000/2530933.stm, date accessed 25 February 2014.
7. See, for example, Alan Clarke, who in diary entry for 28 March 1990, reports of the 'privileged access' enjoyed by 'certain key unelected advisors' (Clark, 2002: 407).
8. The Social Democratic Settlement refers to the postwar consensus that emerged in the wake of the Beveridge Report of 1942 that was put in place by the 1945 Labour government, which championed the values of equality of opportunity, and some redistribution of wealth as underpinned by the safety net of the Welfare State (Hall, 2011).
9. See 'British Gas Ad Tell Sid Postman', YouTube, 2011, http://www.youtube.com/watch?v=nedVpG-GjkE, date accessed 25 February 2014.
10. This theme of patriotism echoed the message of the Conservative Party political broadcasts of the time in which, as the *Guardian* caustically reported: 'Land of Hope and Glory was belted out over a misty picture of Big Ben' (Brown, 2012).
11. See 'UK Party Political Broadcast – May 1987', YouTube, http://www.youtube.com/watch?v=p-3OscH1qK0, date accessed 23 February 2014.
12. *Resentment* is a contested term and its different uses are related to different philosophical traditions. From a psychoanalytic perspective, *resentment* can be used in a similar way to Melanie Klein's concepts of envy and projective identification. For further discussion see: Clarke, Hoggett and Thompson (eds) (2006).

13. See http://www.levesoninquiry.org.uk/, date accessed 27 December 2014.

14. As when, in 2002, *News of the World* journalists hacked into the voicemail of murdered schoolgirl Milly Dowler, giving the impression to the police and her family that she might be alive. For further details, see the above endnote.

15. The counsel, Robert Jay, began to attract a kind of celebrity following in the press and on Twitter, as the style of his questioning, which often involved the use of obscure long words, was viewed as highly seductive and his encounters with the witnesses became an object of fascination for those watching the events unfold (Kennedy, 2012).

16. In particular, see Melanie Klein, who discussed at length the link between the mature love in the 'depressive position' mourning and loss (1940).

17. See Green's (2006) critical essay 'Addendum to Lecture' on the flirtatious cruelty of the psychoanalyst Masud Khan.

18. For discussion of Roosevelt, see Braudy (1986); for Nixon, see Hart (1999) and Sennett (1976); for Reagan, see Ewan (1988); for Clinton, see Van Zoonen (2005); and for Obama, see Sanders (2009).

19. See www.mumsnet.com, date accessed 28 December 2014.

20. This claim was made in a 2008 interview with 'Obama Girl' on MSNBC news: http://www.youtube.com/watch?v=IoYeX1Ngf5Y&feature=related, date accessed 25 June 2009. The first video 'I've got a crush on Obama' was posted in 2007 on YouTube, see: http://www.youtube.com/watch?v=wKsoXHYICqU, date accessed 20 June 2013.

21. See http://www.youtube.com/watch?v=jLSWudoqtWE, date accessed 20 June 2013.

22. For examples of this practice, see the Twitter accounts of Deputy Prime Minister Nick Clegg: https://twitter.com/nick_clegg, Prime Minister David Cameron: https://twitter.com/David_Cameron, and London Mayor Boris Johnson: https://twitter.com/MayorofLondon, date accessed 23 February 2014.

23. Examples of such online responses include websites and blogs by political activists who produce spoof political videos and electioneering posters using comical artwork and captions, as in the recent UK 'Airbrushed for change' e-campaign: http://mydavidcameron.com/; the spoof Twitter accounts of Boris Johnson: https://twitter.com/NotBorisJohnson; spoof 'vile alter ego and inner voice' of Conservative Cabinet Minister Jeremy Hunt: https://twitter.com/Jeremy_Twunt; or the spoof of David Cameron's Tweet from March 2014 that included a 'selfie' of himself on the phone to Barack Obama, discussing the Russian invasion of Ukraine (Chorley, 2014). All the above links accessed 28 December 2014.

24. This power dynamic was illustrated in the 'Yo Blair' episode, when Bush unwittingly spoke to Blair at the 2006 G8 conference in Russia with the microphone still turned on (BBC News, 2006b).

25. Similarly, on the 2007 French election campaign trail – and in contrast to his female rival Ségolène Royal – Nicolas Sarkozy attempted to demonstrate his virility by riding a horse and rounding up cattle (Duval Smith, 2008: 45). His public courtship of Carla Bruni reinforced his performance of flirtatious masculinity, albeit in a less rugged guise.

26. As numerous so-called comical YouTube videos of Berlusconi demonstrate. See, for example: http://www.youtube.com/watch?v=QMX3EgnI6xg, date accessed 12 January 2014.

27. Brown wrongly believed that under his management, New Labour had over-come the contradictions of capitalism and broken the economic cycles of 'boom and bust' (Harvey, 2007; Venn, 2012).
28. The term 'authoritarian populism' was used by Stuart Hall (1979: 15) to refer to the ways in which, at the moment of cultural and political crisis, a new kind of common sense is created in order to ensure active popular consent for 'a new kind of settlement with certain limits'.
29. This neoliberal turn was first presented in a series of essays in the *Orange Book* (2004), edited by David Laws and Peter Marshall, who are associated with the right of the Liberal Party. Orange book liberalism rejects the left-leaning policies associated with what might have been a 'progressive alliance' with New Labour and instead emphasises individualism and the importance of economic free market liberalism.

3   The Dilemmas of Postfeminism and the Fantasies of Political Culture

1. Yet in 1997, only 18.2% of the members of the House of Commons were women. Throughout that period, the presence and public profiles of male politicians remained dominant, and the same is true today, where in the UK, very few women hold senior government posts. Between 1997 and 2012 there was only a 4% increase in the number of female politicians in the UK (Fox, 2012).
2. Third-way politics can be traced back to Bill Clinton (Hall, 2011), but in the UK, a 'version' was adopted by New Labour, with the aim of 'discovering new means to manage both economy and society, working with, rather than against, markets, while nurturing and developing civil society' (Chadwick and Heffernan, 2003: 15). Third-way politics has since been widely critiqued for failing to deal with inequalities of wealth and failing to regulate or even challenge the market system that underpins neoliberalism (for further details, see: Chadwick and Heffernan, 2003; Hall, 1979; Ryner, 2002, 2010).
3. See, for example, Beck et al. (1994); Beck and Beck-Gernsheim (2001); and Giddens (1991).
4. See, for example, www. http://psychologies.co.uk/self/are-we-a-nation-of-workaholics.html, date accessed 22 May 2012.
5. For a useful overview of these developments, see: Munro (2014).
6. *The Reunion: Greenham Common*, BBC Radio 4, Friday, 13 April 2012, http://www.bbc.co.uk/programmes/b01fhnt4; see also *The Reunion: Miss World, 1970'*, BBC Radio 4, http://www.bbc.co.uk/programmes/b00tkpc1, date accessed 27 December 2014.
7. This quotation is printed on the back of the film's DVD cover, alongside a similarly upbeat promotional quotation from the magazine *Glamour*, which tells us that the film 'will have you cheering in your seats'.
8. This same theme regarding the lack of agency can also be found in early feminist critiques of consumption that implied women were in a sense brain-washed like 'Stepford Wives', either by the patriarchal establishment or the capitalist market, or both. For a summary of this work, see Nava (1992) and Lury (1996).

9. Not to mention her appropriation as an object by Tony Blair and Gordon Brown during their times in office as Prime Minister, to augment the centrism of their policies.

10. This speech is also repeated in the magazine *Vanity Fair*, as part of a *homage* to Thatcher (Moore, 2011).

11. As in the Miners Strike (1984–1985) and the 1982 Falklands War, to name but two of her 'battles'.

12. The theme of 'getting back to basics' was first raised in John Major's speech to the Conservative Party conference in Blackpool, 8 October 1993: http://www.johnmajor.co.uk/page1096.html, date accessed 5 January 2015.

13. See, for example, *Kirstie's Homemade Home*, Channel 4, featuring the uppercrust presenter and former advisor to David Cameron on housing matters, Kirstie Allsopp, or the *The Great British Bake Off* (BBC2, 2010–) featuring Mary Berry as a presenter and cook.

14. As I discuss in Chapter 4, this phrase is associated with 'therapy culture' and the reflexive self. Interestingly, the term was also used by Tony Blair in his autobiography, *A Journey* (2011).

15. For a compilation and summary of these reviews, see: 'The Iron Lady Reviews', on the Rotten Tomatoes film web page: http://www.rottentomatoes.com/m/the_iron_lady/reviews/?type=top_critics, accessed 4 January 2015.

4   Political Culture and the Desire for Emotional Wellbeing

1. Parts of this chapter have been published previously in *Free Associations*, 2011, No. 62: 59–84.

2. In August 1997, Tony Blair announced the death of Diana, Princess of Wales to the nation as follows: 'She was the people's princess and that's how she will stay, how she will remain in our hearts and in our memories forever'. A plaque has now been erected outside the church to mark the place where that announcement was made (Mendick, 2013).

3. See, for example, the transcript of talk show host and political commentator Rush Limbaugh's (2008) feature: 'The Clintons Know Fake Crying', 10 January, http://www.rushlimbaugh.com/daily/2008/01/10/the_clintons_know_fake_crying, date accessed 13 March 2014.

4. As I discussed in Chapters 2 and 3, the performance of emotion is a gendered phenomenon.

5. For further discussion of this right-wing stance, see Davison Hunter (1992) and Imber (2004).

6. See Blake Morrison's (2004) critique of this tendency within Furedi's work.

7. The website 'Culture Wars', which is linked to the Battle of Ideas Festival, regularly cites Furedi and in particular the encroachment of therapy culture in education; see http://www.culturewars.org.uk/index.php/site/article/therapy_culture_revisited, date accessed 12 February 2014.

8. Although under-realised as a point of discussion.

9. See, for example, Richard Layard's 2005 government paper 'Mental Health: Britain's Biggest Social Problem?', which discussed the social and economic

costs of mental illness and the need to remedy this in order to get people back to work.

10. See http://www.iapt.nhs.uk/, date accessed 1 April 2014.

11. Edward Bernays was Freud's nephew and allegedly played a key role in psychologically driven advertising campaigns (Yates, 2010).

12. Rieff (1966: 76) argues that previously, therapeutic meaning could be found in the church through religious communities and 'commitment therapy', which he contrasts with 'analytic therapy'.

13. As I discuss later, Freud's approach also contrasts with the certainties of CBT and the current UK government's measurements of happiness in the construction of a 'happiness index' (BBC, 2010).

14. The religious nature of psychoanalysis echoes Foucault's views about psychoanalysis as a secular form of 'confessional', a point developed by Rose (1999) in his critique of therapeutic culture and its techniques which he argues constitute a pernicious form of emotional management in a variety of social and cultural settings.

15. The links between this critique of Lasch and the potentially feminising implications of therapy culture are explored later in this chapter and also in Chapter 5.

16. At the end of the 1999 edition of the book, he asks us to imagine what it might be like if identity were constructed in terms of what we 'do', rather than who we are and how we feel.

17. This plan was also influenced by the New Economics Foundation think tank: http://www.neweconomics.org/, which, in 2006, published their first 'Happy Planet Index' and, in 2009, created a website entitled 'National Accounts of Wellbeing': http://www.nationalaccountsofwellbeing.org; both websites accessed 4 April 2014.

18. Positive psychology became popular in the 1970s and 1980s and was consumed in the mass market of popular psychology thereafter (see Heathcote, 2010, for a brief history of this development).

19. According to his 2009 book, he was at the time of writing in psychotherapy supervision with the renowned psychotherapist Susie Orbach.

20. Some of these original websites have since been removed, however, much of this information has been reproduced at: http://derekdraper1.wordpress.com/2014/02/28/space-the-essential-element-of-great-leadership and www.LabourList.org, date accessed 5 April 2014.

    Draper also had a therapy column in the popular women's journal *Psychologies*, but following 'Smeargate' the link to this journal was removed from his website. However, an archive of his journalist activity can be found on http://www.journalisted.com/derek-draper, date accessed 3 April 2014.

    Draper can also be found on various networking sites, including Twitter: https://twitter.com/derekdraper, and his personal and professional blog webpage: http://derekdraper1.wordpress.com/, both accessed 7 April 2014.

21. See Johnson's 2008 paper, 'Improving Access to Psychological Therapies; Outcomes Toolkit 2008/9', http://ipnosis.postle.net/PDFS/iapt-outcomes-toolkit-2008-november%282%29.pdf, date accessed 23 March 2014. The 2003 government DfES Research Report 'Emotional Well Being', into primary education, also provides an example of this in an educational context (David et al., 2003).

22. See, for example, the petition signed by the 'Coalition Against Over Regulation of Psychotherapy': http://www.psychoanalysis-cpuk.org/HTML/Regulation.htm, date accessed 2 April 2014.

23. Sennett (1976) has discussed the way that the strategy of assigning a sense of authenticity to public figures through the display of intimacy and controlled emotional expression has been used to great effect with politicians such as Richard Nixon.

24. Draper has in fact talked about his 'redemption' and 'finding solace' in spirituality, yoga and prayer. He has also said that he is a practising Christian (Dodd, 2008).

25. See Draper's review of Campbell's novel *All in the Mind*, which addresses the relationship between politics and depression (Draper, 2008).

26. The biggest culprit here is the right-wing political blogger Paul Staines, or 'Guido Fawkes', who was responsible for exposing Draper's role in 'Smeargate'; see http://www.order-order.com/2009/04/mission-accomplished-mcbride-fired/, date accessed 15 December 2014.

27. Draper's psychotherapy qualifications are presented in full on his blog website: http://derekdraper1.wordpress.com/psychotherapy/, date accessed 3 April 2014.

28. The Amazon reviews of his book are mostly negative and often quite vicious: see http://www.amazon.co.uk/Life-Support-Derek-Draper/dp/1848500440, date accessed 12 December 2014.

29. See http://derekdraper1.wordpress.com/psychotherapy/, date accessed 4 April 2014.

30. As also evidenced by proposals for UK state regulation of psychotherapy. For details of the petition set up to oppose this move, see: Letters (2009) 'State Must Stay out of Psychotherapy, *The Guardian*, 9 April, http://www.guardian.co.uk/politics/2009/apr/09/letter-psychotherapy-health-professionals-council, date accessed 15 February 2014.

31. See, for example, the 'Emotional Resilience Toolkit' promoted by the Department of Heath, http://www.kentmindfulemployer.net/Documents/BitC%20Emotional%20Resilience%20toolkit%5b1%5d.pdf, date accessed 5 April 2014.

32. The 2008/9 *Social Trends* survey confirms this perception through interviews, where women were keener than men to discuss their emotions (Anderson et al., 2009).

33. A theme that was also there in his book *Paranoid Parenting* (2001), where he warned against the problems of 'mollycoddling' children.

5   The Absent Parent in Political Culture

1. Some parts of this chapter have been published in *Psychoanalysis, Culture & Society* (2012) Vol. 17, no. 2, pp. 204–221.

2. As the Fawcett Society argued in 28 February 2013: 'benefits make up twice as much of women's income than men's'. See more at: http://www.fawcettsociety.org.uk/benefits/#sthash.1CsKKCiL.dpuf, date accessed 13 April 2014.

3. The proliferation of images of fatherhood can be found in the press and on social networking sites; see, for example, the Fatherhood Institute, http://

www.fatherhoodinstitute.org/, date accessed 6 January 2015. A whole season on 'The Century of Fatherhood' was also scheduled on BBC 4 (2012).

4. See: http://www.youtube.com/watch?v=gTd3j31PIPo, date accessed 1 August 2014.

5. Ibid.

6. Lasch was writing at a time when identity politics was gaining influence in the US and Europe and when feminism was challenging the patriarchal certainties that underpinned the structures of the nuclear family (Tyler, 2007).

7. Murray's ideas were first publicised in the *Sunday Times* in 1989 and were popular with Margaret Thatcher's government (Biressi and Nunn, 2013). The label of the 'underclass' fell out of favour during the New Labour period of government, who instead referred to the 'bottom 5%' in less harsh terms as the 'socially excluded' (Easton, 2011).

8. In 2008, the Conservative Party's so-called 'social policy guru', Iain Duncan Smith, jointly wrote a cross-party document about the need for early forms of social intervention to prevent imminent 'social collapse', describing the so-called 'underclass' as 'a new generation of disturbed and aggressive young people doomed to repeat and amplify the social breakdown disfiguring their lives and others round them' (Allen and Duncan Smith, 2008).

9. Deirdre Kelly from the programme *Benefits Street*, who also suffers from depression, provides a case in point (Cooper, 2014).

10. The significance of mother and baby attachment was a recurring a theme in press reports following the death of celebrity mother Peaches Geldof in 2014, whose role as a mother was seen as her redemption following her earlier years as a 'troubled teenager' and 'wild child'. Peaches Geldof spoke publicly about the importance of her close attachment to her babies and also her own attachment to her mother, who died of an accidental heroine overdose (Brady, 2014). As I discuss later in this chapter, the theme of the unmourned mother is linked to fantasies of attachment, loss and separation, and these links arguably lie behind the fascination with the story of Peaches Geldof which centres on the themes of attachment, motherhood and accidental death.

11. Of course, such resistance isn't confined to the UK Parliament. For example, in Australia, 'former Olympic Skier Kirstie Marshall was evicted from the State parliament for breastfeeding her baby, Charlotte' (Thorne, 2014).

12. The practice of 'self-reflexivity' is 'where agency reflects on itself and there is increased self-monitoring' (Adkins, (2002) cited in Miller (2005: 140)).

13. Self Reflexivity is linked to the concept of 'reflexive modernization' (Beck, et al., 1994) and the rapid changes and structural upheavals associated with the late 20th century, and where the old rules and structures of authority that shaped behaviour have been replaced by the agency of individuals.

14. See their 'Mothers At Home Matter' website: http://www.mothersathome matter.co.uk/latest-news/latest-news/49-in-the-papers/320-my-children-need-my-talent-more-says-laura-perrins, date accessed 13 April 2014.

15. The second-wave feminist emphasis on the workplace as an emancipatory site away from the oppressive sphere of domesticity in the home is not shared by all women. For many black mothers, who face the intersections of prejudice on a number of fronts, the private sphere of the family has been

valued as a sphere where they and their families can escape the experience of everyday racism in the workplace and the public sphere (Hill Collins, 2000).

16. The debates about women's place in the home recall earlier debates about the 'value' or exploitation of women's work in the home (Coulsen et al., 1975).

17. Which, according to the mumpreneuruk.com website, is apparently 'child's play'. See: http://www.mumpreneuruk.com/, date accessed 2 April 2014.

18. See: http://kirstieallsopp.co.uk/, date accessed 12 April 2014.

19. For example, ex-Conservative MP, *Sun* tabloid journalist and web entrepreneur and mother Louise Mensch runs a web business and blog called 'Unfashionista' that carries the bi-line 'Fashion. Feminism. Fitness. And a little Inspiration', (see http://unfashionista.com/about/), thereby providing an example of the neoliberal feminist mother in action (McRobbie, 2013). See also Conservative Party 'Maths Czar', broadcaster, pilot and mother Carol Vorderman; or 'Britain's best-known business woman' and Conservative Party Candidate Karren Brady (Cooper, 2012); or journalist and Conservative Party member Katie Hopkins, whose tweets about working mothers who complain about discrimination include the following: 'Misogyny is just a more concise way of saying that business is too tough for me' (Winter, 2014).

20. See: http://www.mumsnet.com, date accessed 12 April 2014.

21. In 2011, Justine Roberts also set up 'Gransnet': http://www.gransnet.com/, date accessed 14 April 2014.

22. As Roberts (2013) said: 'I wanted Mumsnet to recognise one essential truth. If you're a parent, your children come first, and work second'.

23. For those readers unfamiliar with the style of Boden, see: http://www.boden.co.uk/en-GB/, date accessed 13 April 2014.

24. For a detailed, archived account of that attack and the Mumsnet response, see Louise Pennington's (2013) blog entry: http://elegantgatheringofwhitesnows.com/?cat=78, date accessed 12 April 2014.

25. This law was modelled on 'Megan's Law' in the US, and it made it mandatory that the names of paedophiles in the local area be made available to the public. The campaign for the law was controversial as the *News of the World* 'named and shamed' missing paedophiles, which led to people being attacked by the public. For further details, see Robinson (2011).

26. Cultural Studies scholar Gilbert (2011) argues that the austere appeal for stoical calmness in the face of crisis has been a popular one in the current neoliberal era, where individuals are asked to bear the brunt of economic and social inequality. As discussed in Chapter 1, Gilbert is referring here of course to the ubiquitous 'Keep Calm and Carry On' posters, in which the old wartime slogan becomes overlaid with postmodern irony for the present era.

27. The context for this is further complicated by the fact that Abbott said this as a way to justify sending her son to a fee-paying public school. However, the charges of 'hypocrisy' and of being a 'Champaign Socialist' were more than matched in the press by attacks on her status as a West Indian mother.

28. For example, 45% of women MPs have no children, compared to 28% of male MPs (Campbell and Childs, 2014).

29. See Campbell and Childs' (2014) excellent response to Hurd's speech.

30. At Eton, he was known as 'Hitler Hurd' due to 'his enthusiasm for beating younger boys' (Bedell, 1994).

31. According to journalists Helen Lewis and Laura Pitel, it is often said that such panels choose young men whom they would 'like to have as son-in-laws'. *Woman's Hour*, BBC Radio 4, 14 April 2014.
32. For example, former New Labour Ministers Neil Kinnock, Jack Straw and John Prescott all have sons who have been selected to stand for Parliament in 2015. Tony Blair's son, Euan, also hopes to be selected for the Merseyside seat of Bootle. There are also a number of existing MPs whose fathers were MPs and government ministers, including Conservative MPs Ben Gummer, Douglas Hogg, Francis Maude, Bernard Jenkin and Andrew Mitchell, and Labour MP Hilary Benn (Addley, 2014).

6   Moving Forward to the Past: Fantasies of Nation within UK Political Culture

1. The term 'postnationalism' is contested, but I am using it here to refer loosely to the ways in which the notion of the bounded nation state is undermined by economic, social and cultural factors related to globalisation and mobility (see Beck, 1992; Elliott and Urry, 2010).
2. Who nevertheless promotes a very different politics to Farage.
3. See: http://www.oxforddictionaries.com, 2014.
4. As I discuss later in this chapter, the recent controversy in the UK about the image of an English flag that was draped over the house of a family in the Rochester constituency where UKIP were contesting a seat, provides an example of this process in action.
5. The murder took place on 24 September 2013. For more on the English Defence League, see: http://www.englishdefenceleague.org/mission-statement/, date accessed 30 June 2014.
6. And a longer, more drawn out story about Britain's loss of status in the world as a postcolonial power, following Britain's humiliating role in the Suez crisis ten years previously.
7. I am referring here to Brown's failure to call an election in 2008, which is often called 'the election that never was'. The perception of Brown's 'dithering' in this context set the tone for his leadership and is linked to his unpopularity as Prime Minister (Wintour, 2008). For further details, see Chapter 2.
8. See also David Cameron's 2013 speech on curbing 'non-British benefit claimants' and the need to cut net migration 'radically' (Cameron, 2013).
9. See Lumley's 'Forward' to Peter Carroll's (2012) book *Gurkha: The True Story of a Campaign for Justice.*
10. The British relationship with the Gurkhas can be traced back to the British Indian Army prior to Independence and before that, to the East India Tea Company (Bellamy, 2011; Streets, 2004).
11. As discussed in previous chapters, I am referring here to the UK politicians' expenses scandal, the Leveson Enquiry into the corruption of the press and the police.
12. See BBC News report: http://news.bbc.co.uk/1/hi/8023882.stm, 29 April 2009, date accessed 12 December 2014.
13. The term 'doughty' has been used regularly since 2008 by both Conservative and feminist journalists, who seem seduced by Lumley and her campaigning

methods in equal measure (Suzanne Moore's 2008 article is exemplary in this respect). However, by 2013, the views of some feminist journalists shifted, following Lumley's remarks about drunk women and 'laddettes' who make themselves vulnerable to rape (Gold, 2013).

14. See: http://www.yesscotland.net/news/braveheart-stars-stage-support-indep endence, date accessed 10 October 2014.

15. Many of whom, says Mason (2014), apparently 'despise' the Scottish National Party and Alex Salmond for not being 'radical' enough.

16. The 'Couple Connection' website even intimated that the referendum would lead to an increase in divorces and marital breakdown amongst Scottish couples (Couple Connection, 2014).

17. The English Defence League say that they were formed in opposition to 'Islamic extremism', and on their 'Mission statement' they say they claim to 'oppose religiously-inspired intolerance and barbarity that are thriving amongst certain sections of the Muslim population'; see: http://www. englishdefenceleague.org/mission-statement/, date accessed 30 June 2014.

18. In that speech he said that 'the indigenous population found themselves strangers in their own country'; see YouTube: https://www.youtube.com/ watch?v=6gkBr-qvo-4, date accessed 3 January 2014.

19. As in the notorious incident when a UKIP counsellor blamed the bad weather on gay marriage (BBC News Oxford, 2014).

20. The Pub Landlord's message of 'common sense' can be found at: http://www. dailymail.co.uk/news/article-2916722/I-drink-Farage-table-boasts-Pub-Land lord-Al-Murray-unveils-policies-defeat-Ukip-including-renaming-benefits-scrounge-credits.html, date accessed 20 January 2015.

21. See, for example, 'Women Against UKIP': https://www.facebook.com/ womendefyukip; 'Hope Not Hate': https://www.facebook.com/hope.n. hate; 'Don't Vote UKIP': https://www.facebook.com/pages/Dont-vote-UKIP/ 618809081477853, all accessed 15 January 2015.

7 Reflections on the Psycho-Cultural Dynamics of Political Culture

1. In November 2014, UKIP successfully fielded another Conservative Party 'defector' candidate, Mark Reckless, to stand in a by-election in Rochester and Strood. However, he lost his seat in the 2015 UK General Election.

2. These politicians were Jack Straw (of the Labour Party) and Malcolm Rifkind (of the Conservative Party), who were set up and caught in a press 'sting' by the *Daily Telegraph*, offering privileged use of information and contacts gained in office for the purposes of consultancy work (Ward and Walton, 2015).

3. Wilkinson and Picket's (2010) *The Spirit Level: Why Equality Is Better for Everyone* is a well-known example of such work in the scholarly field. See also Biressi and Nunn's (2013) discussion of class inequality in their *Class and Contemporary British Culture*.

4. As discussed in Chapter 1, the 'post-political moment' has been used to refer to the decline of progressive social democratic politics in the West and the triumph of neoliberalism in all aspects contemporary life (Fisher, 2009; Mouffe, 2005).

5. It is worth noting that such critiques are also linked to scholarly debates about 'post-identity' politics and to critiques of intersectionality (McNay, 2010).
6. As I have discussed, concerns about the absent father are symptomatic of that disillusionment.
7. The film was based on a book by journalist and broadcaster James Naughtie with a title that reinforced the soap opera dimensions of the story, *The Rivals: The Intimate Story of a Political Marriage* (2001). The film was followed by two sequels, *The Queen* (2006) and *The Special Relationship* (2010), which starred the Welsh actor and film star, Michael Sheen as Tony Blair.
8. The Five Star Party also provides a good example of the mediatisation of political culture and the role of new media in harnessing grass roots support. Grillo co-founded the party with 'communications entrepreneur' Gianroberto Casaleggio (Del Savio and Mameli, 2014). As Del Savio and Mameli (2014) point out, Casaleggio provided the party with 'an array of technological platforms, the main one being the website and blog *beppegrillo.it*', which is hugely popular, and is published in several languages and also functions as their 'head quarters'.
9. At the time, Johnson was a Conservative Member of Parliament. In 2004, he was nominated for a BAFTA award for his role in chairing the show. See: http://awards.bafta.org/award/2004/television/entertain ment-performance, date accessed 4 January 2015.
10. See: https://www.youtube.com/playlist?list=PL5BY9veyhGt46KMmgAJYi1LF 0EUkpqcrX, date accessed 15 February 2015. For further discussion of Brand, see Chapter 1.
11. See: http://thepublandlord.com/, date accessed 15 February 2015.
12. See the link in endnote above.
13. As we have just seen, the use of humour by politicians is closely linked to that development.
14. This space first comes into being between mother and infant and is occupied by an actual transitional object, such as a toy, which is a 'me-not-me' object that mitigates against the losses of separation from the mother (Winnicott, 1971).
15. It is worth noting, however, that this plan was contested by another Conservative politician in his own party.
16. Some campaigning cyber feminists of fourth-wave feminism are also active in checking the privilege of others and policing the boundaries of accept able language by other feminists on Twitter, as in the case of feminist journalist Susanne Moore who was accused of transphobia in her *New Statesman* article, 'Seeing Red: The Power of Female Anger' (2013). For the timeline of the subsequent angry 'Twitter storm', see: http://storify.com/ leftytgirl/suzanne-moore-timeline-of-trans-misogynistic-twitt, date accessed 3 January 2014.
17. The 'Big Society' was referred to as 'the big idea' as promoted by Cameron after he was elected as Leader of his party (Norman, 2010). It was an ideology that brought together elements of 'Red Toryism' (Blonde, 2010), communitarianism and civic engagement. According to the Coalition gov ernment Cabinet Office policy document 'Building the Big Society' (2010), they wanted to 'put more power and opportunity into people's hands'.

18. See the endnote 17, above.
19. Zygmunt Bauman (2010: 121) also developed the concept of the inter-regnum to discuss the wider context of globalisation, power and politics and the seeming inability to address 'the new realities of interplanetary interdependency'.
20. The economist Susan Strange (1997) coined the term 'Casino Capitalism' in her book of the same title.
21. See: *Love Actually* (Richard Curtis, 2003).

References

Aaronovitch, D. (2010). *Voodoo Histories; How Conspiracy Theory Has Shaped Modern History*, London: Vintage.

Adams, G. (2014). 'Champagne socialist's property empire: How one £2.9m North London home is just Not enough for sacked "Slob" MP', *Mail Online*, 21 November, http://www.dailymail.co.uk/news/article-2844806/Champagne-socialists-property-empire-Emily-Thornberry-lives-lives-wildest-dreams-working-class-voters-purports-represent.html, date accessed 12 January 2015.

Addley, E. (2012). 'Alastair Campbell back at the Leveson inquiry – and with great clunking balls', *The Guardian*, 14 May, http://www.guardian.co.uk/media/2012/may/14/alastair-campbell-leveson-inquiry, date accessed 24 February 2014.

Addley, E. (2014). 'Neil Kinnock's son joins succession of aspiring political offspring', *The Guardian*, 24 January, http://www.theguardian.com/politics/2014/jan/24/stephen-neil-kinnock-son-labour-aberavon-dynasty, date accessed 12 April 2014.

Addley, E. and Woodward, W. (2007). 'Cameron: Look at me and think of Schwarzenegger', *The Guardian*, 13 October, http://www.theguardian.com/politics/2007/oct/13/conservatives.politics, date accessed 27 December 2014.

Adkins, (2002). *Revisions: Gender and Sexuality in Late Modernity*, Philadelphia: Oxford University Press.

Adorno, T. (1991). *The Culture Industry*, Abingdon, Oxford: Routledge.

Adorno, T. and Horkeimer, M. (1976). *Dialectic of Enlightenment*, London: Continuum International Publishing Group.

Allen, G. and Duncan Smith, I. (2008). *Early Intervention: Good Parents, Great Kids, Better Citizens*, London: The Centre for Social Justice and The Smith Institute.

Allen, N. (2008). 'Joanna Lumley urges Gurkhas on in High Court battle', *The Telegraph*, 18 September, http://www.telegraph.co.uk/news/celebritynews/2969297/Joanna-Lumley-urges-Gurkhas-on-in-High-Court-battle.html, date accessed 10 September 2014.

Allis Simons, J. (2013). 'Diane Abbot's confused attack on men', *The Telegraph*, 17 May, http://blogs.telegraph.co.uk/news/jakewallissimons/100217446/diane-abbotts-confused-attack-on-men/, date accessed 3 March 2014.

Alexander, S. (2014). 'Edwina Curry ordered off Twitter by her husband after saying foodbank users spend spare cash on tattoos and dog food', *Mail Online*, 19 January, http://www.dailymail.co.uk/news/article-2542105/Edwina-Currie-ordered-Twitter-husband-criticised-saying-foodbank-users-spend-spare-cash-tattoos-dog-food.html, date accessed 19 January 2014.

Anderson, B. (1991). *Imagined Communities: Reflections on the Origin and Spread of Nationalism*, London: Verso.

Anderson, S., Brownlie, J. and Given, L. (2009). 'Therapy culture? Attitudes towards emotional support in Britain', in Park, A., Curtice, J., Thomson, K., Phillips, M. and Clery, E. (eds) *British Social Attitudes: The 25th Report*, London: Sage, pp. 155–172.

Anon (2007). 'Vladimir Putin strips for fishing trip with Prince Albert', *Foxnews.com*, 15 August, http://www.foxnews.com/story/0,2933,293341,00. html, date accessed 4 March 2013.

Anon (2009). 'Gordon Brown's You Tube trauma', *Freshworks Blog*, 1 May, http://blog.freshnetworks.com/2009/05/gordon-browns-youtube-trauma/, date accessed 2 April 2014.

Anon (2010). 'Alistair Campbell under fire over attack on Clare Short', *The Guardian*, 22 January, http://www.guardian.co.uk/uk/2010/jan/22/alastair-campbell-clare-short-iraq-inquiry, date accessed 3 March 2014.

Anon (2011). 'Anything Ed can do, Dave can do better', *Daily Telegraph*, 26 September, p. 1.

Anon (2012). 'Did Ken Livingstone's campaign video make you cry?', *The Guardian*, 12 April 2012, http://www.theguardian.com/commentisfree/poll/ 2012/apr/12/ken-livingstone-video-cry, date accessed 12 February 2013.

Anon (2014). 'The truth About Cherie Blair's working class roots', *MailOnline*, 15 March, http://www.dailymail.co.uk/news/article-566925/The-truth-Cherie-Blairs-working-class-roots.html, date accessed 15 March 2014.

Andrejevic, M. (2004). *Reality TV: The Work of Being Watched*, Lanham, MD: Rowman & Littlefield Publishers.

Aslet, C. (2010). 'No Minister: Never mess with Joanna Lumley', *The Telegraph*, 11 March, http://www.telegraph.co.uk/culture/7415768/No-minister-dont-mess-with-Joanna-Lumley.html, date accessed 15 June 2015.

Auestad, L. (2014). *Nationalism and the Body Politic: Psychoanalysis and the Rise of Ethnocentrism and Xenophobia*, London: Karnac Books.

Bainbridge, C. (2008). *A Feminine Cinematics: Luce Irigaray, Women and Film*, Basingstoke: Palgrave Macmillan.

Bainbridge, C. (2010). ' "They've taken her!" – Psychoanalytic perspectives on mediating maternity, feeling and loss', *Studies in the Maternal*, 2 (1–2): 1–18, http://www.mamsie.bbk.ac.uk/bainbridge.html, date accessed 12 March 2014.

Bainbridge, C. and Yates, C. (2005). 'Cinematic symptoms of masculinity in transition: Memory, history and mythology in contemporary film', *Psychoanalysis, Culture & Society*, 10 (3): 299–328.

Bainbridge, C. and Yates, C. (2010). 'On not being a fan: Masculine identity, DVD culture and the accidental collector', *Widescreen*, 2 (1): 1–22.

Bainbridge, C. and Yates, C. (2012). 'Introduction to special issue on media and the inner world: New perspectives on psychoanalysis and popular culture', *Psychoanalysis, Culture & Society*, 17 (2): 113–119.

Bainbridge, C. and Yates, C. (2014). 'Introduction: Psycho-cultural approaches to emotion, media and popular culture', in Bainbridge, C. and Yates, C. (eds) *Media and the Inner World: Psycho-Cultural Approaches to Emotion, Media and Popular Culture*, Basingstoke: Palgrave Macmillan, pp. 1–19.

Bainbridge, C., Radstone, S., Rustin, M. and Yates, C. (eds) (2007). *Culture and the Unconscious*, Basingstoke: Palgrave Macmillan.

Banet-Weiser, S. (2012). *AuthenticTM: The Politics of Ambivalence in a Brand Culture*, New York: University Press.

Barthes, R. (1973). *Mythologies*, London: Paladin.

Baudelaire, C. (1965). 'The Painter in Modern Life' in: *The Painter of Modern Life and Other Essays*, trans. and ed. Jonathan Mayne (London: Phaidon).

Bauman, Z. (2007). *Liquid Times: Living in an Age of Uncertainty*, Cambridge: Polity Press.

Bauman, Z. (2010). *44 Letters From the Liquid Modern World*, Cambridge: Polity Press.

Benjamin, J. (1990). *The Bonds of Love; Psychoanalysis, Feminism, and the Problem of Domination*, London: Virago Press.

Barkham, P. (2012). 'Why do politicians cry in public?' *The Guardian*, http://www.theguardian.com/politics/shortcuts/2012/apr/11/why-do-politicians-cry-in-public, date accessed 2 April 2014.

Barnett, S. and Gaber, I. (2001). *Westminister Tales; The Twenty-First Century Crisis in Political Journalism*, London: Continuum.

BBC Home (1978). 'On this day: March 1978: Tories recruit advertisers to win votes', http://news.bbc.co.uk/onthisday/hi/dates/stories/march/30/newsid_2530000/2530933.stm, date accessed 3 March 2014.

BBC News (2000). 'Baby Blair makes his debut', *BBC News*, 22 May, http://news.bbc.co.uk/1/hi/uk/758999.stm, date accessed 12 September 2011.

BBC News (2006). 'Brown speech promises Britishness', *BBC News*, 14 April, http://news.bbc.co.uk/1/hi/uk_politics/4611682.stm, date accessed 12 July 2014.

BBC News Channel (2006b). 'Transcript: Bush and Blair's Unguarded Chat', 18 July, http://news.bbc.co.uk/1/hi/world/americas/5188258.stm, date accessed 12 June 2009.

BBC News (2007). 'Polls didn't sway me, says Brown', *BBC News*, 8 October, http://news.bbc.co.uk/1/hi/uk_politics/7033084.stm, date accessed 14 February 2010.

BBC News (2009). 'No.10 'Smear' messages published', *BBC News*, 12 April, http://news.bbc.co.uk/1/hi/7995515.stm, date accessed 12 October 2013.

BBC News, (2009b). 'Brown defeated over Gurkha rules', *BBC News*, 29 April, http://news.bbc.co.uk/1/hi/8023882.stm, date accessed 6 December 2014.

BBC News (2010). 'Plan to measure happiness not woolly – Cameron', *BBC News*, 25 November, http://www.bbc.co.uk/news/uk-11833241, date accessed 13 April 2014.

BBC News (2010b). 'Cameron "Proud Dad" after Wife Samantha has a baby girl', *BBC News*, 24 August, http://www.bbc.co.uk/news/uk-11074163, date accessed 23 September 2013.

BBC News (2011). 'Cameron and how runaway dads should be shamed', *BBC News*, 19 June, http://www.bbc.co.uk/news/uk-13825737, date accessed 13 August 2014.

BBC News (2013). 'Twitter Trolls: Police probe tweets to MP Stella Creasy', *BBC News*, 30 July, http://www.bbc.co.uk/news/uk-23500190, date accessed 30 July 2013.

BBC News (2014). 'Vote 2014: England council results', *BBC News*, 22 May, http://www.bbc.co.uk/news/events/vote2014/england council election results, date accessed 26 July 2014.

BBC News (2015). 'Election 2015', http://www.bbc.co.uk/news/election/2015/results, date accessed 20 June, 2015.

BBC Newsnight (2013). 'Paxman versus Brand, full interview', *BBC*, 23 October, YouTube, https://www.youtube.com/watch?v=3YR4CseY9pk, date accessed 12 February 2015.

BBC News Europe (2013). 'Profile: Francois Hollande', *BBC.co.uk*, 15 May, http://www.bbc.co.uk/news/world-europe-15311645, date accessed 23 February 2014.

BBC News Oxford (2014). 'UKIP Councillor blames storms and floods on gay marriage', *BBC News Oxford*, 18 January, http://www.bbc.co.uk/news/uk-england-oxfordshire-25793358, date accessed 12 January 2015.

BBC News Politics (2012). 'MP Dorries calls PM and Chancellor 'arrogant posh boys', 23 April, http://www.bbc.co.uk/news/uk-politics-17815769, date accessed 12 July 2014.

Beard, M. (2014). 'Oh do shut up dear! Mary Beard on the public voice of women', *BBC*, Radio Four, 17 March.

Beaumont, P. (2012). 'Europe's new insurgents: Rising rebels spurn the era of bling', *The Observer*, 20 May, http://www.theguardian.com/world/2012/may/20/europe-new-leaders-generation-normal, date accessed 24 February 2014.

Beck, U. (1992). *Risk Society: Towards a New Modernity*, London: Sage.

Beck, U. and Beck-Gernsheim, E. (2001). *Individualization: Institutionalized Individualism and Its Social and Political Consequences*, London: Sage.

Beck, U., Giddens, A. and Lash, S. (1994). *Reflexive Modernization: Politics, Tradition and Aesthetics in the Modern Social Order*, Cambridge: Polity Press.

Beck, U., Bonss, W. and Lau, C. (2003). 'The theory of reflexive modernization', *Theory, Culture & Society*, April, 20 (2): 1–33.

Becket, A. (2014). 'Tony Blair, from New Labour to political embarrassment', *The Guardian*, 26 February, http://www.theguardian.com/politics/2014/feb/26/tony-blair-new-labour-hero-political-embarrassment-murdoch, date accessed 2 March 2014.

Bedell, G. (1994). 'A smooth operator, Eton, Cambridge and the diplomatic service. Douglas Hurd is a Conservative of the old school', *The Independent*, 29 May, http://www.independent.co.uk/arts-entertainment/the-smooth-operator-eton-cambridge-and-the-diplomatic-service-douglas-hurd-is-a-conservative-of-the-old-school-is-he-a-statesman-who-could-unite-a-bitterly-divided-party-or-does-his-civilised-veneer-conceal-too-limited-a-vision-of-the-world-1439340.html, date accessed 12 April 2014.

Bell, S. (2013). 'Steve Bell at the Lib Dem conference, "Bride of Cleggenstein" – Video', 19 September, http://www.theguardian.com/commentisfree/video/2013/sep/19/steve-bell-lib-dem-conference-2013-video, date accessed 4 March 2014.

Bellamy, J. (2011). *The Gurkhas; Special Force*, London: John Murray.

Ben-Shahar, T. (2008). *Happier*, Maidenhead, Berkshire: McGrawHill: The Open University Press.

Bennett, C. (2007). 'In this age of the political man-beast, what has become of our dreams of more women in power?', *The Guardian*, 6 December, http://www.guardian.co.uk/commentisfree/2007/dec/06/women.comment, date accessed 13 January 2014.

Benjamin, J. (1990). *The Bonds of Love*, London: Virago Press.

Benjamin. W. (1999). *Selected Writings II 1927–1934*. Trans. Rodney Livingstone et al., ed. M. W. Jennings, H. Eiland, and G. Smith. Cambridge, MA: Harvard.

Benjamin, W. (1992). (Trans. H. Zohn, 1955) 'On some motifs in Baudelaire', in Benjamin, W. (ed.) *Illuminations*, London: Fontana Press, pp. 152–192.

Benjamin, W. (2008) *The Work of Art in the Age of Mechanical Reproduction*, London: Penguin Books. Trans. J.A. Underwood. [First published, 1936].

Bennett, C. (2009). 'Anyone seeking help from Derek Draper needs therapy: If you wonder why psychotherapy is in urgent need of regulation, just consider the actions of this practitioner', *The Observer*, 19 April, 27.

Bennett, W. L. and Entman, R. M. (eds) (2001). *Mediated Politics: Communication in the Future of Democracy*, Cambridge: Cambridge University Press.

Bentley, P. and Duell, M. (2014). ' "We can't be running away from history": Hilary Mantel goes on the offensive as she attacks critics of her fantasy to assassinate Margaret Thatcher', *MailOnline*, 21 September, http://www.dailymail.co.uk/news/article-2764520/Hilary-Mantel-unrepentant-backlash-grows-fantasies-assassinating-Margaret-Thatcher.html, date accessed 2 January 2015.

Berlant, L. (2008). *The Female Complaint: The Unfinished Business of Sentimentality in American Culture*, Durham NC: Duke University Press.

Berlinsky, C. (2008). *There Is No Alternative*, New York: Basic Books.

Bernays, E. L. (1928). *Propaganda*, New York: I G Publishing. 2005.

Billig, M. (1995). *Banal Nationalism*, London: Sage.

Bingham, J. (2012). 'Failure to treat tens of thousands of mothers creating riots generation', *The Telegraph*, 18 May, http://www.telegraph.co.uk/health/healthnews/9272927/Failure-to-treat-tens-of-thousands-of-mothers-creating-riots-generation.html, date accessed 3 April 2014.

Birrell, I. (2013). 'Tory strategist Lynton Crosby would do well to read those deleted speeches', 14 November, http://www.theguardian.com/commentisfree/2013/nov/14/lynton-crosby-deleted-conservative-speeches, date accessed 3 March 2014.

Biressi, A. and Nunn, H. (eds) (2008). *The Tabloid Culture Reader*. Maidenhead and New York: McGraw Hill/OU.

Biressi, A. and Nunn, H. (2013). *Class and Contemporary British Culture*, Basingstoke: Palgrave Macmillan.

Biressi, A. and Nunn, H. (eds) (2008). *The Tabloid Culture Reader*, Maidenhead and New York: McGraw Hill/OU University Press.

Blair, T. (1998). *The Third Way; New Politics for the New Century*, London: The Fabian Society.

Blair, T. (1995). 'Leader's speech Brighton', *British Political Speech, Speech Archive*, 3 October, http://www.britishpoliticalspeech.org/speech-archive.htm?speech=201, date accessed 12 July 2014.

Blair, T. (2010). *A Journey*, London: Random House.

Blonde, P. (2010). *Red Tory: How Left and Right have Broken Britain and How We Can Fix It*, London: Faber and Faber.

Bly, R. (1996). *The Sibling Society*, New York: Vintage Books.

Bollas, C. (1987). *The Shadow of the Object: Psychoanalysis of the Unthought Known*, London: Free Association Books.

Bollas, C. (1992). *Being a Character: Psychoanalysis and Self Experience*, Abingdon, Oxford: Routledge.

Bradshaw, P. (2010). 'Made in Dagenham', *The Guardian*, 30 September, http://www.guardian.co.uk/film/2010/sep/30/made-in-dagenham-film-review, date accessed 4 March 2014.

Bradshaw, P. (2012). 'The Iron Lady – review', *The Guardian*, 5 January, http://www.theguardian.com/film/2012/jan/05/the-iron-lady-film-review, date accessed 12 December 2014.

Brady, T. (2014). ' "I am not about to let my sons down for anyone or anything": Peaches Geldof's haunting last interview – less than a month before she was found dead', *MailOnline*, 7 April, http://www.dailymail.co.uk/news/article-2599122/I-not-let-sons-not-How-Peaches-spoke-children-credited-making-just-month-death.html, date accessed 12 April 2014.

Braidotti, R. (2002). *Metamorphoses: Towards a Feminist Theory of Becoming*, Cambridge: Polity Press.

Bramall, R. (2013). *The Cultural Politics of Austerity: Past and Present in Austere Times*, Basingstoke: Palgrave Macmillan.

Brammell, R. (2013). *The Cultural Politics of Austerity; Past and Present in Austere Times*, Palgrave Macmillan, Kindle Edition.

Brand, R. (2013a). 'Brand on revolution: "We no longer have the luxury of tradition" ', *New Statesman*, 24 October, http://www.newstatesman.com/politics/2013/10/russell-brand-on-revolution, date accessed 23 November 2014.

Brand, R. (2013b). 'Russell Brand on Margaret Thatcher: I always felt sorry for her children', *The Guardian*, 9 April, http://www.theguardian.com/politics/2013/apr/09/russell-brand-margaret-thatcher, date accessed 10 April.

Brand, R. (2014). *Revolution*, London: Century.

Brand, R. (2015) 'Russell Brand calls on his folllowers to vote labour on Election Day- Video', *The Guardian*, 4 May, http://www.theguardian.com/politics/video/2015/may/04/russell-brand-followers-vote-labour-election-day-video, date accessed 15 June 2015.

Braudy, L. (1986). *The Frenzy of Renown*, Oxford: Oxford University Press.

Briddon, L. (2013). 'Margaret Thatcher's alternative funeral at Goldthorpe. Effigy burned, full video', *YouTube*, https://www.youtube.com/watch?v=j6VEzGtf5FY, date accessed 12 December 2014.

Brown, D. (2012). 'From the archive, 18 May 1978: Tories turn to Saatchi & Saatchi to help them win election', *The Guardian*, 18 May, http://www.theguardian.com/theguardian/2012/may/18/archive-1978-saatchi-tory-advertising, date accessed 23 February 2014.

Brown, G. (2007). 'Gordon Brown's speech in full', *BBC News*, 24 September, http://news.bbc.co.uk/1/hi/uk_politics/7010664.stm, date accessed 10 May 2014.

Brown, G. (2014). 'The Referendum is not Scotland versus Britain. It's about a patriotic alternative to the SNP', *The Guardian*, 9 June, http://www.theguardian.com/commentisfree/2014/jun/09/scottish-referendum-not-britain-v-scotland, date accessed 12 June 2014.

Burrell, I. (2013). 'Johnnie Boden: Anti-fashion for all the family', *The Independent*, 8 November, http://www.independent.co.uk/news/people/profiles/johnnie-boden-antifashion-for-all-the-family-8929879.html, date accessed 12 August 2014.

Burstow, P. (2010) 'Speech by Paul Burstow MP, Minister of State for Care'. *Psychological Therapies in the NHS, 4th Annual Conference*, Savoy Place, London, 2 December.

Burstow, P. (2010). 'Speech by Paul Burstow MP, Minister of State for Care', Series, 2 December: New Savoy Partnership (Psychological Therapies), http://webarchive.nationalarchives.gov.uk/+/www.dh.gov.uk/en/MediaCentre/Speeches/DH_122375, date accessed 2 April 2014.

Butler, J. (1991). *Gender Trouble: Feminism and the Subversion of Identity*, Abingdon: Routledge.

Butler, P. (2015) 'Do foreigners come to the UK to get HIV Treatement?' *The Guardian*, 3 April, ULR: ww.theguardian.com/politics/reality-check/2015/apr/03/do-foreigners-come-to-uk-to-get-hiv-treatment, date accessed 20 June 2015.

Byrne, C. (2004). 'Sun turns on "Killjoy Short" in page 3 row', *The Guardian*, 14 January, http://www.guardian.co.uk/media/2004/jan/14/pressandpublishing.politicsandthemedia, date accessed 12 September 2014.

Cabinet Office (2010). 'Building the big society', *Cabinet Office – Gov.UK*, https://www.gov.uk/government/uploads/system/uploads/attachment_data/file/78979/building-big-society_0.pdf, date accessed 12 February 2015.

Cameron, D. (2005). 'Full text of David Cameron's victory speech', *The Guardian*, 6 December, http://www.guardian.co.uk/politics/2005/dec/06/toryleadership2005.conservatives3, date accessed 18 February 2014.

Cameron, D. (2011). 'England riots Witney speech', in Sparrow, J. (ed) 'England Riots: Cameron and Milliband Speeches and Reaction – Monday 15 August 2011', *The Guardian*, 15 August, http://www.theguardian.com/politics/blog/2011/aug/15/england-riots-cameron-miliband-speeches, date accessed 15 April 2014.

Cameron, D. (2011a). 'PM's speech on the fight-back after the riots', *Number 10.gov*, 15 August, 2011, http://www.number10.gov.uk/news/pms-speech-on-the-fightback-after-the-riots/, date accessed 28 December 2014.

Cameron, D. (2011b). 'A Wake-up call for the UK', *The Guardian*, 15 August, http://www.guardian.co.uk/uk/video/2011/aug/15/david-cameron-riots-uk-video, date accessed 27 December 2014.

Cameron, D. (2013). 'David Cameron's immigration speech', *Gov.UK*, 25 March, https://www.gov.uk/government/speeches/david-camerons-immigration-speech, date accessed 12 August 2014.

Cameron, D. and Clegg, N. (eds) (2010). 'The coalition: Our programme for government', *HM Government*, https://www.gov.uk/government/uploads/system/uploads/attachment_data/file/78977/coalition_programme_for_government.pdf, date accessed 3 March 2014.

Campbell, C. (1987). *The Romantic Ethic and the Spirit of Modern Consumerism*, Oxford: Blackwell Publishers.

Campbell, A. (2008). *The Blair Years: Extracts From the Alastair Campbell Diaries*, London: Arrow Books Ltd.

Campbell, A. (2009). *All in the Mind*, London: Arrow Books Ltd.

Campbell, R. and Childs, S. (2014) 'Parents in Parliament: Where's mum?' *The Political Quarterly*, 85 (4):487–492.

Campbell, R. and Childs, S. (2014). 'This ludicrous obsession, parents in parliament: The parenthood trap', *Huffington Post*, 16 January, http://www.huffingtonpost.co.uk/dr-rosie-campbell/women-in-politics_b_1608418.html, date accessed 12 April 2014

Cannadine, D. (2006). 'Taking the strain', *BBC News*, 31 July, http://news.bbc.co.uk/1/hi/magazine/5230612.stm, date accessed 10 June 2014.

Carr, D. (2012). 'Hashtag activism and its limits', *New York Times*, 25 March, http://www.nytimes.com/2012/03/26/business/media/hashtag-activism-and-its-limits.html?pagewanted=all&_r=0, date accessed 12 March 2014.

162   *References*

Castells, M. (1997). *The Power of Identity (The Information Age: Economy, Society and Culture, Volume II)*, Oxford: Blackwell Publishers.

Castells, M. (2000). *The Rise of the Network Society: Economy, Society and Culture*, 2nd edition, Oxford: Blackwell Publishers.

Castells, M. (2009). *Communication Power*, Oxford: Oxford University Press.

Castells, M. (2012). *Networks of Outrage and Hope: Social Movements in the Internet Age*, Cambridge: Polity Press.

Cecil, N. (2009). 'Derek Draper urged to get off the political stage', *Evening Standard*, 15 April, http://www.standard.co.uk/news/derek-draper-urged-to-get-off-the-political-stage-6872511.html, date accessed 13 March 2014.

Chakelian, A. (2015). 'The Granola pact: Is there a rift between Natalie Bennett and Caroline Lucas?' *The Staggers*, 4 March, http://www.newstatesman.com/politics/2015/03/granola-pact-there-rift-between-natalie-bennett-and-caroline-lucas, date accessed 6 March 2015.

Chadwick, A. and Heffernan, R. (eds) (2003). *The New Labour Reader*, Cambridge: Polity Press.

Chadwick, A. and Heffernan, R. (2003). 'Introduction: The New Labour phenomenon', in Chadwick, A. and Heffernan, A. (eds) *The New Labour Reader*, Cambridge: Polity Press, pp. 1–26.

Chadwick, A. and Heffernan, R. (2003). 'A new Whitehall style? New Labour in government', in Chadwick, A. and Heffernan, A. (eds) *The New Labour Reader*, Cambridge: Polity Press, pp. 267–270.

Channel 4 News (2010). 'Gordon Brown's politics of emotion', *Channel 4 News*, 12 February, http://www.channel4.com/news/articles/politics/domestic_politics/gordon%2Bbrownaposs%2Bpolitics%2Bof%2Bemotion/3538537.html, date accessed 12 January 2015.

Chapman, J. (2009). 'The boy who shaped a Tory leader', *MailOnline*, 26 February, http://www.dailymail.co.uk/news/article-1155008/The-boy-shaped-Tory-leader-Tributes-David-Camerons-disabled-son-Ivan.html, date accessed 2 April 2014.

Chapman, J. (2010). 'SamCam back on the school run, as David says death of son Ivan last year prompted them to try for a new baby', *MailOnline*, 23 March, http://www.dailymail.co.uk/news/article-1259940/Samantha-Cameron-expecting-baby-September.html, date accessed 27 December 2014.

Chapman, L. (2012). 'Evidenced based practice, talking therapies and the new Taylorism', *Psychotherapy and Politics International*, 10 (1): 33–44.

Chorley, M. (2014). 'David Cameron ditches the phone, after serious selfie mockery to tweet a picture of himself meeting Bill Clinton face to face', *MailOnline*, 7 March, http://www.dailymail.co.uk/news/article-2574745/Camerons-selfie-phone-Obama-mocked-online-comedians-animals-actor-Patrick-Stewart.html, date accessed 12 March 2014.

Claasen, R. C. (2007). 'Floating voters and floating activists', *Political Research Quarterly*, 60 (1): 124–134.

Clark, A. (2002). *The Last Diaries: In and Out of the Wilderness*. London: Phoenix. [Edited and transcribed]

Clark, T. and Mason, R. (2013). 'Fury with MPs is main reason for not voting', *The Guardian*, 26 December, http://www.theguardian.com/politics/2013/dec/26/fury-mps-not-voting-poll, date accessed 10 January 2014.

Clarke, N. (2009). 'So why DO they call me the Minister for sexy Skirts?...You tell us, Caroline Flint', *MailOnline*, 29 May, http://www.dailymail.co.uk/femail/article-1182928/So-DO-Minister-Sexy-Skirts—You-tell-Caroline-Flint.html, date accessed 28 December 2014.

Clarke, S., Hoggett, P. and Thompson, S. (eds) (2006). *Emotions, Politics and Society*, Basingstoke: Palgrave Macmillan.

Clarke, P., Hoggart, P. and Thompson, S. (eds) (2006). *Emotion, Politics and Society*, Basingstoke: Palgrave Macmillan.

Classen, R. L. (2007). 'Floating voters and floating activists: Political change and information', *Political Research Quarterly*, March, 60 (1): 124–1.

Cochrane, K. (2012). 'Louise Mensch the heir to Thatcher? Really?' *The Guardian*, 3 January, http://www.theguardian.com/politics/shortcuts/2012/jan/03/louise-mensch-thatcher, date accessed 21 March 2014.

Cockerell, M. (2007). 'David Cameron's incredible journey', *BBC News*, 20 December, http://newsbbc.co.uk/1/hi/uk_politics/7153406.stm, date accessed 6 January 2014.

Cohen, L. (2001) 'Citizen Consumers in the United States in the Century of Mass Consumption', in: M. Daunton and M. Hilton (eds.) *The Politics of Consumption*. Oxford: Berg. pp. 203–222.

Cohen, N. (2014). 'Revolution by Russell Brand review – The barmy credo of a Beverly Hills buddhist', *The Observer*, 27 October, http://www.theguardian.com/books/2014/oct/27/revolution-review-russell-brand-beverly-hills-buddhist, date accessed 27 December 2014.

Collier R. S. (2009). 'Fathers' rights, gender and welfare: Some questions for family law', *Journal of Social Welfare and Family Law*, 31 (4): 357–371.

Collin, R. (2012). 'Oscars 2012: The Iron Lady, review', *The Telegraph*, 27 February, http://www.telegraph.co.uk/culture/film/filmreviews/8995679/Oscars-2012-The-Iron-Lady-review.html, date accessed 3 January 2015.

Conlan, T. (2014). 'Channel 4 Benefits Street producers struggle to cast second series', *The Guardian*, 16 April, http://www.theguardian.com/media/2014/apr/16/channel-4-benefits-street-second-series-stockton-opposition, date accessed 16 April 2014.

Cooper, A. and Lousada, J. (2010). 'The shock of the real: Psychoanalysis, modernity, survival', in Lemma, A. and Patrick, M. (eds) *Off the Couch: Contemporary Psychoanalytic Applications*, London: Taylor and Francis, pp. 33–45.

Cooper, G. (2012). 'Karren Brady: Emotion is not part of my make up', *The Telegraph*, 25 April, http://www.telegraph.co.uk/women/mother-tongue/9223539/Karren-Brady-Emotion-is-not-part-of-my-make-up.html, date accessed 15 April 2014.

Cooper, R. (2014). 'The only person who should be depressed is the taxpayer', *MailOnline*, 19 February, http://www.dailymail.co.uk/news/article-2563069/Questions-Benefits-Streets-White-Dee-appear-TV-ill-work.html, date accessed 14 April 2014.

Corner, J. and Pels, D. (eds) (2003). *Media and the Restyling of Politics*, London: Sage Publications.

Couldry, N. (2012). *Media, Society, World: Social Theory and Digital Media Practice*, Cambridge: Polity.

Couldry, N., Livingstone, S. and Markham, T. (2010). *Media Consumption and Public Engagement*, Basingstoke: Palgrave Macmillan.

Coulsen, M., Magaš, C. and Wainwright, H. (1975). 'The housewife and her labour under capitalism', *New Left Review*, (83), 1–89, January–February.
Couple Connection (2014). 'Could Scottish independence lead to rise in divorce?', *Couple Connection, Where Couples Work It Out*, 8 September, http://thecoupleconnection.net/blog/could-scottish-independence-lead-to-rise-in-divorce#, date accessed 12 November 2014.
Craib, I. (1995). *The Importance of Disappointment*, Abingdon, Oxford: Routledge.
Craig, G. (2004). *The Media, Politics and Public Life*, Crows Nest: Allen & Unwin.
Cummings, D. (2003). 'You're so vain, you probably think this book is about you. Therapy culture and the therapistas', *Culture Wars*, 5 December, http://www.culturewars.org.uk/index.php/site/article/youre_so_vain_you_probably_think_this_book_is_about_you/, date accessed 5 June 2014.
Curtis, P. (2010). 'Gordon Brown calls Labour supporter a bigotted woman', *The Guardian*, 28 April, http://www.theguardian.com/politics/2010/apr/28/gordon-brown-bigoted-woman, date accessed 12 July 2014.
Daily Mail Reporter (2010). 'Brown breaks his pledge to meet more "ordinary voters" with speech to room full of Labour activists', *MailOnline*, 25 April, http://www.dailymail.co.uk/news/article-1268684/Vote-Lib-Dem-youll-Cameron-Mandelson-warns-Labour-voters-flirt-Nick-Clegg.html, date accessed 14 March 2014.
Daily Mail Reporter (2010a). 'Tory plans to give tax breaks to married couples blasted as social engineering', *MailOnline*, 18 January, http://www.dailymail.co.uk/news/article-1243981/Tory-plans-tax-breaks-married-couples-blasted-social-engineering.html, date accessed 4 September 2014.
Daily Mail Reporter (2010b). 'That's how to build a cabinet: David Cameron and Nick Clegg reveal they formed DIY coalition to build new cupboard for baby Florence', *MailOnline*, 18 September, http://www.dailymail.co.uk/news/article-1313223/Thats-build-cabinet-David-Cameron-Nick-Clegg-reveal-formed-DIY-coalition-build-new-cupboard-baby-Florence.html#ixzz1eG5fjXM0, date accessed 2 May 2014.
Daily Mail Reporter (2011). 'Children whose mothers suffer baby blues FOUR Times as likely to suffer depression', *MailOnline*, 18 June, http://www.dailymail.co.uk/health/article-2004627/40-children-mothers-experience-baby-blues-suffer-depression-16.html, date accessed 12 January 2015.
Daily Mail Reporter (2012). 'Coulson would have profited from shares if BskyB takeover was approved', *MailOnline*, 6 May, http://www.dailymail.co.uk/news/article-2140290/BSkyB-scandal-David-Cameron-fears-Rebekah-Brooks-texts-public-Leveson-Inquiry.html, date accessed 3 March 2014.
David, T., Gooch, K., Powell, S. and Abbott, L. (2003). Emotional Well Being', DfES Research Report Number 444: Birth to Three Matters: A Review of the Literature, Nottingham, Queen's Printer, pp. 127–131.
Davison Hunter, J. (1992) *Culture Wars: The Struggle to Define America*. New York: Basic Books.
Davis, A. (2002). *Public Relations Democracy: Public Relations, Politics and the Mass Media in Britain*, Manchester: Manchester University Press.
Day, E. (2009). 'The day I interviewed a feisty Caroline Flint for that photoshoot', *The Observer*, 7 June, http://www.theguardian.com/politics/2009/

jun/07/caroline-flint-photoshoot-women-cabinet, date accessed 28 December 2014.

Day Sclater, S., Jones, D. W., Price, H. and Yates, C. (eds) (2009). *Emotion: New Psychosocial Perspectives*, Basingstoke: Palgrave Macmillan.

Deans, J. and Plunkett, J. (2014). 'Cameron's spin doctors more obsessive than Tony Blair's, says Adam Boulton', *The Guardian*, 3 February, http://www.theguardian.com/media/2014/feb/03/adam-boulton-cameron-spin-doctors-alastair-campbells, date accessed 3 March 2014.

De Benedictis, S. (2012). ' "Feral" Parents: Austerity parenting under neoliberalism', *Studies in the Maternal*, 4 (2), www.mamsie.bbk.ac.uk, date accessed 12 December 2014.

Del Savio, L. and Mameli, M. (2014). 'Anti-representative democracy: How to understand the Five Star movement', *Open Democracy*, 4 July, https://www.opendemocracy.net/can-europe-make-it/lorenzo-del-savio-matteo-mameli/antirepresentative-democracy-how-to-understand-fi, date accessed 12 February 2015.

Delli Carpini, M. and Williams, B. (2001). 'Let us infotain you', in Bennett, L. and Entman, R. W. (eds) *Mediated Politics*, Cambridge: Cambridge University Press, pp. 160–181.

Department of Education (2010). *Health and Wellbeing*, http://www.education.gov.uk/childrenandyoungpeople/healthandwellbeing, date accessed 4 March 2013.

Dermody, J. and Hanmer-Lloyd, S. (2011). 'An introspective, retrospective, future-spective analysis of the attack advertising in the 2010 British General Election', *Journal of Marketing Management*, 27 (7–8): 736–761.

Doane, M. A. (1991). *Femmes Fatales*, Abingdon, Oxford: Routledge.

Dodd, C. (2008). 'Derek Draper, Mark Oaten and Christine Ohuruoghu talk about redemption', *The Times*, http://women.timesonline.co.uk/tol/life_and_style/women/celebrity/article3592620.ece, date accessed 4 January 2014.

Dominiczak, P. (2013). 'UKIP Eastleigh candidate calls for moratorium on immigration', *The Telegraph*, 12 February, http://www.telegraph.co.uk/news/politics/9864970/Ukip-Eastleigh-candidate-calls-for-moratorium-on-immigration.html, date accessed 12 September 2014.

Dominiczak, P. (2014). 'David Cameron announces immigration benefits crackdown', *The Telegraph*, 29 July, http://www.telegraph.co.uk/news/uknews/immigration/10996721/David-Cameron-announces-immigration-benefits-crackdown.html, date accessed 12 August 2014.

Dominiczak, P., Spence, P. and Johnson, S. (2014). 'Stay with us: David Cameron's desperate plea to Scots', *The Telegraph*, 9 September, http://www.telegraph.co.uk/news/uknews/scottish-independence/11086060/Stay-with-us-David-Camerons-desperate-plea-to-Scots.html, date accessed 12 September 2014.

Donzelot, J. (1997). *The Policing of Families*, London: The John Hopkins Press Ltd. [Translated by R. Hurley]. 1979.

Dowd, M. (2007). 'She's not buttering him up', *New York Times*, 25 April, http://www.nytimes.com/2007/04/25/opinion/25dowd.html?hp&_r=0, date accessed 24 January 2014.

Dowling, T. (2009). 'David Cameron takes the biscuit', *The Guardian*, 19 November, http://www.theguardian.com/politics/2009/nov/19/david-cameron-mums net-biscuits, date accessed 15 April 2014.

Draper, D. (2007). 'The road to wellbeing. British political discourse is undergoing a sea-change as last night's debate showed', *The Guardian*, 22 February, http://www.guardian.co.uk/commentisfree/2007/feb/22/wherenextforwellbeing, date accessed 2 May 2014.

Draper, D. (2008). 'Inside the sick world of the spin doctor', *The Observer*, 9 November, http://www.theguardian.com/books/2008/nov/09/review-alastair-campbell, date accessed 4 April 2014.

Draper, D. (2009a). 'So is Labour doomed? And what therapy would you offer Brown?', *Independent*, 23 February 2009, p. 38.

Draper, D. (2009b). 'Chore wars: Tin hats on! Kate Garraway's hubby is spoiling for a fight', *Mail Online*, 19 March, http://www.dailymail.co.uk/femail/article-1163024/Chore-wars-Tin-hats-Kate-Garraways-hubby-spoiling-fight.html, date accessed 3 May 2014.

Draper, D. (2009c). *Life Support: A Survival Guide for the Modern Soul*, London: Hay House.

Draper, D. (2009d). 'Is cognitive behavioural therapy really the answer to Britain's depression "epidemic"?', *Daily Mail*, 17 March, http://www.dailymail.co.uk/health/article-1162512/Is-Cognitive-Behavioural-Therapy-really, date accessed 2 May 2009.

Drury, I. and Hickley, M. (2009). 'Dame Joanna, Gurkha heroine: Brown set to honour a new forces sweetheart', *Daily Mail*, 22 May, http://www.dailymail.co.uk/news/article-1184803/Dame-Joanna-Gurkha-heroine-Brown-set-honour-new-Forces-sweetheart.html, date accessed 23 January 2015.

DuBois, E. C. (1998). *Woman Suffrage and Women's Rights*, New York: University Press.

Duval Smith, A. (2008). 'France begins to grow weary with the Sarkozy soap opera', *The Observer*, 13 January, p. 45.

Easton, M. (2011). 'English riots: The return of the underclass', *BBC News UK*, 11 August, http://www.bbc.co.uk/news/uk-14488486, date accessed 12 March 2014.

Ecclestone, K. and Hayes, D. (2008). *The Dangerous Rise of Therapeutic Education*, Abingdon, Oxford: Routledge.

Economist, The (2005). 'Italy: The real sick man of Europe', *The Economist*, 19 May, http://www.economist.com/node/3987219, date accessed 23 February 2014.

Edmonson, N. (2012) 'Fathers 4 Justice Stage Naked Mumsnet Protest in Marks & Spencer, Oxford Street', *International Business Times*, 19 March. http://www.ibtimes.co.uk/fathers-4-justice-naked-protest-marks-spencer-316172, date accessed: 14 June 2015.

Elliott, A. (1996). *Subject to Ourselves*, Cambridge: Polity Press.

Elliott, A. and Urry, J. (2010). *Mobile Lives*, Abingdon, Oxford: Routledge.

Evans, J. (2009). '*As if*' intimacy? Mediated persona, politics and gender', in Day Sclater, S., Jones, D.W., Price, H. and Yates, C. (eds) *Emotion: New Psychosocial Perspectives*, Basingstoke: Palgrave Macmillan, pp. 72–85.

Evans, J. and Hesmondhalgh, D. (2005). *Understanding Media: Inside Celebrity,* Maidenhead, Berkshire: Open University Press.

Ewen, S. (1988). *All Consuming Images: The Politics of Style in Contemporary Culture,* New York: Basic Books.

Fairclough, N. (2000). *New Labour, New Language?,* Abingdon, Oxford: Routledge.

Faludi, S. (1991). *Backlash: The Undeclared War Against American Women,* New York: Crown.

Faludi, S. (2000). *Stiffed: The Betrayal of the American Man,* New York: Harper Collins.

Farage, N. (2014). *Flying High,* London: Back Bite Publishing.

Farrell, N. (2012). 'Celebrity politics: Bono, product (RED) and the legitimising of philanthrocapitalism', *British Journal of Politics and International Relations,* 14 (3): 392–406.

Fawcett Society (2013). 'Equal Pay Day 2013', *Fawcett Society Blog,* 7 November 2013, http://www.fawcettsociety.org.uk/equal-pay-day-2013/, date accessed 2 March 2014.

Fawcett Society (2014) 'Stats and facts on women in power', *Fawcett Society Blog,* http://www.fawcettsociety.org.uk/2013/02/stats-and-facts-on-women-in-power/, date accessed 12 February 2015.

Featherstone, M. (2007). *Consumer Culture and Postmodernism,* 2nd edition, London, Sage Publications Ltd.

Ferguson, G. (2011). 'The family on reality television: Who's shaming whom?' *Television and New Media,* March 2010, 11 (2): 87–102.

Ferguson, M. (1992). *Subject to Others: British Women Writers and Colonial Slavery, 1670–1834,* Abingdon, Oxford: Routledge.

Fielding, S. (2014). *A State of Play: British Politics on Screen, Stage and Page; From Anthony Trollope to the Thick of It,* London: Bloomsbury Academic.

Fisher, M. (2009). *Capitalist Realism Is There No Alternative?* Winchester, UK: Zero Books.

Fisher, M. (2013). 'Exiting the vampire castle', 25 November, *Our Kingdom, Power and Liberty in Britain,* https://www.opendemocracy.net/ourkingdom/mark-fisher/exiting-vampire-castle, date accessed 12 January 2015.

Flint, C. (2009). 'European minister Caroline Flint on why she resigned', *The Sun,* 12 June, http://www.thesun.co.uk/sol/homepage/news/2478043/Europe-minister-Caroline-Flint-on-why-she-resigned.html, date accessed 13 January 2014.

Foley, M. (2000). *The British Presidency, Tony Blair and Politics of Public Leadership,* Manchester: Manchester University Press.

Ford, R. and Godwin, M. J. (2014). *Revolt on the Right: Explaining Support for the Radical Right in Britain,* Abingdon, Oxford: Routledge.

Forsyth, B. (1968). 'I'm Backing Britain', written by Tony Hatch and Jackie Trent, Pye Records YouTube: https://www.youtube.com/watch?v=rT8LsRVN7C4, date accessed 13 July 2014.

Foucault, M. (2008). *The Birth of Biopolitics: Lectures at the Collège de France 1978–9,* Basingstoke: Palgrave Macmillan.

Fox, R. (2012). 'Women at the top: Politics and public life in the UK (revised and updated)', *Hansard Society Briefing Paper,* 11 January 2012.

Frank, D. and Manson, A. (2008) 'Foreword'. In: P. Rieff, *Charisma: The Gift of Grace and How It Has Been Taken Away from Us.* New York: Vintage Books: ix–x.

Franklin, B. (2004). *Packaging Politics: Political Communications in Britain's Media Democracy*, 2nd edition, London: Arnold.

Fraser, N. (2013). *Fortunes of Feminism: From State-Managed Capitalism to Neoliberal Crisis*, London: Verso Books.

Freedland, J. (2014). 'If Britain loses Scotland it will feel like an amputation', *The Guardian*, 5 September, http://www.theguardian.com/commentisfree/2014/sep/05/britain-scotland-independence, date accessed 6 September 2014.

Freen, A. (2012). 'Conservative women to bankroll new iron ladies', *The Times*, 7 May, http://www.thetimes.co.uk/tto/news/world/americas/article3406638. ece, date accessed 13 May 2014.

French, P. (1968). 'Put out less flags', *New Statesman*, 19 January, p. 85.

Freud, S. (1900). *The Interpretation of Dreams: Penguin Freud Library, No. 4* (1991), ed. A. Richards, trans. J. Strachey, London: Penguin Books.

Freud, S. (1905). *Jokes and Their Relation to the Unconscious*, London: White Press, 1991.

Freud, S. (1910) 'A special type of choice of object made by men (Contributions to the Psychology of Love 1)'. In: S. Freud (1977) *The Pelican Freud Library Volume 7: On Sexuality*, Harmondsworth, Middlesex: Penguin Books. [Ed. A. Richards, Trans. J. Strachey], pp. 227–242.

Freud, S. (1913). *Totem and Taboo*, trans. J. Strachey (1960), London: Routledge Kegan Paul.

Freud, S. (1915). 'Thoughts on war and death. Our attitude towards death', in Richards, A. (ed.) and Stachey, J. (trans.) (1991) *Penguin Freud Library 12, Civilization, Society and Religion: Group Psychology, Civilization and its Discontents and other Works*, Harmondsworth, Middlesex: Penguin Books, pp. 57–89.

Freud, S. (1920). 'Beyond the pleasure principle', in Richards, A. (ed.) and Strachey, J. (trans.) *Penguin Freud Library, 11 On Metapsychology, The Theory of Psychoanalysis*, Harmondsworth, Middlesex: Penguin Books, pp. 269–339.

Freud, S. (1921). 'Group psychology and the analysis of the ego', in Richards, A. (ed.) and Strachey, J. (trans.) *Penguin Freud Library, 12, Civilization, Society and Religion: Group Psychology, Civilization and its Discontents and other Works*, London: Penguin Books, pp. 91–167.

Freud, S. (1930). 'Civilisation and its discontents', in Dickson, A. (eds) and Strachey, J. (trans) *Penguin Freud Library 12, Civilisation, Society and Religion*, London: Penguin Books, pp. 251–340.

Freud, S. (2014) 'On Narcissism: An Introduction', in *Pelican Freud Library Volume 11, On Metapsychology, The Theory of Psychoanalysis*, Harmondsworth, Middlesex: Penguin Books 1984. Ed. A. Richards, Trans. J. Strachey, pp. 59–99.Furedi, F. (2001). *Paranoid Parenting: Why Ignoring the Experts May be Best For Your Child*, London: Continuum International Publishing Group.

Furedi, F. (2004). *Therapy Culture: Cultivating Vulnerability in an Uncertain Age*, Abingdon, Oxford: Routledge.

Gamble, A. (1994). *The Free Economy and the Strong State: The Politics of Thatcherism*, Basingstoke: Palgrave Macmillan.

Gibbon, G. (2010). 'Clegg cartoons: Harmless fun for the Lib Dems?' *Channel 4 News*, 1 August, http://www.channel4.com/news/articles/politics/domestic_politics/clegg+cartoons+harmless+fun+for+the+lib+dems/3730777.html, date accessed 20 December 2014.

Giddens, A. (1991). *Modernity and Self-Identity: Self and Society in the Late Modern Age*, Cambridge: Polity Press.

Giddens, A. (1992). *The Transformation of Intimacy*, Cambridge: Polity Press.

Giddens, A. (1998). 'The third way: The renewal of social democracy', in Chadwick, A. and Heffernan, R. (eds) *The New Labour Reader*, Cambridge: Polity Press, pp. 28–34.

Gilbert, J. (2011). 'Sharing the Pain: The emotional politics of austerity', *OpenDemocracy*, 28 January, http://www.opendemocracy.net/ourkingdom/jeremy-gilbert/sharing-pain-emotional-politics-of-austerity, date accessed 12 March 2014.

Gilbert, J. (2013). 'What kind of thing is neoliberalism?', *New Formations: Special Issue: Neoliberal Culture*, 80/81: 7–22.

Gilbert, J. (2014). 'Populism and the left, does UKIP matter? Can democracy be saved?', *Our Kingdom*, 21 October, https://www.opendemocracy.net/ourkingdom/jeremy-gilbert/populism-and-left-does-ukip-matter-can-democracy-be-saved, date accessed 3 January 2015.

Gill, R. (2008). 'Culture and subjectivity in neoliberal and postfeminist times', *Subjectivity*, 25: 432–445.

Gilroy, P. (2004). *Postcolonial Melancholia*, New York: Columbia University Press.

Gimson, A. (2009). ' "Joanna Lumley is coming": The Gurkhas' traditional battle cry', *Daily Telegraph*, 22 May, http://www.telegraph.co.uk/news/politics/5363695/Joanna-Lumley-is-coming-the-Gurkhas-traditional-battle-cry.html, date accessed 12 March 2015.

Giroux, H. (2014). *Politics in the Age of Casino Capitalism*, New York: Peter Lang

Glynos, J. and Stavrakakis, Y. (eds) (2010). 'Politics and the unconscious', *A Special Edition of Subjectivity*, 3 (3): 225–323.

Gold, T. (2013). 'Joanna Lumley is foolish for laying rape at drunken feet', *The Guardian*, 25 January, http://www.theguardian.com/commentisfree/2013/jan/25/joanna-lumley-foolish-rape-drunken-feet, date accessed 12 September 2014.

Goodman, P. (2014). 'Is Cameron really set to produce "a new policy to curb immigrants and benefits every week"?', *Conservativehome*, 19 January, http://www.conservativehome.com/thetorydiary/2014/01/is-cameron-really-set-to-produce-a-new-policy-to-curb-immigrants-and-benefits-every-week.html, date accessed 2 March 2014.

Goodwin, M. (2010). 'The angry white men and their motives', *Social Policy Network*, June, www.policy-network.net, date accessed 25 June 2014.

Gould, P. (1998). *The Unfinished Revolution: How the Modernisers Saved the Labour Party*, London: Little Brown.

Gramsci, A. F., Nowell Smith, G. and Hoare, Q. (1971). *Selections from the Prison Notebooks of Antonio Gramsci*, London: Lawrence and Wishart.

Green, A. (2006). *Play and Reflection in Donald Winnicott's Writings: The Donald Winnicott Memorial Lecture Given by André Green*, London: Karnac Books.

Griffin, N. (2009). 'BNP defends policy on race', *BBC News*, 23 April, http://news.bbc.co.uk/1/hi/uk/politics/8011878.stm, date accessed 12 July 2014.

Guardian, The (2009). 'Damian McBride resignation. Sex, lies and the videos that did not exist', *The Guardian*, 13 April, http://www.guardian.co.uk/politics/2009/apr/13/damian-mcbride-derek-draper-emails, date accessed 23 October 2014.

Guardian, The (2014). 'Russell Brand talks revolution with Owen Jones', *The Guardian*, 23 October, http://www.theguardian.com/culture/live/2014/oct/23/guardian-live-russell-brand-revolution-owen-jones-live-debate, date accessed 23 December 2014.

Guardian, The (2015). 'Where to now after the Malcolm Rifkind scandal?', *The Guardian*, 24 February, http://www.theguardian.com/politics/2015/feb/24/where-now-after-malcolm-rifkind-jack-straw-cash-access-scandal, date accessed 25 February 2015.

Guardian.co.uk (2010). 'General election campaign in 2010 posters', 15 April, http://www.guardian.co.uk/politics/gallery/2010/mar/30/general-election-2010-labour, date accessed 10 January 2010.

Habermas, J. (1989). *The Structural Transformation of the Public Sphere. An Enquiry into a Category*, Cambridge: Polity Press.

Habermas, J. (2001). *The Postnational Constellation: Political Essays*. Cambridge: Polity Press.

Hall, M. (2014). 'Inside politics: Sibling rivalry between Ed and David Miliband', *Daily Express*, 21 June, http://www.express.co.uk/comment/columnists/macer-hall/483864/Ed-David-Miliband-David-Cameron-still-fights-EU-Angela-Merkel, date accessed 15 February 2015.

Hall, S. (1979). 'The great moving right show', *Marxism Today*, January, pp. 14–20.

Hall, S. (1996) 'Introduction: Who needs "Identity"?' in Hall, S. and Du Gay, P. (eds.) *Questions of Cultural Identity*, London: Sage.

Hall, S. (2006). 'Notes on deconstructing the popular', in Storey, J. (ed.) *Cultural Theory and Popular Culture: A Reader* (3rd ed.), Harlow: Pearson Education Limited, pp. 498–508.

Hall, S. (2011). 'The neoliberal revolution', *Cultural Studies*, 25 (6): 707–728.

Hall, S., Critcher, C., Jefferson, T., Clarke, J. and Roberts, B. (1978). *Policing the Crisis: Mugging the State, and Law and Order*, London: Macmillan.

Hall, S., Massey, D. and Rustin, M. (2013). 'Chapter 1 framing statement. After neoliberalism: Analysing the oresent', in Hall, S., Massey, D. and Rustin, M. (eds) *After Neoliberalism? The Kilburn Manifesto*. London: Soundings, http://www.lwbooks.co.uk/journals/soundings/manifesto.html, date accessed 26 December 2014.

Hall, S., Massey, D. and Rustin, M. (eds) (2013). *After Neoliberalism? The Kilburn Manifesto*, London: Soundings, http://www.lwbooks.co.uk/journals/soundings/manifesto.html, date accessed 26 December 2014.

Hall, S. and O'Shea, A. (2013). 'Common-sense neoliberalism', in Hall, S., Massey, D. and Rustin, M. (eds) *After Neoliberalism? The Kilburn Manifesto*, London: Soundings, http://www.lwbooks.co.uk/journals/soundings/manifesto.html, date accessed 26 December 2014.

Harman, I. (2013). 'Nadine Dorries interview: Why I want to run as a UKIP-Tory joint candidate', 18 May, http://www.spectator.co.uk/features/8910521/the-prodigal-daughter/, date accessed 12 July 2014.

Harris, J. (2010a). 'Welcome to the first e-election', *The Guardian, G2*, 17 March, 6.

Harris, J. (2010b). *The Last Party: Britpop, Blair and the Demise of English Rock*, 2nd edition, London: Harper Perennial.

Harris, J. (2014). 'Labour encounters emotion on the doorstep', *The Guardian*, 21 May, 7.

Hart, R. P. (1999). *Seducing America; How Television Charms the Modern Voter,* London: Sage Publications.

Harvey, D. (2007). *A Brief History of Neoliberalism,* Oxford: Oxford University Press.

Hasan, M. (2014). 'Yes New Labour got it wrong about immigration. But not in the way that its front benchers think', *New Statesman,* 27 January, http://www.newstatesman.com/2014/01/labour-got-it-wrong-about-immigration-not-way-its-frontbenchers-seem-think, date accessed 23 February 2014.

Hattenstone, D. (2014). 'UKIP defector Douglas Carswell on leaving the Tories: They think *Love Actually* is actually a manual on how to govern the country', *The Observer,* 19 October, http://www.theguardian.com/politics/2014/oct/19/ukip-douglas-carswell-mp-clacton, date accessed 13 February 2015.

Hawkins, R. (2010). 'David Cameron's father dies in hospital', *BBC News,* 8 September, http://www.bbc.co.uk/news/uk-politics-11227525, date accessed 4 September 2014.

Heathcote, E. (2010). 'Does the happiness formula really add up?', *The Independent,* 20 June, http://www.independent.co.uk/life-style/health-and-families/features/does-the-happiness-formula-really-add-up-2004279.html, date accessed 5 January 2015.

Heller, M. (2010). *Paths to Post-Nationalism: A Critical Ethnography of Language and Identity,* Oxford: Oxford University Press.

Hennessy, P. (2001). *The Prime Minister: The Office and Its Holders Since 1945,* New York: Palgrave.

Hennessy, P. (2011). 'Runaway fathers are like drink-drivers blasts Cameron', *The Telegraph,* 18 June, http://www.telegraph.co.uk/news/politics/david-cameron/8583752/Runaway-fathers-are-like-drink-drivers-blasts-David-Cameron.html, date accessed 8 August 2014.

HeraldScotland (2014). 'Cameron urges Scots: Don't rip apart UK and break my heart', *HeraldScotland,* 10 September, http://www.heraldscotland.com/politics/referendum-news/cameron-urges-scots-dont-rip-apart-uk-with-a-leap-in-the-dark.1410332546, date accessed 12 September.

Hern, A. (2013). 'The Conservatives website purge has destroyed history', *The Guardian,* 14 November, http://www.theguardian.com/commentisfree/2013/nov/14/conservatives-website-purge-history-tory-party-speeches-internet, date accessed 12 March 2015.

Hill, J. (1999). *British Cinema in the 1980s,* Oxford: Clarendon Press.

Hill Collins, P. (2000). *Black Feminist Thought: Knowledge, Consciousness, and the Politics of Empowerment,* 10th Anniversary edition, Abingdon, Oxford: Routledge.

Hinsliff, G. (2014). 'Who would be a woman in politics?' *The Observer,* 9 February, http://www.theguardian.com/politics/2014/feb/09/women-politics-female-politicians-rape-threats-patronising-comments, date accessed 10 February 2014.

Hirsch. D. and Miller, J. (2004). 'Labour's welfare reform, progress to date', *Joseph Roundtree Foundation,* 17 November, http://www.jrf.org.uk/publications/labour%E2%80%99s-welfare-reform-progress-date, date accessed 1 October 2014.

Hoffmann, E. T. A. (1816). 'The Sandman', in. Hollingdale, R. J. (ed. and trans.) (1982) *Tales of Hoffmann*, London: Penguin Books, pp. 85–127.

Hopkins, K. (2013). 'Feisty Katie Hopkins lets us know her opinions in her first column for the Sun', *The Sun*, 1 November, http://www.thesun.co.uk/sol/homepage/suncolumnists/5235627/Feisty-Katie-Hopkins-lets-us-know-her-opinions-in-her-first-column-for-The-Sun.html, date accessed 21 March 2014.

Hornby, N. (2005). *About a Boy*, London: Penguin Books.

Hochschild, A. (2012). *The Managed Heart: Commercialization of Human Feeling*, 3rd revised edition, Berkely and Los Angeles: University of California Press.

Howard, P. N. and Hussain, M. (2013). *Democracy's Fourth Wave? Digital Media and the Arab Spring*, Oxford: Oxford University Press.

Huffington Post (2014). 'Nigel Farage says Enoch Powell's "Rivers of Blood Speech" right in principle', *Huffington Post UK*, 21 January, http://www.huffingtonpost.co.uk/2014/01/05/ukip-nigel-farage-enoch-powell_n_4545681.html, date accessed 23 August 2014.

Imber, J. B. (ed.) (2004). *Therapeutic Culture: Triumph and Defeat*, New Brunswick, NJ: Transaction Publishers.

Irigaray, I. (1981). 'The bodily encounter with the mother', in Whitford, M. (ed) and Macey, D. (trans.) *The Irigaray Reader*, Oxford: Basil Blackwell, pp. 34–46.

Irigaray, L. (1993). *Sexes and Genealogies* (trans. Gill, G. C.), New York: Columbia University Press.

Isaaman, G. (2013). 'Claire Perry praises Margaret Thatcher', *Marlborough News Online*, 11 April, http://www.marlboroughnewsonline.co.uk/news/all-the-news/1633-claire-perry-praises-lady-thatcher-while-pointing-out-her-mistakes-from-which-we-, date accessed 20 March 2014.

Isaby, J. (2010). 'Priti Patel uses her maiden speech to praise the Thatcherite free market policies which allowed small businesses to flourish', *Conservative Home*, 29 July, http://s477308942.websitehome.co.uk/parliament/2010/07/priti-patel-uses-her-maiden-speech-to-praise-the-that cherite-free-market-policies-which-allowed-smal.html, date accessed 21 March 2014.

ITV News (2012). 'Government has put a stop to Labour's mass immigration', 14 December, http://www.itv.com/news/update/2012-12-14/this-government-has-put-a-stop-to-labours-mass-immigration/, date accessed 10 August 2014.

Jensen, T. (2012). 'Tough love in tough times', *Studies in the Maternal*, 4 (2), http://www.mamsie.bbk.ac.uk, date accessed 23 February 2014.

Jensen, T. (2014). 'Welfare common sense, poverty porn and doxosophy', *Sociological Research Online*, 19 (3): 3, http://www.socresonline.org.uk/19/3/3.html, date accessed 12 November 2014.

Jeory, T. (2009). 'The Gurkhas guarding Olympic site for little more than Olympic pay', *Sunday Express*, 10 May, http://www.express.co.uk/news/uk/100087/The-Gurkhas-guarding-Olympic-site-for-little-more-than-minimum-pay, date accessed 10 September 2014.

Johnson, A. (2014). *This Boy: A Memoir of a Childhood*, London: Corgi.

Jones, D. (2014). 'A Braveheart fiction Scots would regret for ever', *Daily Mail*, 31 August, http://www.dailymail.co.uk/debate/article-2738802/A-Braveheart-fiction-Scots-regret-former-trade-minister-Digby-Jones, date accessed 10 September 2014.

Jones, E. (1929). 'Jealousy', in Jones, E. (ed.) *Papers on Psychoanalysis, 5th edition*, London: Balliere, Tindall & Cox, pp. 325–40.

Kahr, B. (2014). 'Television as Rorschach: The unconscious use of the cathode nipple', in Bainbridge, C., Ward, I. and Yates, C. (eds) *Television and Psychoanalysis; Psycho-Cultural Perspectives*, London: Karnac Books, pp. 31–46.

Kantor, J. (2012). *The Obamas: A Mission, A Marriage*, London: Penguin Books.

Katz, C. (2008). 'Barack Obama sorry for "sweetie gaffe" ', *Daily News Politics*, 15 May, http://www.nydailynews.com/news/politics/2008/05/15/2008-05-15_barack_obama_sorry_for_sweetie_gaffe.html, date accessed 10 June 2014.

Kay, R. and Arkell, H. (2014). 'Stay at home mothers, who never go out at night RUINED my business, complains city "Superwoman" Nicola Horlick', *Daily Mail*, 8 January, www.dailymail.co.uk/news/article-2535760/Stay-home-mothers-never-night-RUINED-business-complains-superwoman-Nicola-Horlick.html, date accessed 2 April 2014.

Kaye, R. A. (2002). *The Flirt's Tragedy: Desire Without End in Victorian and Edwardian Fiction*, Charlottesville and London: University Press of Virginia.

Kennedy, M. (2012). 'Robert Jay QC seduces with the language of Leveson', *The Guardian*, 10 May, http://www.theguardian.com/media/2012/may/10/robert-jay-qc-language-leveson, date accessed 23 February 2014.

Kirkup, J. (2014). 'Immigration shock: You, dear reader, are a member of the wealthy metropolitan elite', *The Telegraph*, 6 March, http://blogs.telegraph.co.uk/news/jameskirkup/100262397/immigration-shock-you-dear-reader-are-a-member-of-the-wealthy-metropolitan-elite/, date accessed 12 September 2014.

Klein, M. (1937). 'Love, guilt and reparation', in Klein, M. (ed.) *Love, Guilt and Reparation and Other Works, 1921–1945*, London: Virago, pp. 306–344.

Klein, M. (1946). 'Notes on some schizoid mechanisms', in Klein, M. (1988) *Envy and Gratitude and Other Works 1946–1963*, London: Virago Press, pp. 1–24.

Klein, M. (1940). 'Mourning and its relation to manic-depressive states', in Klein, M. (ed.) *Love, Guilt and Reparation and other Works, 1921–1945*, London: Virago, pp. 344–370.

Klein, M. (1957) 'Envy and gratitude', in Klein, M. (1988) *Envy and Gratitude and other Works, 1946–1963*. London: Virago, pp. 176–236.

Kohut, H. (1971). *The Analysis of the Self: A Systematic Approach to the Psychoanalytic Treatment of Narcissistic Personality Disorders*, London: The University of Chicago Press.

Kristeva, J. (1992). *Black Sun*, New York: Columbia University Press.

Kristeva, J. (1993). *Nations Without Nationalism*, New York: Columbia University Press.

Kuenssberg, L. (2011). 'David Cameron criticized for "calm down dear" jibe: Analysis', *BBC News*, 27 April, http://www.bbc.co.uk/news/uk-politics-13211577, date accessed 23 March 2014.

Kuhn, W. (2006). *The Politics of Pleasure: A Portrait of Benjamin Disraeli*, London: The Free Press.

Lacan, J. (1977). *The Four Fundamental Concepts of Psycho-Analysis*, London: Tavistock.

Lammy, D. (2011). 'Black fatherhood in the 21st Century', 'David Lammy' Website, http://www.davidlammy.co.uk, date accessed 4 September 2014.

Lasch, C. (1991). *The Culture of Narcissism*, New York: Norton Paperbacks.

Layard, R. (2005). 'Mental health: Britain's biggest social problem?, Strategy Unit Seminar on Mental Health'. 20 January, *LSE Research Online*, Date Deposited: November 2012, http://eprints.lse.ac.uk/47428/, date accessed 2 April 2014.

Layard, R. (2011) *Happiness: Lessons from a New Science*, 2nd Edition. London: Penguin Books.

Layton, L. (2004). *Who's That Girl? Who's That Boy? Clinical Practice Meets Postmodern Gender Theory*, London: The Analytic Press.

Layton, L. (2007). 'What psychoanalysis, culture and society mean to me', *Mens Sana Monographs*, 1–5 (1): 146–157.

Layton, L. (2010). 'Irrational exuberance: Neoliberal subjectivity and the perversion of truth', *Subjectivity*, 3: 303–322.

Layton, L. (2011). 'Something to do with a girl named Marla Singer: Capitalism, narcissism, and therapeutic discourse in David Fincher's *Fight Club*', *Free Associations, Psychoanalysis and Culture, Media, Groups, Politics*, September, 62: 111–134.

Layton, L. (2013) 'Relational No More. Defensive Autonomy in Middle Class Women' in J. A. Winer; J. W. Anderson and C.C. Kieffer, *The Annual of Psychoanalysis, Volume 32. 2004: Psychoanalysis and Women*. London: Routledge

Leader, D. (2008) A Quick fix for the soul. *The Guardian*, 9 September, http://www.guardian.co.uk/science/2008/sep/09/psychology.humanbehaviour, date accessed 18 June 2015.

Leadsome, A. (2012). 'The case for solid early foundations', Andrea Leadsome MP, Conservative Party blog, 12 December, http://www.andrealeadsom.com/working-for-you/andrea%27s-blog/the-case-for-solid-early-foundation/471, date accessed 12 March 2015.

Lears, J. (1995) *Fables of Abundance: A Cultural History of Abundance in America*. New York: Basic Books.

Lennon-Patience, S. (2013). 'Measuring a nation's well-being: A psycho-cultural investigation', *Free Associations, Psychoanalysis and Culture, Media, Groups, Politics*, 64: 14–36, http://www.freeassociations.org.uk, date accessed 12 December 2014.

Letts, Q. (2008a). 'Hello boys! Meet Caroline Flint: The flirtatious minister who has turned Downing Street into her very own catwalk', *MailOnline*, 14 May, http://www.dailymail.co.uk/femail/article-1019770/Hello-boys-Meet-Caroline-Flint-flirtatious-MP-whos-turned-Downing-Street-catwalk.html, date accessed 28 December 2014.

Letts, Q. (2008b). 'A feminist firebrand. A sexbomb who flirted with Ted Heath. This is how the BBC's controversial film sees the young Mrs. Thatcher – Maggie the Minx', *MailOnline*, 18 May, http://www.dailymail.co.uk/news/article-1020345/A-feminist-firebrand-A-sex-bomb-flirted-Ted-Heath-This-BBCs-controversial-new-film-sees-young-Mrs-Thatcher–Maggie-The-Minx.htm, date accessed 21 March 2014.

Levy, G. (2013). 'As the Labour leader reacts angrily to our critique of his Marxist father ... We repeat: This man did hate Britain', *MailOnline*, 1 October, http://www.dailymail.co.uk/debate/article-2439565/As-Ed-Miliband-reacts-angrily-critique-Marxist-father–We-repeat-This-man-did-hate-Britain.html, date accessed 11 February 2015.

Lewis, J. (2002). 'The problem of fathers: Policy and behaviour in Britain', in Hobson, B. (ed.) *Men, Masculinities and the Social Politics of Fatherhood*, Cambridge: Cambridge University Press, pp. 125–149.

Lewis, H. (2015). 'When Labour comes to terms with embarrassing Uncle Tony, It can finally start to defend its record', *The New Statesman*, 26 March, http://www.newstatesman.com/politics/2015/03/when-labour-comes-terms-embarrassing-uncle-tony-it-can-finally-start-defend-its, accessed 15 June 2015.

Lewis, H. and Pitel, L. (2014) 'New Women's Minister Nicky Morgan', *Woman's Hour*, Radio 4, 14 April, http://www.bbc.co.uk/programmes/b040hhnf, date accessed 16 June 2015.

Lievrouw, L. A. and Livingstone, S. M. (eds) (2006). *The Handbook of New Media*, London: Sage Publications.

Lilleker, D. G. (2012). *Key Concepts in Political Communication*, London: Sage.

Lilleker, D. G., Jackson, N. A. and Scullion, R. (eds) (2007). *The Marketing of Political Parties: Political Marketing at the 2005 Election*, Manchester and New York: Manchester University Press.

Lindsay, C. (2014). 'Should MPs be allowed to take their babies into the voting lobby?', *Liberal Democrat Voice*, 9 January, http://www.libdemvoice.org/should-mps-be-allowed-to-take-their-babies-into-the-voting-lobby-37775.html, date accessed 12 April 2014.

Lister, R. (1996). 'Introduction: In search of the underclass', in Murray, C. (ed.) *Charles Murray and the Underclass: The Developing Debate*, London: The IEA Health and Welfare Unit in Association with The Sunday Times, London, pp. 1–19.

Little, B. (2013). 'Parties, causes and political power', *Soundings*, Winter (55): 25–39.

Littler, J. (2008). 'Gendering anti-consumerism: alternative genealogies, consumer whores and the role of ressentiment', in Soper, K., Ryle, M. and Thomas, L. (eds) *The Politics and Pleasures of Consuming Differently*, Basingstoke: Palgrave Macmillan, pp. 171–188.

Livingston, K. (2005). 'London United', *YouTube*, 14 July, https://www.youtube.com/watch?v=6BSIBPsbL9c, date accessed 12 July 2014.

Livingstone, K. (2005) 'Ken Livingston: London United', https://www.youtube.com/watch?v=6BSIBPsbL9c, date accessed 15 June 2015.

Livingstone, S. (2009). 'On the mediation of everything: ICA Presidential address', *Journal of Communication*, 59 (1): 1–18.

Lumley, J. (2012). 'Forward', in Carroll, P. (ed.) *Gurkha: The True Story of a Campaign for Justice*, Google eBook, Biteback Publishing.

Lury, C. (1996). *Consumer Culture*, Cambridge: Polity Press.

Macintyre, B. (2014). *A Spy Among Friends; Kim Philby and the Great Betrayal*, London: Bloomsbury Press.

Macnab, G. (2009). 'Films that make you feel good', *The Independent*, 16 January, http://www.independent.co.uk/arts-entertainment/films/features/films-that-make-you-feel-good-1380271.html, date accessed 12 January 2015.

McNay, L. (2010). 'Feminism and post-identity politics: The problem of agency', *Constellations*, 17 (4): 512–525.

McRobbie, A. (2004). 'Feminism and popular culture', *Feminist Media Studies*, 3 (4): 255–264.

McRobbie, A. (2009). *The Aftermath of Feminism; Gender, Culture and Cultural Change*, London: Sage.

McRobbie, A. (2013). 'Feminism, the family, and the new mediated maternalism', in *New Formations*: 80/81, pp. 119–137.

MacRury, I. (2012). 'Humour as "social dreaming": Stand up comedy as therapeutic performance', *Psychoanalysis, Culture and Society*, 17 (2): 185–203.

MacRury, I. and Rustin, M. J. (2013). *The Inner World of Doctor Who: Psychoanalytic Reflections in Time and Space*, London: Karnac Books.

McTague, T. (2015). 'Senior Tory Slams Cameron's illegal and unworkable plan to force fat people to go on a diet or lose benefits', *Mailonline*, 16 February, http://www.dailymail.co.uk/news/article-2955682/Senior-Tory-slams-Cameron-s-illegal-unworkable-plan-force-fat-people-diet-lose-benefits.html, date accessed 20 February 2015.

McTague, T. and Chorley, M. (2014). 'Miliband takes giant step towards Number 10: Cameron admits "big UKIP vote puts Labour in power" ', *Daily Mail Online*, 10 October, http://www.dailymail.co.uk/news/article-2786919/Douglas-Carswell-set-make-history-UKIP-s-elected-MP-votes-counted-Clacton-election.html, date accessed 12 October 2014.

Mail Online Reporter (2010). '*Brokeback Mountain*? Cameron says he prefers *True Grit*, (because it's what the coalition needs)', *MailOnLine*, 30 July, http://www.dailymail.co.uk/news/article-1298677/Brokeback-Mountain-Cameron-says-prefers-True-Grit.html, date accessed 12 February 2015.

Major, J. (1993). 'Mr Major's Speech to 1993 Conservative Party Conference', 8 October, http://www.johnmajor.co.uk/page1096.html, date accessed 5 January 2015.

Mandelson, P. (2010). *The Third Man: Life at the Heart of New Labour*, London: Harper Press.

Mansfield, C. (2006). *Manliness*, New Haven, CT: Yale University Press.

Mardel, M. (2014). 'Disconnected generation ready to make Westminster pay', *BBC News*, 6 November, http://www.bbc.co.uk/news/29915542, date accessed 27 December 2014.

Maresfield Report (2012). 'The Maresfield Report on the Regulation of Psychotherapy in the UK', http://www.psychoanalysis-cpuk.org/PDF/MaresfieldReport.pdf, date accessed 4 March 2015.

Marsden, S. (2012). 'MPs reveal their battles with depression', 14 June, http://www.telegraph.co.uk/news/politics/9332575/MPs-reveal-their-battles-with-depression.html, date accessed 6 April 2014.

Marshall, O. and Laws, D. (eds) (2004). *The Orange Book*, London: Profile Books.

Marshall, P. D. (1997). *Celebrity and Power: Fame in Contemporary Culture*, Minniapolis: University of Minnesota Press.

Martin, I. (2009). 'Morality is making a comeback', *The Telegraph*, 6 January, http://www.telegraph.co.uk/comment/columnists/iainmartin/4127282/Morality-is-making-a-comeback-and-thats-bad-news-for-Gordon-Brown.html, date accessed 6 January 2015.

Martinson, J. (2012). 'Lynne Featherstone: I have the powers of high-level nagging', 10 March, http://www.theguardian.com/theguardian/2012/mar/10/lynne-featherstone-equality-women-feminism, date accessed 12 December 2014.

Mason, P. (2014). 'Something incredible is happening in Scotland', *The Guardian*, 31 August, http://www.theguardian.com/commentisfree/2014/aug/31/scottish-independence-yes-vote-turnout-polls, date accessed September 2014.

Mattinson, D. and Tyndal, Z. (2013). 'Meet the swing voters', progress online, 1 December, http://www.progressonline.org.uk/2013/12/01/meet-the-swing-voters/, date accessed 17 February 2015.

Maughan, B. (2010). 'Tony Blair's asylum policies: The narratives and conceptualisations at the heart of New Labour's restrictionism', Working Paper Series, No. 69, Refugee Centre, Oxford Department of International Development, University of Oxford, pp. 1–34.

Memon, A. (2014). 'Why a divorce from Scotland could be the ruin of us all', *Daily Mail*, 7 September, http://www.dailymail.co.uk/news/article-2746514/Why-divorce-Scotland-ruin-Mortgages-Pensions-The-pound-pocket-worth-90p-ll-pay-water, date accessed 12 November 2014.

Mendick, R. (2013). 'Tony Blair's "people's princess" speech honoured', *The Telegraph*, 16 November, http://www.telegraph.co.uk/news/politics/tony-blair/10454599/Tony-Blairs-peoples-princess-speech-honoured.html, date accessed 1 April 2014.

Mensch, L. (2015). 'Unfashionista', Louise Mensch blog, http://unfashionista.com/about/, date accessed 15 April 2014.

Merrick, J. and Bell, M. (2009) No. 10 aide fired over obscene email smears. *The Independent*, 12 April, http://www.independent.co.uk/news/uk/politics/no-10-aide-fired-over-obscene-em-smears-1667519.html, date accessed 15 June 2015.

Messler Davies, J. (1998). 'Thoughts on the nature of desires: The ambiguous, the transitional and the poetic: Reply to commentaries', *Psychoanalytic Dialogues*, 8 (6): 805–824.

Midgley, C. (1995). *Women Against Slavery: The British Campaigns, 1780–1870*, Abingdon, Oxford: Routledge.

Millard, R. (2009). 'Dolly's out to play again', *Sunday Times*, 22 March, 6.

Miller, M. C. (2005). 'Introduction', in Bernays, E. L. (1928) *Propaganda*. New York: IG Publishing, pp. 1–9.

Miller, T. (2005). *Making Sense of Motherhood, A Narrative Approach*, Cambridge: Cambridge University Press.

Minsky, R. (1998). *Psychoanalysis and Culture*, Cambridge: Polity Press.

Mitchell, J. and Rose, J. (eds) (1982). *Feminine Sexuality: Jacques Lacan and the École Freudienne*, Basingstoke: Macmillan.

Moore, C. (2011). 'The invincible Mrs. Thatcher', *Vanity Fair*, December, http://www.vanityfair.com/politics/features/2011/12/margaret-thatcher-201112, date accessed 12 April 2013.

Moore, S. (2008). 'Joanna Lumley is absolutely fabulous and absolutely right', *MailOnline*, 20 September, http://www.dailymail.co.uk/news/article-1058821/SUZANNE-MOORE-Joanna-Lumley-absolutely-fabulous-absolutely-right, date accessed 12 July 2014.

Moore, S. (2013). 'Seeing red: The power of female anger', *The NewStatesman.com*, 8 January, http://www.newstatesman.com/politics/2013/01/seeing-red-power-female-anger, date accessed 8 January 2013.

Morrison, B. (2003). 'Pull your self together', *The Guardian*, 20 December, http://www.guardian.co.uk/books/2003/dec/20/featuresreviews.guardianreview7, date accessed 20 January 2015.

Mouffe, C. (ed.) (2005). *On the Political*, Abingdon, Oxford: Routledge.

Mulholland, H. (2010). 'David Cameron's father dies after a stroke', *The Guardian*, 8 September, http://www.guardian.co.uk/uk/2010/sep/08/david-cameron-father-dies, date accessed 2 October 2014.

Mullen, C. (2010). *Decline and Fall; Diaries 2005–2010*, London: Profile Books.

Mullin, C. (2009) *A View from the Foothills: The Diaries of Chris Mullin*. London: Profile Books.

Munro, E. (2014). 'Feminism, a fourth wave?', *Political Insight*, http://www.psa.ac.uk/print/934, date accessed 12 March 2014.

Murray, C. (1990). *The Emerging British Underclass*, London: Institute of Economic Affairs.

Naughtie, J. (2001). *The Rivals: The Intimate Story of a Political Marriage*, London: Fourth Estate Ltd.

Nava, M. (1992). *Changing Cultures, Feminism, Youth and Consumerism*, London: Sage.

Nava, M. (2002). 'Cosmopolitan modernity: Everyday imaginaries and the register of difference', *Theory, Culture and Society*, 19 (1–2): 81–99.

Neale, A. (2009) 7 Days: My week. *The Observer*, 5 April: 37.

Negra, D. and Tasker, Y. (eds) (2014). *Gendering the Recession; Media and Culture in an Age of Austerity*, Durham & London: Duke University Press.

Negrine, R. and Stanyer, J. (eds) (2008). *The Political Communication Reader*, Abingdon, Oxford: Routledge.

Nicolson, N. (ed.) (2005). *The Harold Nicolson Diaries 1907–1964: 1907–1963*, New edited edition, London: Weidenfeld and Nicolson.

Nikkaha, R. (2010). 'Labour poster backfires on Tories', *The Telegraph*, 3 April, http://www.telegraph.co.uk/news/election-2010/7549078/Labour-poster-attack-on-Tories-backfires.html, date accessed 7 April 2014.

Nolan Jr., J. L. (ed.) (1996) *The American Culture Wars; Current Contests and Future Prospects*. Charlottesville: University of Virginia Press.

Norman, J. (2010). *The Big Society*, Buckingham: The University of Buckingham Press.

Nunn, H. (2002). *Thatcher, Politics and Fantasy. The Political Culture of Gender and Nation*, London: Lawrence and Wishart.

Nunn, H. and Biressi, A. (2010). ' "A trust betrayed": Celebrity and the work of emotion', *Celebrity Studies*, 1 (1): 49–64.

O'Carroll, L. (2012). 'Jeremy Hunt criticised for failure to oversee advisor', *The Guardian*, 14 May, http://www.theguardian.com/politics/2012/may/14/jeremy-hunt-criticised-failure-adviser, date accessed 20 February 2015.

Oliver, J. (2006). 'David Cameron's kitchen sink drama', *MailOnline*, http://www.dailymail.co.uk/news/article-407825/David-Camerons-kitchen-sink-drama.html, date accessed 5 September 2014.

Oliver, J. (2008). 'David Cameron tries to unravel the female mind', *The Sunday Times*, 19 October, http://www.thesundaytimes.co.uk/sto/Test/politics/article242809.ece, date accessed 15 June 2015.

O'Neill, B. (2009). 'Turning Gurkhas into a new victim race', *Spiked*, 11 May, http://www.spiked-online.com/newsite/article/6648#.VDE2CedxxPU, date accessed 12 September 2014.

Orr, D. (2014). 'A lack of mothers in the cabinet is bad for everyone – Not just lefty feminists', *The Guardian*, 11 April, http://www.theguardian.com/commentisfree/2014/apr/11/lack-of-mothers-cabinet-bad-for-everyone, date accessed 12 April 2014.

Ortega Breton, H. (2014). 'Coping with a crisis of meaning: Televised paranoia', in Bainbridge, C. and Yates, C. (eds) *Media and the Inner World: Psycho-Cultural Approaches to Emotion, Media and Popular Culture*, Basingstoke: Palgrave Macmillan, pp. 113–134.

Osborne, G. (2010). *Comprehensive Spending Review*, London: Crown Copyright, Oxforddictionaries.com (2014). 'Nationalism', http://www.oxforddictionaries.com/definition/english/nationalism, date accessed 14 July 2014.

Pace, J. (2011). 'Obama readies for MLK speech as President, Father', *Yahoo News*, Associated Press, http://news.yahoo.com/, 14 October, date accessed 16 October 2014.

Painter, A. (2012). 'The debate on Englishness can no longer be avoided', *Our Kingdom*, 26 January, https://www.opendemocracy.net/ourkingdom/anthony-painter/debate-on-englishness-can-no-longer-be-avoided, date accessed 12 August 2014.

Park, A., Curtice, J., Thomson, K., Phillips, M. and Clery, E. (eds) (2009). *National Centre for Social Research: British Social Attitudes, the 25th report, 2008/9 Edition*, London: Sage Publishing.

Parker, K. (2014). 'The shock of Hillary Clinton as ambitious', 12 February, http://www.washingtonpost.com/opinions/kathleen-parker-the-shock-of-hillary-clinton-as-ruthless/2014/02/11/1e27a8a2-9356-11e3-84e1-27626c5ef5fb_story.html, date accessed 12 March 2015.

Parris, M. (2007). 'A nation asks: 'How were we taken in?', *The Times*, 11 August, 15.

Patterson, J. (2006). 'Family values don't stretch far enough', *The Independent*, 29 July, 16.

Pennington, L. (2013). 'Fathers4Justice, Mumsnet and me: Shouting back', Louise Pennington's blog: *My Elegant Gathering of White Snows*, http://elegantgatheringofwhitesnows.com/?cat=78, date accessed 12 April 2014.

Perrins, L. (2013). 'Hands off our maternity leave', *The Telegraph*, 5 August, www.telegraph.co.uk/women/mother-tongue/10222797/Hands-off-our-maternity-leave-IPPR.html, date accessed 12 April 2014.

Phillips, A. (1994). *On Flirtation*, London and Boston: Faber and Faber.

Phillips, C. (2004). 'Ethnic inequalities under New Labour: Progress or entrenchment', *LSE Research Online*, http://eprints.lse.ac.uk/9578/1/Ethnic_inequalities_under_New_Labour_(LSERO).pdf, date accessed 1 August 2014.

Pimlot, B. (1993). *Harold Wilson*, London: Harper Collins

Powell, H. (2011). 'The affect of looking backwards: An analysis of the emotional labour of advertising in times of recession', *Free Associations: Psychoanalysis and Culture, Media, Groups, Politics*, September, 62: 134–150.

Powell, H. (2013). *Promotion and Convergence: Markets, Methods, Media*, London: Routledge.

Power, N. (2009). *One Dimensional Woman*, Winchester: Zero Books.

Prabhakar, R. (2011). 'What is the legacy of New Labour?', in Lee, S. and Beech, M. (eds) *The Cameron-Clegg Government: Coalition Politics in an Age of Austerity*, Basingstoke: Palgrave Macmillan.

Prior, M. (2007). *Post Broadcast Democracy: How Media Choice Increases Inequality in Political Involvement and Polarizes Elections*, Cambridge: Cambridge University Press.

Quin, B. (2013). 'Nick Hurd "grit" comments meet with storm of protest', *The Guardian*, 21 August, http://www.theguardian.com/society/2013/aug/21/nick-hurd-youth-unemployment-storm, date accessed 12 April 2014.

Radstone, S. (1995). 'Too straight a drive to the tollbooth: Masculinity, mortality and Al Pacino', in Kirkham, P. and Thumim, J. (eds) *Me Jane: Masculinity, Movies and Women*, London: Lawrence and Wishart, pp. 148–165.

Radstone, S. (2007). *The Sexual Politics of Time*, Abingdon, Oxford: Routledge.

Rainy, S. (2014). 'Emotional resilience: it's the armour you need for modern life', 25 February, http://www.telegraph.co.uk/health/wellbeing/10660556/Emotional-resilience-its-the-armour-you-need-for-modern-life.html, date accessed 4 April 2014.

Rawnsley, A. (2010a). *Servants of the People: The Inside Story of New Labour*, London: Penguin Books.

Rawnsley, A. (2010b). 'Why all these emails from Barack Obama make me feel cheap', *The Observer*, 21 March, 39.

Rayner, G. (2010). 'David Cameron: From the depths of despair to the delight of a beautiful baby girl', *The Telegraph*, 25 August, http://www.telegraph.co.uk/news/politics/david-cameron/7963101/David-Cameron-from-the-depths-of-despair-to-the-delight-of-a-beautiful-baby-girl.html, date accessed 2 September 2014.

Rendall, J. (ed.) (1987). *Equal or Different: Women's Politics 1800–1914*, Oxford: Blackwell.

Rentoul, J. (2001). *Tony Blair*, London: Little Brown.

Rentoul, J. (2011). 'Threatened, isolated, under siege: The UK's working class today', *The Independent*, 26 June, http://www.independent.co.uk/news/uk/home-news/threatened-isolated-under-siege-the-uks-working-class-today-2302850.html, date accessed 10 June 2014.

Richards, B. (1989). *Images of Freud, Cultural Responses to Psychoanalysis*, London: J. M. Dent and Sons Ltd.

Richards, B. (2000). 'The real meaning of spin: compression and containment in the therapeutic age', *Soundings*, 14: 161–170.

Richards, B. (2007). *Emotional Governance: Politics, Media and Terror*, Basingstoke: Palgrave Macmillan.

Richards, B. (2015). *Pleasure and Restraint in Popular Culture: What Is Holding Us Together?*, London: Karnac Books.

Richards, B. and Brown, J. (2011). 'Media as drivers of a therapeutic trend', *Free Associations: Psychoanalysis and Culture, Media, Groups, Politics*, 62, 18–30.

Riches, C. (2014). 'Benefits mum slammed by neighbours for boasting about a life on welfare', *The Express*, 17 April, http://www.express.co.uk/news/uk/470863/Benefits-mum-slammed-by-neighbours-for-boasting-about-life-on, date accessed 17 April 2014.

Rieff, P. (1966). *The Triumph of the Therapeutic: Uses of Faith after Freud*, London: Chatto and Windus.

Rieff, P. (2007). *Charisma: The Gift of Grace and How It Has Been Taken Away from Us*, New York: Vintage Books.

Riviere, J. (2009) 'Womanliness as a Masquerade', in: V. Burgin, J. Donald & C. Kaplan (1986) (eds) *Formations of Fantasy* ,London: Methuen. pp. 35–44.

Roberts, J. (2013). 'Mumsnet founder, Justine Roberts, talks maternity leave and flexible working', 19 November, http://www.theguardian.com/women-in-leadership/2013/nov/19/justine-roberts-maternity-leave-mumsnet,   date accessed 15 April 2014.

Robinson, J. (2011). 'Sara Pain and Rebekah Brooks: Fresh test for friendship', *The Guardian*, 28 July, http://www.theguardian.com/uk/2011/jul/28/sara-payne-rebecca-brooks-friendship, date accessed 12 April 2014.

Roch, E. (2013). 'Amanda Holden hits at Mumsnet critics', *Express.co.uk*, 8 April, http://www.express.co.uk/news/showbiz/390164/Amanda-Holden-hits-at-Mumsnet-criticswithout, date accessed 15 April 2014.

Rose, J. (1988). 'Margaret Thatcher and Ruth Ellis', *New Formations*, 6, 1–26.

Rose, J. (2014). 'We need a bold, scandalous feminism', *The Guardian*, 17 October, http://www.theguardian.com/books/2014/oct/17/we-need-bold-scandalous-feminism-malala-yousafzai, date accessed 12 January 2015.

Rose, N. (1999). *Governing the Soul: The Shaping of the Private Self*, 2nd edition, Abingdon, Oxford: Routledge.

Roseneil, S. and Budgeon, S. (2004). 'Cultures of intimacy and care beyond "the family": Personal life and social change in the early 21st century', *Current Sociology*, 52 (2): 135–149.

Royle, N. (2003). *The Uncanny*, Manchester and New York: Manchester University Press.

Rustin, M. (1991). *The Good Society and The Inner World: Psychoanalysis, Politics and Culture*, London: Verso Books.

Rustin, M. (1994) 'Incomplete modernity'. *Radical Philosophy*, 67 (Summer): 10.

Rustin, M. (2001). *Reason and Unreason: Psychoanalysis, Science and Politics*, London: Continuum.

Rustin, M. (2007). 'What's wrong with happiness?', *Soundings*, 36: 67–84.

Rustin, M. (2010). 'The politics of "pain" in an age of austerity', 8 December, UEL Centre for Cultural Studies research seminar, https://rikowski.wordpress.com/2010/11/20/the-politics-of-pain-in-an-age-of-austerity/, date accessed 12 January 2014.

Rustin, M. (2013). 'A relational society – the Kilburn manifesto', *Open Democracy*, 17 September, https://www.opendemocracy.net/transformation/mike-rustin/relational-society-kilburn-manifesto, date accessed 15 January 2015.

Rymer, M. (2002). *Capitalist Restructuring, Globalisation and the Third Way: Lessons from the Swedish Model*, Abingdon, Oxford: Routledge.

Rymer, M. (2010). 'An obituary for the third way: The financial crisis and social democracy in Europe', *Political Quarterly*, 81 (4): 554–63.

Samuels, A. (1993). *The Political Psyche*, Abingdon, Oxford: Routledge.

Samuels, A. (2001). *Politics on the Couch: Citizenship and the Internal Life*, New York: Other Press LLC.

Sanai, L. (2014). 'The assassination of Margaret Thatcher by Hilary Mantel, book review: Author conjures sinister forces', *The Independent*, 18 October, http://www.independent.co.uk/arts-entertainment/books/reviews/the-assassination-of-margaret-thatcher-by-hilary mantel book review author conjures sinister forces-9802818.html, date accessed 2 January 2015.

Sandberg, S. (2013). *Lean In: Women, Work and the Will to Lead*, New York: Random House.

Sandbrook, D. (2012). *Seasons in the Sun*, London: Allan Lane.

Sanders, K. (2009). *Communicating Politics in the 21st Century*, Basingstoke: Palgrave Macmillan.

Sanghani, R. (2014). 'If these silly modern female MPs can't cope, they shouldn't be there', *The Telegraph*, 20 February, http://www.telegraph. co.uk/women/womens-politics/10649213/Former-Tory-MPs-If-these-silly-modern-female-MPs-cant-cope-they-shouldnt-be-there.html, date accessed 21 March 2014.

Savigny, H. (2016) *Political Communication, a Critical Introduction*. London: Palgrave, forthcoming.

Schiesari, J. (1992). *The Gendering of Melancholia: Feminism, Psychoanalysis and the Symbolics of Loss in Renaissance Literature*, New York: Cornell University.

Schuster, J. (2013). 'Invisible feminists? Social media and young women's political participation', *Political Science*, 65 (1): 8–24.

Scialabba, G. (2007) Charisma: The gift of grace and how it has been taken from us by PhilipRieff (Review). *Boston Review* 23 July, http://www.georgescialabba.net/mtgs/2007/07/charisma-the-gift-of-grace-and.html, date accessed 26 April 2015.

Scullion, R., Jackson, D. and Molesworth, M. (2013). 'Performance, politics and media: How the 2010 British General Election leadership debates generated "talk" amongst the electorate', *Journal of Political Marketing*, 12 (2–3): 226–243.

Sebbagh, D. (2012). 'Rebekah Brooks tells Leveson of more meetings with David Cameron', *The Guardian*, 11 May, http://www.theguardian.com/media/2012/may/11/rebekah-brooks-leveson-cameron-meetings, date accessed 3 March 2014.

Segal, L. (1994). *Is the Future Female? Troubled Thoughts on Contemporary Feminism*, London: Virago Press.

Seligman, M. (2004). *Authentic Happiness: Using the New Positive Psychology to Realise Your Potential for Lasting Fulfillment*, London and New York: Free Press.

Sennett, R. (1976). *The Fall of Public Man*, New York: W.W. Norton & Company.

Seymour, R. (2010). *The Meaning of David Cameron*, Winchester, UK: Zero Books.

Shengold, L. (1982). 'The symbol of telephoning', *Journal of the American Psychoanalytic Association*, 30: 461–471.

Siddique, H. (2014). 'BBC Recruits BBC's "Gobby" as Communications Director', *The Guardian*, 7 December, http://www.theguardian.com/politics/2014/dec/07/ukip-bbc-gobby-communications-director-paul-lambert-nigel-farage, date accessed 4 January 2015.

Simmel, G. (1903) 'The Metropolis and Mental Life', Adapted by D. Weinstein from trans. K. Wolff (1950) *The Sociology of Georg Simmel*, New York: Free Press, pp. 409–424.

Simmel, G. (1909). 'Flirtation', in: Simmel, G. and Trans, Oakes G. (eds) *On Women, Sexuality and Love*, New Haven, CT: Yale University Press, pp. 133–153.

Simons, N. (2014). '"There is a danger this feminism thing is getting a bit ludicrous" warns Lord Hurd', *Huffington Post*, 15 January, http://www.huffingtonpost.co.uk/2014/01/14/lord-hurdfeminism_n_4598256.html?utm_hp_ref=uk, date accessed 12 April 2014.

Sin, H. W. (2010). *Casino Capitalism: How the Financial Crisis Came About and What Needs to be Done*, Oxford: Oxford University Press.

Skeggs, B. (2004). *Class, Self, Culture*, Abingdon, Oxford: Routledge.

Skey, M. (2009). 'The national in everyday life: A critical engagement with Michael Billig's thesis of banal nationalism', *Sociological Review*, 58: 331–364.

Sky News (2011). 'Tackling gangs new national priority', *Sky News*, 15 August, http://news.sky.com/home/politics/article/16050003, date accessed 30 August 2014.

Smith, M. (2013). 'Samantha Cameron turns Red for Comic Relief Bake', *The Guardian*, 5 March, http://www.theguardian.com/politics/2013/mar/05/samantha-cameron-turns-red-comic, date accessed 11 March 2014.

Soodin, V. (2009). 'Flint: PM treated me as window dressing', *The Sun*, 5 June, http://www.thesun.co.uk/sol/homepage/news/2467348/Fuming-Caroline-Flint-savages-Brown-as-she-quits-the-Cabinet.html, date accessed 21 June 2013.

Sparrow, A. (2011). 'England riots: Cameron and Miliband speeches and reaction', *The Guardian*, 15 August, http://www.guardian.co.uk/politics/blog/2011/aug/15/england-riots-cameron-miliband-speeches, date accessed 1 September 2014.

Spears, G., Seydegart, K. and Gallagher, M. (2000). *Who Makes the News? Global Media Monitoring Project 2000*, London: World Association for Christian Communication.

Standing, G. (2011a). *The Precariat: The New Dangerous Class*, London: Bloomsbury Press.

Standing, G. (2011b). 'Who will be the voice for the emerging Precariat?', *The Guardian*, 1 June, http://www.theguardian.com/commentisfree/2011/jun/01/voice-for-emerging-precariat, date accessed 13 September 2014.

Standing, G. (2014). *A Precariat Charter: From Denizens to Citizens*, London: Bloomsbury Press.

Stears, M (2011). 'Family breakdown and the riots', *New Statesman*, 22 August, http://www.newstatesman.com/society/2011/08/family-breakdown-riots, date accessed 23 September 2014.

Stone, J. (2013). 'How Margaret Thatcher transformed the world of modern political communications', *The Drum*, 9 April, http://www.thedrum.com/opinion/2013/04/09/how-margaret-thatcher-transformed-world-modern-political-communications, date accessed 25 February 2014.

Storey, J. (2014). *From Popular Culture to Everyday Life*, Abingdon: Oxford.

Strange, S. (1997). *Casino Capitalism*. Manchester: Manchester University Press.

Straw, J. (2013). *Last Man Standing: Memoirs of a Political Survivor*, London: Pan.

Street, J. (1997). *Politics and Popular Culture*, Cambridge: Polity Press.

Street, J. (2001). *Mass Media, Politics and Democracy*, London: Macmillan.

Street, J. (2003). 'The celebrity politician: Political style and popular culture', in Corner, J. and Pels, D. (eds) *Media and the Restyling of Politics*, London: Sage, pp. 85–99.

Street, J., Hague, S. and Savigny, H. (2008). 'Playing to the crowd: The role of music and musicians in political participation', *British Journal of Politics and International Relations*, 10 (2): 269–285.

Street Porter, J. (2010). 'This smug Mumsnet mafia won't get my vote', *MailOnline*, 15 February, http://www.dailymail.co.uk/femail/article-1251003/JANET-STREET-PORTER-This-smug-Mumsnet-mafia-wont-vote.html, date accessed 15 April 2014.

Streets, H. (2004). *Martial Races: The Military, Race and Masculinity in British Imperial Culture, 1857–1914*, Manchester and New York: Manchester University Press.

Sylvester, R. (2006). 'Iraq has tested Mr. Blair's interventionism to destruction', *The Telegraph*, 23 May, http://www.telegraph.co.uk/comment/personal-view/3625149/Iraq-has-tested-Mr-Blairs-interventionism-to-destruction.html, date accessed 4 June 2014.

Tasker, Y and Negre, D. (eds) (2007). *Interrogating Post-Feminism, Gender and the Politics of Popular Culture*, Durham and London: Duke University Press.

Tasker, Y. and Negra, D. (eds) (2014). *Gendering the Recession; Media and Culture in an Age of Austerity*, Durham and London: Duke University Press.

Thatcher, M. (1976). 'Speech to Finchley conservatives', *Margaret Thatcher Foundation*, Thatcher Archive, 31 January, http://www.margaretthatcher.org/document/102947, date accessed 12 April 2014.

Thompson, J. P. (1995). *The Media and Modernity: A Social Theory of the Media*, Cambridge: Polity.

Thorne, F. (2014). 'Banned: the MP and her breastfed baby', *MailOnline*, 15 April, http://www.dailymail.co.uk/news/article-167422/Banned-MP-breastfed-baby.html, date accessed 15 April 2014.

Toynbee, P. (2005). 'How could Cherie Blair do this without blushing?' *Theguardian.com.* 5 June 2005, http://www.theguardian.com/politics/2005/jun/08/labour.cherieblair, date accessed 12 March 2014.

Traister, R. (2008). 'What's so bad about "Sweetie" anyway?' *Salon.com*, 16 May, http://www.salon.com/life/broadsheet/2008/05/16/sweetie/print.html, date accessed 17 January 2014.

Tran, M. (2007). 'Thatcher visits Brown for tea at No.10', *The Guardian*, 13 September, http://www.guardian.co.uk/politics/2007/sep/13/politicalnews.uk, date accessed 10 February 2015.

Travis, A. and Stratton, A. (2011). 'David Cameron's solution for broken Britain: Tough love and tougher policing', *The Guardian*, 16 August, http://www.guardian.co.uk/uk/2011/aug/15/david-cameron-broken-britain-policing, date accessed 1 September 2014.

Treneman, A. (2014). 'The *Über-Mutter*, a tightrope walker who gives away nichts', *The Times*, 28 February, 4.

Trewin, I. (ed.) (2009). *Alan Clark: The Biography*, London: Weidenfield and Nicholson.

Trewin, I. (ed.) (2010). *Alan Clark, a Life in His Own Words; The Edited Diaries 1972–1999*, London: A Phoenix Paperback.

Turner, G. (2004). *Understanding Celebrity*, London: Sage.

Tyler, I. (2007). 'From the me decade to the me millennium: The cultural history of narcissism', *The International Journal of Cultural Studies*, 10 (3): 343–363.

Tyler, I. (2008). 'Chav mum, chav scum: Class disgust in contemporary Britain', *Feminist Media Studies*, 8 (1). 17–34.

Tyler, I. (2013). *Revolting Subjects: Social Abjection and Resistance in Neoliberal Britain*, London: Zed Books.

Van Dijk, J. (2006). *The Network Society*, 2nd edition, London: Sage.

Van Zoonen, L. (2005). *Entertaining the Citizen: When Politics and Popular Culture Converge*, Oxford and New York: Rowan & Littlefield Publishers, Inc.

Van Zoonen, L. (2006). 'The personal, the political and the popular, a woman's guide to celebrity politics', *European Journal of Cultural Studies*, 9 (3): 287–301.

Venn, C. (2012). 'Protocols for a post capitalist world. Section 8, the crash, debt, accumulation, financial capitalism', *CouzeVenn1, Scribd*, 16 February, http://www.scribd.com/doc/81803134/Protocols-for-a-Post-Capitalism-World-Section-8-the-Crash-Debt-Accumulation-Financial-Capitalism#scribd, date accessed 15 February 2015.

Vincent, J. (2013). 'Mining village celebrates Margaret Thatcher's funeral', *BBC News, Sheffield & South Yorkshire*, 17 April, http://www.bbc.co.uk/news/uk-england-south-yorkshire-22183736, date accessed 4 January 2015.

Wahl-Jorgensen, K. (2000) 'Constructing Masculinities in the US Presidential Campaign: The Case of 1992', in Sreberny, A. and Van Zoonen, L. (eds) *Gender Politics and Communication*. Creskill NJ: Hampton Press, pp. 53–78.

Walker, K. (2010). 'Diane Abbott plays the race card to excuse her decision to send her son to private school', *MailOnline*, 22 June, http://www.dailymail.co.uk/news/article-1288358/Diane-Abbott-plays-race-card-excuse-decision-send-son-private-school.html, date accessed 12 April 2014.

Walker, P. (2014). 'Boris Johnson backs new era tenants' battle with US landlord over rent rises', *The Guardian*, 17 November, http://www.theguardian.com/society/2014/nov/17/boris-johnson-backs-new-era-tenants, date accessed 27 December 2014.

Walters, S. (2010). 'Gordon Brown weeps on TV as he talks about death of Jennifer', *MailOnline*, 7 February, http://www.dailymail.co.uk/news/article-1249089/Gordon-Brown-weeps-television-talks-death-Jennifer.html, date accessed 23 July 2011.

Wanell, G. (2008) 'Joanna's Dad and a Very British Hero Called Pun', *Daily Mail Online*, 18 September, http://www.dailymail.co.uk/news/article-1057401/Joannas-dad-British-hero-called-Pun-Why-Major-Lumley-overwhelmed-shame-British-Governments-treatment-Gurkhas.html, date accessed 16 June 2015.

Ward, V. and Walton, G. (2015). 'Malcom Rifkind and Jack Straw cash for access scandal: As it happened', *The Telegraph*, 23 February, http://www.telegraph.co.uk/news/politics/11429144/Cash-for-access-scandal-the-reaction.-Live.html, date accessed 24 February 2015.

Warsi, W. (2013). 'The Muslim news: Baroness Warsi tribute to Margaret Thatcher', *The Baroness Warsi Blog*, 30 April, http://sayeedawarsi.com/2013/04/30/the-muslim-news-baroness-warsi-tribute-to-baroness-thatcher/, date accessed 12 March 2014.

Washbourne (2010). *Mediating Politics: Newspapers, Radio, Television and the Internet*, Maidenhead: McGraw-Hill Open University Press.

Waterfield, B. (2014). 'Italy's Bebbe Grillo joins Nigel Farage's 'people's army', *The Telegraph*, 12 June, http://www.telegraph.co.uk/news/worldnews/europe/eu/10896432/Italys-Beppe-Grillo-joins-Nigel-Farages-peoples-army.html, date accessed 12 January 2015.

Watt, N. (2010. 'David Davis pub talk reveals Tory unease at the "Brokeback Coalition" ', *The Guardian*, 24 July, http://www.theguardian.com/politics/2010/jul/24/david-davis-brokeback-coalition-pub-talk, date accessed 12 January 2015

Watt, N. (2010). 'Television debate, Brown Clash, but politely', *The Guardian*, 16 April 2010. http://www.theguardian.com/politics/2010/apr/16/television-debate-brown-cameron-clegg, date accessed 16 June 2015.

Watt, N. (2013). 'The Lynton Crosby effect: dog whistles and jewellery jokes', *The Guardian*, 29 September, http://www.theguardian.com/politics/2013/sep/29/lynton-crosby, date accessed 4 March 2014.

Watt, N. (2014). 'Keep HIV positive migrants out of Britain says UKIP's Nigel Farage', *The Guardian*, 10 October, http://www.theguardian.com/politics/2014/oct/10/nigel-farage-keep-hiv-positive-migrants-out-britain, date accessed 20 October 2014.

Weatherill, R. (2004). *A Last Great Illusion: A Radical Psychoanalytical Critique of Therapy Culture*, Exeter, UK: Imprint Academic.

Wernick, A. (1991). *Promotional Culture*, London: Sage.

Wheeler, B. (2005). 'Who are Britain's hardworking families?' *BBC News*, 19 April, http://news.bbc.co.uk/1/hi/uk_politics/vote_2005/frontpage/4458273.stm, date accessed 24 February 2014.

White, M. (2009). 'Gurkhas Vote: Gordon Brown never stood a chance against Joanna Lumley', *The Guardian*, 29 April, http://www.theguardian.com/politics/blog/2009/apr/29/gordon-brown-joanna-lumley-gurkhas, date accessed 12 September 2014.

White, J. (2013) 'Tony Blair is the embarrassing uncle of British Politics', *The Huffington Post*, http://www.huffingtonpost.co.uk/john-wight/tony-blair-syria_b_3878993.html, date accessed 15 June 2015.

Wieland, C. (1996). 'Matricide and destructiveness: Infantile anxieties and technological culture', *British Journal of Psychotherapy*, 12 (3): 300–313.

Wight, J. (2013). 'Tony Blair is the embarrassing uncle of British politics', *Huffington Post*, 7 September, http://www.huffingtonpost.co.uk/john-wight/tony-blair-syria_b_3878993.html, date accessed 2 March 2014.

Wilkes, D. (2014). 'Jobless mum advises her daughter, 19 to get pregnant – for an easy life on benefits', *MailOnline*, 16 April, http://www.dailymail.co.uk/news/article-2605677/Mother-two-never-worked-encouraged-daughter-pregnant-council-house-easy-life-benefits.html, date accessed 15 April 2014.

Wilkinson, R. and Picket, K. (2010). *The Spirit Level: Why Equality Is Better for Everyone*, London: Penguin.

Williams, R. (1976). *Keywords: A Vocabulary of Culture and Society*, London: Fontana Paperbacks.

Williams, R. (1977). *Marxism and Literature*, Oxford: Oxford University Press.

Williams, R. (1982). *Culture and Society, 1780–1950*, London: The Holgarth Press.

Wilson, H. (1967). 'Pound in your pocket speech', *YouTube*, https://www.youtube.com/watch?v=-IHVQU9BSks, date accessed 12 July 2014.

Wilson, S. (2014). *Stop Making Sense: Music from the Perspective of the Real*, London: Karnac Books.

Winnicott, D. W. (1971). *Playing and Reality*, London: Tavistock.

Winter, K. (2014). 'Full time mummy is not an occupation. It is merely a biological status. Katie Hopkins attacks stay at home mothers on Twitter', *Daily Mail*, 28 January, http://www.dailymail.co.uk/femail/article-2547349/Full-time-mummy-not-occupation-It-merely-biological-status-Katie-Hopkins-attacks-stay-home-m, date accessed 15 April 2014.

Wintour, P. (2008). 'A huge price paid for the election that never was', *The Guardian*, 26 June, http://www.theguardian.com/politics/2008/jun/26/gordonbrown.labour, date accessed 12 September 2014.

Wintour, P. (2009). 'Joanna Lumley confronts Phil Woolas over Gurkhas', *The Guardian*, 7 May, http://www.theguardian.com/uk/2009/may/07/gurkhas-joanna-lumley-phil-woolas, date accessed 10 September 2014.

Wintour, P. (2011). 'UK riots: Four days of chaos that re-shaped the political landscape', *The Guardian*, 11 August, http://www.theguardian.com/uk/2011/aug/11/uk-riots-cameron-miliband-aftermath, date accessed 12 March 2014.

Wintour, P. and Watt, N. (2014). 'Ed Milliband urged to harden stance on immigration after slim by-election win', *The Guardian*, 10 October, http://www.theguardian.com/politics/2014/oct/10/ed-miliband-labour-immigration-policy-ukip-byelection, date accessed 12 October 2014.

Wiseman, A. (2014). 'Meryl Streep to play suffragette leader Emmeline Pankhurst', *Screendaily.com*, 19 February, http://www.screendaily.com/news/meryl-streep-to-join-suffragette/5067887.article, date accessed 14 April 2014.

Withnail, A. (2014). 'Russell hailed by New Era estate protest that saved 93 estate families from eviction: I don't think we'd be here now without his support', *The Independent*, 21 December, http://www.independent.co.uk/news/people/russell-brand-saves-93-families-from-eviction-with-downing-street-campaign-i-dont-/, date accessed 27 December 2014.

Wolfsfeld, G. (2011). *Making Sense of Media and Politics: Five Principles in Political Communication*, Abingdon, Oxford: Routledge.

Woman's Hour (2014). 'Nigel Farage and UKIP's sexism towards women', *Woman's Hour*, BBC Radio, 4, 14 February, http://www.bbc.co.uk/programmes/b03ttg7z, date accessed 12 September 2014.

Woodhouse Hart, J. (2014). 'Programmes for people who are paranoid about the way they look: Thoughts on paranoia, recognition, mirrors and makeover television', in Bainbridge, C. and Yates, C. (eds) *Media and the Inner World: Psycho-Cultural Approaches to Emotion, Media and Popular Culture*, Basingstoke: Palgrave Macmillan, pp. 135–154.

Worley, C. (2005). ' "It's not about race, it's about community". New Labour and "community cohesion" ', *Critical Social Policy*, 25: 483–496.

Wyatt, D. (2014). 'Benefits Street White Dee to join Katie Hopkins in live televised benefits debate', *The Independent*, 3 February, http://www.independent.co.uk/arts-entertainment/tv/news/benefits-streets-white-dee-to-join-katie-hopkins-in-live-televised-benefits-debate-9103733.html, date accessed 12 January 2015.

Yates, C. (2007a). *Masculine Jealousy and Contemporary Cinema*, Basingstoke: Palgrave Macmillan.

Yates, C. (2007b). ' "I am a feminist but". The paradoxes of postfeminism in Rosalind Gill's Gender and the Media', *The European Journal of Women's Studies*, 14 (4): 365–367.

Yates, C. (2009). 'Masculinity, flirtation and political communication in the UK', in Day Sclater, S., Jones, D. W., Price, H. and Yates, C. (eds) *Emotion: New Psychosocial Perspectives*, Basingstoke: Palgrave Macmillan, pp. 85–97.

Yates, C. (2010). 'Spinning, spooning and the seductions of flirtatious masculinity in contemporary politics', *Subjectivity*, 3 (3): 282–302.

Yates, C. (2011). 'Charismatic therapy culture and the seductions of emotional well-being', *Free Associations: Psychoanalysis and Culture, Media, Groups, Politics*, 62: 59–84.

Yates, C. (2012). 'Fatherhood, political culture and the new politics', *Psychoanalysis, Culture & Society*, 17 (2): 204–221.

Yates, C. (2014a). 'Political sport and the sport of politics: A psycho-cultural study of play, the antics of Boris Johnson and the London 2012 Olympic Games', in Bainbridge, C. and Yates, C. (eds) *Media and the Inner World: Psycho-Cultural Approaches to Emotion, Media and Popular Culture*, Basingstoke: Palgrave Macmillan. pp. 34–53.

Yates, C. (2014b). 'Psychoanalysis, television, towards a psycho-cultural approach', in Bainbridge, C., Ward, I. and Yates, C. (eds) *Television and Psychoanalysis: Psycho-Cultural Perspectives*, London: Karnac Books, pp. 1–28.

Yates, C. and Day Sclater, S. (2000). 'Culture, psychology and transitional space', in Squire, C. (ed.) *Culture in Psychology*, London: Routledge, pp. 135–146.

Young, R. M. (1994). *Mental Space*, London: Process Press.

Young, T. (2009). 'Leave alone', coffee house: *The Spectator Blog*, 16 April, http://blogs.spectator.co.uk/coffeehouse/2009/04/leave-derek-alone/, date accessed 7 March 2015.

Younge, G. (2012). 'Michelle Obama, reluctant presidential consort', *The Guardian*, 13 January, http://www.theguardian.com/commentisfree/cifamerica/2012/jan/13/michelle-obama-reluctant-first-lady, date accessed 3 March 2014.

YouTube (2008). 'Bill Clinton fakes crying at Ron Brown's funeral', http://www.youtube.com/watch?v=lf8TOGrq8Bo, date accessed 1 April 2014.

Yuval-Davis, N. (2011). *The Politics of Belonging: Intersectional Contestations*, London: Sage.

Žižek, S. (2009). *The Ticklish Subject: The Absent Centre of Political Ontology*, London: Verso, New Ed. Edition.

Žižek, S. (2014). *Event: A Philosophical Journey Through a Concept*, London: Penguin Books.

Films and Television Programmes

A Century of Fatherhood (BBC, Channel 4, UK, 2012).
A Very British Coup (TV Mini-Series, Channel 4, UK, 1988).
Benefits Street (Channel 4, UK, 2014–).
Billy Elliott (S. Daldry, UK/France, 2000).
Borgen (BBC4, UK, 2012–2013).
Braveheart (M. Gibson, US, 1995).
Bremner, Bird and Fortune (Channel 4, UK, 1999–2010).
Bridget Jones's Diary (S. Maguire, UK/France, 2001).
Britain's Got Talent (ITV, UK, 2007–).
Captain America, The First Avenger (J. Johnston, US, 2011).
Celebrity Big Brother (Channel 4, UK, 2001–2010).
Chariots of Fire (H. Hudson, UK, 1981).
East Enders: 'When Peggy Met Boris' (BBC1, UK, 13 September 2010).
Have I Got News For You (BBC2, UK, 1990–2000; BBC2, UK, 2000–).
House of Cards (TV Mini-Series, BBC1, UK, 1990).
House of Cards (NetFlix, US, 2013–).
I'm a Celebrity, Get Me Out of Here (ITV, UK, 2012 & 2014).
Kirstie's Homemade Home (IWC Media for Channel 4, UK, 2009–).
Love Actually (R. Curtis, UK/USA, 2003).

Made in Dagenham (N. Cole, UK, 2010).
Margaret Thatcher: The Iron Lady (A. Byron, UK, 2012).
Miliband of Brothers (More4, UK, 2010).
Mo (P. Martin, Channel 4, UK, 2010).
Newsnight: Jeremy Paxman Talks to Russell Brand (BBC2, UK, 23 October 2013).
Noah (D. Aronofsky, US, 2014).
Only Fools and Horses (BBC1, UK, 1981–2003).
Passport to Pimlico (H. Cornelius, UK, 1949).
Piers Morgan's Life Stories (ITV, UK, 2009–2011).
Pride (M. Warchus, UK, 2014).
Red Nose Day with Catherine Tate and Tony Blair (BBC1, UK, 16 March 2007).
The Deal (S. Frears, Channel 4, UK, 2003).
The Edge of Darkness (TV Mini-Series, ITV, UK, 1985).
The Full Monty (P. Cattaneo, UK, 1997).
The Ghost Writer (R. Polansky, France/Germany UK, 2010).
The Great British Bake Off (BBC2, UK, 2010–).
The Iron Lady (P. Law, UK/France, 2011).
The Long Walk to Finchley (N. MacCormick, BBC4, UK, 2008).
The News Quiz (BBC Radio 4, UK, 1977–).
The Politician's Husband (TV Mini-Series, BBC2, UK, 2013).
The Special Relationship (S. Frears, Chanel 4, UK, 2010).
The Thick of It (BBC4, UK, 2005–09; BBC2, UK, 2009–2012).
The Wizard of Oz (V. Fleming, US, 1939).
The Wolf of Wall Street (M. Scorsese, 2013, US).
The Queen (S. Frears, Channel 4, UK, 2006).
Question Time (BBC1, UK, 1979–)
Wall Street; When Money Never Sleeps (O. Stone, US, 2010).
We Pay Your Benefits (BBC1, UK, 2013).
When Boris Met Dave (Channel 4, UK, 2009).
Yes Minister (BBC1, UK, 1980–1984).
Yes, Prime Minister (BBC1, UK, 1986–1987).
10 O'Clock Live (Channel 4, UK, 2011–2013).

Index

194   *Index*

Printed and bound by CPI Group (UK) Ltd, Croydon, CR0 4YY